Britain in Decline

Also by Andrew Gamble

From Alienation to Surplus Value (with Paul Walton)
The Conservative Nation
Capitalism in Crisis (with Paul Walton)
An Introduction to Modern Social and Political Thought
The British Party System and Economic Policy 1945–83
      (with Stuart Walkland)
The Free Economy and the Strong State
Developments in British Politics 4 (co-editor)

Britain in Decline

Economic Policy, Political Strategy and
the British State

FOURTH EDITION

Andrew Gamble

St. Martin's Press

© Andrew Gamble 1981, 1985, 1990, 1994

Published in Great Britain by
THE MACMILLAN PRESS LTD
Houndmills, Basingstoke, Hampshire RG21 2XS
and London
Companies and representatives
throughout the world

A catalogue record for this book is available
from the British Library.

ISBN 0-333-61440-2 hardcover
ISBN 0-333-61441-0 paperback

Printed in China

First edition 1981
Reprinted 1983, 1984
Second edition 1985
Reprinted 1986, 1988, 1989
Third edition 1990
Reprinted 1991, 1992, 1993
Fourth edition 1994

Published in the United States of America by
Scholarly and Reference Division,
ST. MARTIN'S PRESS, INC.,
175 Fifth Avenue,
New York, N.Y. 10010

ISBN 0-312-12239-X

Library of Congress Cataloging-in-Publication Data
Gamble, Andrew.
Britain in decline : economic policy, political strategy, and the British state / Andrew Gamble. — 4th ed.
  p.   cm.
Includes bibliographical references and index.
ISBN 0-312-12239-X
1. Great Britain—Economic policy—1945-   2. Great Britain-
-Politics and government—1945-   I. Title.
HC256.6.G35   1994
338.941—dc20   94-16020
                                                      CIP

In memory of A. N. Silver

The purely British causes of the economic depression are complex, but they can be summed up in a single sentence. English manufacturing costs are among the highest in the world. If this situation continues, any economic structure based on exports is faced with inevitable ruin . . . England is trying to compete in international markets, and at the same time provide her people with a wage level and a standard of living which does not permit costs to be low enough either to export profitably, or to attract the capital necessary for the development and upkeep of her manufacturing.

André Siegfried, *England's Crisis* (1931)

What with our sentimentality, our Party system, our government by committee, our 'Mandarins', our 'Society', and our Generals . . . the game is just hopeless . . . Our political organisation is thoroughly rotten, almost non-existent. It is Carthaginian – really the only comparison I can think of. Never was there such an absurd waste of power, such ridiculous inconsequence of policy – not for want of men but for want of any effective central authority or dominant idea to make them work together.

Lord Milner (1909)

Shame is a kind of anger turned in on itself. And if a whole nation were to feel ashamed it would be like a lion recoiling in order to spring. I admit that even this shame is not yet to be found in Germany; on the contrary the wretches are still patriots. But if the ridiculous system of our new knight does not disabuse them of their patriotism, then what will? . . . The state is too serious a business to be subjected to such buffoonery. A Ship of Fools can perhaps be allowed to drift before the wind for a good while; but it will still drift to its doom precisely because the fools refuse to believe it possible. This doom is the approaching revolution.

Karl Marx (1843)

Contents

Acknowledgements

The author and publishers wish to thank the following who have kindly given permission for the use of copyright material: Banco Nazionale Del Lavoro for data from an article 'Phases of Capitalist Development' by A. Maddison, published in the June 1977 issue of the Bank's *Quarterly Review*; The Controller of Her Majesty's Stationery Office for data from Royal Commission on Trade Unions and Employers' Associations, *Report* and *Employment Gazette*; National Institute of Economic and Social Research for tables from *Review*; Organisation for Economic Co-operation and Development for tables from OECD Reports, National Accounts 1961–7 and *Economic Outlook*, July 1979 and June 1993.

Preface

This book was a product of the 1970s and first appeared in 1981 at the beginning of the great economic and political shakeout which accompanied the Thatcher Government's attempt to reverse British decline. The second and third editions were prepared and appeared during the Thatcher era. This fourth edition has been prepared after its end. Much has changed since the book was first written, and my perspective on many of the issues discussed in these pages has changed also. In all the later editions, however, I have kept changes to the main chapters to a minimum, leaving them as a commentary on the debates and the solutions proposed in the 1970s. The main changes over the four editions have been to the Introduction, to Chapter 1 and to the Conclusion. The final chapter has been completely rewritten, and in this fourth edition offers an assessment of the achievements and the significance of the Thatcher Government in the context of the long debate on British decline.

The original title of the book was *The Politics of Decline*, which in certain respects expresses more accurately the contents and approach of the book. It is a study of how decline has been perceived and the perceptions of decline and of the political struggles to reverse decline, rather than of decline as an external objective process. Whether there has been a decline and whether it can be measured depends on whether there is such an entity as the British national economy. In the era of national protectionism in the world economy which has now ended, the British political elite certainly believed there was such an entity, and perceived Britain to be in decline both as a world power and as a national economy. It is this perception and the historical experience which informs it which is the main subject of this book.

Many people helped me write it. I owe a great deal to

xii *Preface*

students at Sheffield who attended my course on political
economy. I also learnt much from discussion with friends and
colleagues and I would particularly like to thank Jerry Agnew,
Anthony Arblaster, David Baker, Peter Duff, Brian Duncan,
Stephen George, Ankie Hoogvelt, Eddie Jachcel, Steve
Ludlam, David Marquand, Bryan Mason, Tony Payne, Ben
Rosamond, Quentin Rudland, Patrick Seyd, Martin Smith,
Ian Taylor and Stuart Walkland.

My wider intellectual debts are too many to mention. They
are apparent on every page of this book. Its judgements and
arguments lean heavily on the work of others. This book
would not have been possible without the pioneering work of
Perry Anderson and Tom Nairn in their seminal essay in *New
Left Review* in the 1960s which opened up a new range of
questions about the interpretation of English history. Henry
Drucker, Martin Jacques and Ralph Miliband encouraged me
to develop in essay form some of the ideas explored in this
book. Henk Overbeek and Bob Jessop, through their writings
on decline, stimulated me to clarify some of my conceptions,
as, did two conferences organised by Michael Mann in
Cambridge in 1988 and Uffe Ostergaard in Aarhus in 1991.

The book was nursed into life by four Macmillan editors:
Shaie Selzer, Rob Shreeve, John Winckler and Steven
Kennedy. I owe a great deal in particular to Steven Kennedy
for his special and much appreciated assistance and advice.
Thanks are also due to Keith Povey, who has been an
extremely efficient and helpful copy-editor for all four
editions; and to Hazel Watson, who prepared the original
typescript. My family gave me great support throughout the
writing of this book, as did Neil Lyndon, even if it turned out
rather differently from what he expected.

I owe a special debt to Yoshi Ogasawara, who studied with
me in Sheffield and undertook the laborious task of translating
the book into Japanese. The Japanese take a special interest in
the question of Britain's decline, perhaps in the spirit of
Marx's advice to the Germans that they heed the lessons of
British development – 'De Te Fabula Narratur.'

Sheffield   Andrew Gamble
November 1993

Introduction

It is remarkable to see how relatively numerous in declining empires are the people capable of making the right diagnosis and preaching some sensible cure. It is no less remarkable, however, that wise utterances generally remain sterile, because, as Gonzales de Cellorigo forcefully put it while watching impotently the decline of Spain, 'those who can will not and those who will cannot'.

Carlo Cipolla[1]

Britain has now been in decline for a hundred years. It has become the most observed and analysed decline in modern history, provoking a speculative literature of enormous dimensions. Few explanations have not been proffered, few causes not dissected, few remedies not canvassed at least twice. The decline has been the central fact about British politics for a century, a major preoccupation of its public intellectuals and intermittently but increasingly of its political leaders. Two processes stand out – the absolute decline in the power and status of the British imperial state, and the relative decline of the British economy with its long-standing failure to match the rates of expansion of its rivals.

The starting point of Britain's decline was the position of unrivalled dominance it had achieved during the nineteenth century. By 1900 Britain controlled over one-fifth of the world's land surface and ruled one-quarter of the world's population. Its land forces remained small but its navy was still maintained at a level where it would be superior to the two next most powerful navies combined. The foundations of this empire had been the commercial and strategic policies pursued by the British state for 250 years. Its consolidation and further extension in the nineteenth century had been the result of the industrial and technological lead Britain established by being the first major economy to industrialise. The height of Britain's industrial domination of the world was reached in the middle decades of the nineteenth century. At that time one third of the world's output of manufactured goods came from Britain. Britain produced half the world's coal and iron, half the world's cotton goods, almost half its steel. From this position Britain conducted one-quarter of the world's trade and built up a massive commercial and financial predominance. Even in 1900 Britain still accounted for one-third of the world's exports of manufactures, and the registered tonnage of British shipping was more than the tonnage of the rest of the world combined. London was the unchallenged commercial and financial centre of the new capitalist world economy. The international monetary system was centred upon the gold standard and the pound sterling, and British foreign investments had risen by 1914 to the remarkable total of £4000 million.

By the last decade of the twentieth century a very different picture presented itself. The British Empire had disappeared. Only a few last outposts such as Hong Kong and the Falkland Islands remained. Britain retained some of the trappings of a great power. It still had a nuclear arsenal, substantial and well-equipped armed forces, and a permanent seat on the UN Security Council. But it was no longer the kind of global power it had been in the first half of the century, and its proud tradition of sovereign independence was increasingly circumscribed by the new realities and requirements of interdependence. The security and economic relationships forged with the United States and Western Europe after 1945 were indications of how limited British sovereignty had become.

The British economy was incomparably richer and more productive in 1990 than in 1900 but it was no longer the world leader or the powerhouse of the world economy. It remained one of the richest economies in the world, but its position and performance relative to other economies in the leading group had substantially weakened. On a range of indicators Britain had slipped behind and despite several determined attempts showed no signs of being able to catch up.

The slope of Britain's descent has not been constant. There

have been periods of recovery, even of advance and success, but they do not affect the overall judgement that Britain in the twentieth century has been a state in decline and that the efforts of its governing class have failed to arrest that decline. The problems surrounding Britain's future have accumulated while the reserves for meeting them have dwindled.

There is a vast literature on decline but little agreement about how decline should be defined and still less about how it should be explained. This is hardly surprising. Decline is to an important extent a matter of political perception rather than an objective reality. To study decline is to study the perceptions and responses of the British governing class during the last hundred years. For many of them the decline in world power and the relative decline in economic performance are inextricably linked. They are part of the same process.

The crucial contexts which have shaped the domestic debates on decline and what to do about it have been formed by Britain's changing place in the world order. There have been three key debates, which are examined in this book – the debate on National Efficiency before 1914; the debate on modernisation from the 1920s through to the 1960s; and the debate on social democracy from the 1960s through to the present. These debates succeed one another chronologically, although they also overlap, and arguments and positions from the earlier debates often reappear in the later ones.

One of the most persistent aspects of the discourse on decline is the belief in a 'British disease', a malady whose causes lie deep in British psychology and British culture. A popular diagnosis of this 'disease' in the 1960s and 1970s was that the country was living beyond its means. The British consumed too much and worked too little. As one Labour minister memorably put it: 'For generations this country has not earned an honest living'.[2]

What made such assertions plausible were repeated economic crises – over the balance of payments,[3] public expenditure, and pay. The nation it was said was importing more than it exported, the government was spending more than it raised in taxes, and the workers were demanding the distribution of a bigger cake than the one they were producing. The consequences of such behaviour was placing Britain's future prosperity and its traditional freedoms in danger.

The favourite political scapegoat for the British disease used to be the trade unions. Their behaviour was most frequently cited as the reason why Britain's payments would not balance, why public expenditure was out of control and was beginning to encroach on 'our plural society',[4] and why inflation was accelerating.[5] Sir Keith Joseph summed up twenty years of anti-union criticism in the title of a speech delivered in 1979 during the Winter of Discontent: 'Solving the trade union problem is the key to Britain's economic recovery.'[6]

When Margaret Thatcher left office in 1990 trade unions had been weakened by a decade of high unemployment and anti-union legislation. The Government claimed the change in the climate of industrial relations as one of their greatest successes. Management had regained the power to manage. But the symptoms of the British disease appeared little affected. The public finances and the balance of payments were once again out of control and heading for record deficits. Inflation was rising sharply and the economy was moving back into recession. Solving the trade union problem, it seems, was not enough.

Many writers on decline had never thought it was. Some have attempted to explain Britain's post-war failure in terms of the cyclical patterns at work in the history of all great empires. Parallels for Britain's experience have been sought in the declines of other great imperial powers – Rome, Venice, Spain. As in other small states which have created empires the qualities and attitudes which assisted Britain to rise and expand were discarded or neglected by the later generations which inherited the imperial position. They developed instead tastes, needs, and activities which were sustainable only so long as Britain retained its economic and military leadership, yet which tended to undermine the basis of that strength. Britain's rise to world power was followed by the development of a pervasive 'anti-enterprise' culture and a social conservatism at all levels, particularly in education and business management, which persistently blocked successful modernisation and adaptation.

Trade unions are part of this 'anti-enterprise culture' but not the only or the most important part. The real source of Britain's decline is traced to the attitudes and the behaviour of political elites.[7] Such is the argument of two of the most influential books published on British decline in recent years – Corelli Barnett's *The Audit of War* and Martin Wiener's *English Culture and the Decline of the Industrial Spirit, 1870–1980*. Both were cited by Thatcherite ministers as evidence that Britain required a radical change in the climate of ideas, a cultural revolution, to rebuild a vibrant capitalist economy.

Barnett argued in his study of the shortcomings of British industry in the second world war that the problems of poor management, overmanning, restrictive practices, low investment, and low productivity were rife throughout British industry even during the war-time economy, which according to official accounts had been one time when the British economy had performed well. Barnett argued that the euphoria of victory allowed these failings to be ignored. Postwar reconstruction was fatally flawed by being directed on the one hand to the building of a universal welfare state, a New Jerusalem, a project which had come to dominate the thinking of the bulk of the British political elite, and on the other hand to the preservation of Britain's world role. Both New Jerusalem and the world role assumed a strong economy which no longer existed. Their spending programmes were therefore erected on very shaky foundations.

Critics of this cultural or 'declinist' thesis have argued that the evidence for it is highly selective; that the whole notion of decline is an illusion; and that it has often been used as a way of justifying technocratic and authoritarian policy solutions.[8] The standpoint of this book is rather different. The cultural thesis often presents an exaggerated and misleading picture of the British economy and its performance, but its critics are sometimes in danger of asserting the contrary – that there has been no decline at all, and that all the problems dealt with as problems of decline are no more than normal problems of change and adjustment. This book analyses decline in two main ways: first as a discourse which was constituted by the particular ideas and assumptions of those participating in it; secondly as a historical process, a set of circumstances and constraints which defined the limits within which the debate proceeded.

Understanding British decline as a historical process requires analysis of the complex interplay between the decline in British power and the decline in British competitiveness. What was different about Britain's Empire compared with the great empires of the past was that it became inextricably linked with a global process of capital accumulation which resulted in the creation of an interdependent world economy and a rate of growth of population and material wealth far surpassing any levels previously achieved in human history.[9]

Britain's expansion may have been launched upon foundations that were similar to those of many previous empires, but it reached its zenith and was consolidated under very different ones. When earlier empires that arose from a self-sufficient agricultural base collapsed, the imperial state was forced back to this base, once decline had reached a certain point. That possibility disappeared for Britain during the nineteenth century. At a certain stage of its development Britain abandoned such foundations, merging its future irrevocably with the wider world economy.

All discussion of British decline must start from Britain's relationship to the world economy that was the means of Britain's rise, which was transformed in the course of that rise, and to which Britain remains tied. What has to be explained is why the most dynamic and expansionist nation in modern European history, the organiser of the largest world empire, the pioneer of industrialisation, and the country renowned above all others for continuity of its institutions and the political skill of its ruling class, should have lost out during the last thirty years in competition with Germany, France, and Japan. The eclipse of British military power by the United States and Russia was widely forecast as early as the 1840s because of the much greater human and physical resources they could command. What was not anticipated was the relative inability of the British *economy* to maintain its dynamism and compete with its rivals.

A central problem for British historiography in the twentieth century has been why the British economy proved so weak and why political attempts to overcome this weakness were not successful. The unevenness of the development of different economies and regions within the world economy has been a noted feature of the modern era. Recognition of backwardness has acted as a spur for states to modernise themselves and catch up with the economic leaders. According to this argument the disappearance of Britain's lead over its competitors was entirely predictable. What is not so easily explained is the feebleness of the British response. Charles Feinstein has argued that 'the leader who falls behind will ultimately respond to the changed circumstances and in particular to the increased threat to markets and jobs created by the formerly backward economies.'[10] Yet although Britain had clearly lost its economic leadership to the United States by 1914, and had fallen behind other competitors in the 1950s and 1960s the response was a very long time in coming.

One explanation is that for most of the period of its decline the British state has proved able to negotiate a gradual descent. At no point did failing power threaten a major rupture in institutional continuity or an irreversible collapse of British prosperity. The decline in the world power of the British state occurred in stages. The continuing expansion of the British economy helped to compensate for that decline and to limit its impact. The British state used its considerable political, ideological, economic and financial resources, which had been accumulated during the period of British dominance of the world economy, to buy time, to stave off challenges and to delay adjustments. When crises shook the world economy, the British state and the British economy were strong enough to ride them out. But this success reduced the will to tackle many internal weaknesses which gradually became more significant as Britain's relative position deteriorated.

During the world economic downturn in the 1970s, the relative weakness of the British economy, tolerated for so long, became increasingly unsupportable, and brought growing political and social tensions. The world recession changed the political climate by threatening to turn relative decline into absolute decline. Some observers argued that there was no general crisis of capitalism, only a crisis of capitalism in Britain. But general crises always take the form of national crises, and their impact is uneven depending on the ability of each state to protect itself, drawing on whatever resources and strengths it has. The consequences of a recession like the consequences of a boom are unevenly distributed because the world economy is an interdependent economic system rather than a group of self-contained national economies. To analyse the economic policy of a nation-state like Britain it is important to place Britain in the context of the wider world system.

In the 1970s Britain came to be widely perceived as a weak link among the leading economic powers. The worries about the balance of payments, inflation, and public spending were symptoms of wider anxieties about Britain's economic future, because of the apparently unstoppable tide of imports and the inability of so many sectors of British industry to compete. The extent of the shakeout which took place in the 1970s and 1980s prompted many people to ask how much further the contraction could go. What would be the end of it? A Britain with no industry at all? Unemployment and destitution of an unimaginable scale? Exports insufficient even to pay for the imports needed to feed the population? The fears were not new. Joseph Chamberlain, Radical, Imperialist, and Tariff Reformer, declared in 1903:[11]

> Agriculture, as the greatest of all trades and industries of this country, has been practically destroyed. Sugar has gone; silk has gone; iron is threatened; wool is threatened; cotton will go! How long are you going to stand it?

Many found it difficult to comprehend how a nation that was on the winning side in two world wars could lose the peace and succumb to the commercial challenge of rivals defeated on the battlefield. How could a nation that showed such unity in the Second World War, and was so long renowned for its traditions of civility and consensus, appear so disunited and racked by conflict, envy, and cynicism in the 1960s and 1970s? Why was Britain, unable to achieve an economic miracle in the 1950s, still unable to achieve one in the 1960s when so many faults had been identified and so many remedies proposed, and when, for a time, all parties and all major interests subscribed to growth and a strategy for modernising the British economy?

What we call decline is a product of political perception and definition. The ways in which it is explained are often not independent of the political remedies proposed to deal with it. This book is about the various ways in which decline has been defined and explained, and the political strategies that have emerged to tackle it. It offers an account of Britain's historical development not as a unique self-contained experience but as the interaction between the external expansion of the state and the internal formation of its principal classes and institutions. Only if Britain is viewed as part of the world economic and political system can the national aspects of British development be properly located. Without a world system perspective the real 'peculiarities' of British development are lost to view.[12]

This book is divided into three parts. Part I explores the concept of decline, examines how it might be measured, and discusses how it has been perceived in the major intellectual debates. Part II discusses the specific historical roots of decline; the history of the British state and the dominant patterns of external expansion and internal compromise; and the history of the working class.

Part III explores three perspectives – market, state, and class – which have dominated debates on decline and which have helped to form political strategies and programmes for overcoming it. Chapter 4 considers the modernisation programmes of the 1960s and 1970s. Chapters 5 and 6 look at the new strategies which emerged in the 1970s in response to the apparent failure of modernisation, the free market strategy of the right and the alternative economic strategy of the left.

The term 'strategy' is here used to mean a discourse on economic policy and political action which is unified and bounded by certain shared assumptions about the desirable relationship between the state and the economy. It identifies long-term objectives and means of achieving them. A strategy in this sense is different from the political programme of a particular party, although it may influence it.

The final chapter assesses whether the Thatcher era is best understood as the long-awaited political response which restructured the economy and brought the decline to an end, or as merely the latest episode in that decline.

PART 1

DECLINE

1

The hundred years' decline

This nation has to be mobilised and rallied for a tremendous effort . . . If that effort is not made we may soon come to crisis, to a real crisis. I do not fear that so much, for this reason, that in a crisis this nation is always at its best. This people knows how to handle a crisis, it cools their heads and steels their nerves. What I fear much more than a sudden crisis is a long, slow, crumbling through the years until we sink to the level of a Spain, a gradual paralysis, beneath which all the vigour and energy of this country will succumb. That is a far more dangerous thing and far more likely to happen unless some effort is made.

Oswald Mosley[1]

To speak of British decline is to isolate a national economy and a state that are British and are declining. But decline should not be confused with decay, nor with a process of internal decomposition. During its rise to world power the British state abandoned self-sufficiency and became dependent for its survival on the wider world economy. British decline is not therefore primarily an internal question of morals and customs, but depends on perceiving the British state and national economy within the world political and economic order, which Britain helped to construct and of which the British economy remains an integral part. Britain's successes and failures are accordingly measured against the successes and failures of other states in the world system, and much of the writing on decline is a deliberate attempt to identify what is peculiar to British experience.

1.1 Britain and the world economy

This world economy into which Britain was integrated has passed through a number of stages in its development. During the long mercantilist period which began in the fifteenth century, a world market arose based upon colonies, sea power and a protected trade in primary commodities and slaves. It was followed in the nineteenth century by a brief era of free trade, which was made possible by the development of capitalist industry in Britain. It encouraged a division of labour between different parts of the world economy based on the exchange of manufactured goods for primary products. Britain exploited its advantage as the first industrial nation to the full by throwing open its markets and attempting to persuade or force all other states to do the same. Agriculture was sacrificed for the greater gains that flowed from specialising in manufactures. The history of the world economy was increasingly determined by the worldwide accumulation of capital. This involved a progressive widening and deepening of the world division of labour. The world market embraced more and more countries and the pressures of competitive accumulation enforced ever greater degrees of specialisation and ever greater interdependence of production. The emergence of this new world economy is the major historical event of modern times.

The free-trade period was succeeded by a national protectionist period after 1880, marked by intense commercial and strategic rivalry between the great powers, strong pressures towards the formation of blocs, and two world wars. After 1945 the world economy was split into two major competing blocs which enjoyed considerable internal unity. The capitalist bloc was unified under American leadership and competition between national economies and nation-states receded as the leading sectors of industry began to be organised transnationally and pressures developed for the convertibility of currencies and the reduction of tariff barriers. A further development of the division of labour became evident in the new pattern of trade which emerged. Trade between the advanced industrial countries grew fastest during the long post-war boom, and soon became more important than the complementary trade between the producers of manufactures and the producers of food and raw materials.[2] It was evident also in the changing character of the capitalist enterprise. The main agent of capital accumulation in the early industrial revolution had been the businesses based upon small work-shops and single factories. Competitive accumulation had seen these give way in sector after sector, first to multi-divisional and multi-product national firms, and then to international companies. These now operated globally, were highly diversified, and could deploy huge financial and productive resources.[3] Dominating the world economy, they were no longer tied to a single national base. National economies and nation-states still remained, but their import-ance and their independence were qualified by this new interpenetration of the production empires of capital.

With the collapse of communism in eastern Europe and the Soviet Union between 1989 and 1991, and the rapid develop-ment of capitalism in China a new period of development of the world economy has commenced. The world economy has been reunified, and there are strong pressures towards the re-establishment of global free trade and the extension of global finance and global production. At the same time there are pressures towards the formation of regional identities and institutions, particularly in Europe and North America. Both these tendencies are reducing the former scope and importance of the nation-state as a decision-making centre.

British decline both as a historical process and as a political discourse belong to the national protectionist period of world economic development. In the years since 1880 three main phases of decline can be identified, although it is important to recognise that since 'decline' depends upon political perception the 'hundred years decline' means not that there has been a continuous downward trend in British economic performance and military power, but that decline has been a key preoccupation of the political elite for one hundred years.

The first phase of decline understood in this sense was between 1880 and 1914 when Britain first suffered major competition from industrial rivals, and shortcomings in British industry began to be noticed. A major but unsuccessful challenge to the ruling free-trade policy of the British state was mounted by Joseph Chamberlain and the Social Imperialists. The second phase – between the two world wars – saw a much weakened Britain attempting and failing to rebuild its world power, but managing to avoid the worst effects of the world slump of the 1930s. The internal challenge of the Labour movement was contained for the moment, and the lesser challenge of Fascism resisted. In the third phase after 1945 Britain, now subordinate financially and militarily to the United States, and shorn of a substantial part of its accumulated wealth, was forced to withdraw from its empire, and failed to grow or invest at the same rate as other capitalist national economies during the long post-war boom. As a result its position grew steadily more vulnerable.

The period of decline had seen Britain change from a position of world leadership and dominance to one of weakness and dependence, its fortunes increasingly linked to a world economic system over which the British state could exert less and less control. For a long time the seriousness of Britain's position was concealed by the prosperity and buoyancy of the post-war western economy. But with the downturn in the 1970s a new phase opened both in the history of the world economy and in Britain's decline. Britain entered it with heavy burdens and facing daunting tasks.

1.2 The long boom

A major world recession erupted in 1974–5. It marked the decisive end of the longest and most rapid period of continuous expansion world capitalism has ever enjoyed, and opened a period of much more uncertain and uneven economic progress. Because the boom was so prolonged and so general there is a paradox in speaking of British 'decline' since 1945, since in absolute terms the British economy had never been so prosperous, nor had it ever expanded so fast.[4] This boom was unannounced and largely unexpected, but once it was properly under way many came to believe it could be a boom without end. The general downturn that began at the end of 1973 was not widely accepted at first as the turning point it has since been acknowledged to be.[5]

The widespread predictions made after 1945 of an early return to the slow growth, stagnant demand and high unemployment of the 1930s proved false because of major changes which the world war had brought about. It created a new set of investment opportunities, new social relations between capital and labour, and new political relations between the leading capitalist states, which helped to create for almost twenty-five years a most favourable environment for accumulation. These conditions were fortuitous in the sense that no central authority designed them or planned them, although their coming into being had always been possible, since there was never any doubt that there was great scope for a further development of the productive forces under capitalism. Capitalist development has never proceeded smoothly but always unevenly, in great uncontrollable spurts followed by equally uncontrollable periods of slump and stagnation.

As an economic system capitalism has always been marked by instability, which arises principally from its own internal compulsion to expand. Capital accumulation is an immensely powerful mode of production, yet it has become increasingly fragile. It has expanded material wealth far more than any previous mode of production, and has made possible the construction of a world economy that is based not just on trade but upon a world division and specialisation of labour. On both counts it marks a crucial watershed in human history. In its quest for profits capital seeks to overcome all obstacles in the path of its accumulation. That is why competitive capital accumulation between individual enterprises has no resting place short of the complete automation of the production process and the industrialisation of the whole world. But its progress towards these limits has been interrupted by great crises of over-production, because the accumulation of capital constantly tends to race ahead of the conditions that can sustain it. Capitalism as a world system has suffered twenty such general crises of over-production since 1825.[6] They have become progressively more severe, because the scale of production and degree of interdependence have grown during every period of expansion.[7]

The great post-war expansion that finally ended in 1973

rested on conditions that released once more the springs of capitalist advance.[8] A wide range of new investment opportunities emerged, particularly in cars, electronics, and construction, which boosted average profitability in a wide band of industrial sectors. There was a plentiful supply of labour, and in many countries, particularly in those which had suffered Fascist rule, labour was weakly organised. There were also many new supplies of labour as yet untapped in agriculture, amongst women, and in less developed regions of the world economy, and there were abundant and cheap supplies of energy and raw materials. Political regimes were now quite ready to extend government involvement in the economy and to remove many costs and insecurities from the shoulders of individual enterprises.[9]

But there was another condition which was crucial. Despite the fact that capitalism was a world economic system with a tendency to expand to its limit, the world economy has always been fragmented by the existence of national economies and nation states. Capital accumulation was still organised within territorial units, and each government claimed sovereignty over its own economy, the right to pursue and support the economic interests of its own industries, and the capacity to maintain the minimal conditions for internal capital accumulation: in particular, a national economic market, effective laws on property, contract and labour, a stable currency, and the ability to raise taxes. Responsibility for maintaining the conditions for the functioning of the world market was accepted by no one. Yet from the beginning the prosperity of capitalist economies depended crucially on the delicate networks of the world economy, its markets and its division of labour, and on the free flow of goods, capital, and labour.[10]

In the history of world capitalism this responsibility has been borne by two states, Britain and the United States, because each for a time was the unchallenged industrial and financial centre of the world economy. The United States after 1945 took over the role Britain had been performing with increasing difficulty, and set out to rebuild the shattered international monetary system and trading network of the capitalist world, as well as to unify it politically and militarily against the Soviet Union. The stability of the western world and the pace of its economic advance owed much to the challenged leadership and domination of the United States which was able as a result to impose its own terms and its own solutions.[11]

The factories which made the boom possible and sustained it eventually became exhausted. The intensive exploitation of the new investment opportunities eventually led to their exhaustion. New technological systems of the same scope which might form the leading sectors of a future expansion were not available. Supplies of cheap labour that are easily or safely available had been used up, and in the advanced western states the working class had become highly organised and highly paid. State expenditure and state involvement in the economy had been pushed to the point where they created a fiscal crisis of expenditures outrunning revenues, and accelerating inflation. Finally, the very success of the United States in creating the conditions in the world economy for the boom led directly to the recovery of rivals, particularly Germany and Japan, and the closing of the productivity gap between them and the United States. The levels of American foreign investment and overseas military spending were only supportable indefinitely so long as the allies of the United States agreed to finance them. Their refusal caused the downfall of the dollar and the eventual disintegration in 1971 of the international monetary system which the Americans had designed and upheld after the war.[12] It signalled the end of a phase of development of world capitalism which the recession in 1974–6 confirmed.

If capitalism is seen as a world system as well as a collection of national economies, the division between the leading group of capitalist states and the rest of the world economy is what is most striking. The relative strengths and weaknesses of the members of the leading group are problems of much smaller magnitude than the gulf between the developed and the underdeveloped. It is important to remember this throughout the discussion in this book. Amidst all the talk of British decline it is sometimes possible to forget that Britain remains one of the wealthiest countries in the world.

When Britain is placed in the context of the world economy, its apparently peculiar and special problems often lose their uniqueness and are seen to be problems shared by all the leading capitalist states. Periods of boom and periods of recessions affect all economies. So do changes in prices of primary commodities and energy. There are significant differences between states, but these arise within a context of common institutions and common structures, such as the increasing scale of industrial enterprises; the application of science to production; the widening of the market to embrace all occupations, social groups and nations; the great expansion of the state; the growth of trade unions and the establishment of mass democracy. These have generated many common problems, of which the most important in recent years has been to find ways to fund state expenditures, which have risen inexorably and apparently irreversibly in every state, and at the same time to contain the inflation which has become since the war a permanent feature of western capitalist economies.[13] The key to both has long been seen as engineering a faster rate of growth, because it effortlessly generates higher tax revenues and permits demands to be more easily reconciled with resources at lower levels of inflation. But it is precisely growth that can no longer be relied upon or stimulated in the old ways. In the 1970s Britain's leisurely relative decline in economic performance threatened to turn into something potentially much more serious.

1.3 The measurement of decline

British decline can only be understood, and in some sense only perceived, when it is related to the world economy which Britain once dominated and to which it has remained chained long after its dominance has passed away. The British have little to learn about uneven development in the world economy, although they have been more used to finding the advantages rather than the disadvantages stacked in their favour. Since they were the first nation to develop modern industry and to embrace most whole-heartedly the new division of labour it made possible, with all its consequences for social structure, the British established a marked lead over other states, even those like France which had initially a larger population, a more extensive land area, and greater resources. Marx argued in a famous passage that 'the country that is more developed industrially only shows to the less developed the image of its own future'. He had England in mind, and it was the British model of development that countries like Germany strove to emulate and to surpass. The history of capitalism as a world economic and political system has involved not simply relentless competition between capitalist enterprises in their drive for high and secure profits. It has also increasingly involved competition between states. Nations have organised themselves to catch up with those states that have forged ahead, and nationalism has become an ideology for galvanising and reorganising societies to take advantage of the opportunities for military power and material wealth that industrialisation and the world economy have created. Once one country had industrialised and opened up a significant lead, all others were gradually drawn in to the race, for it became clear that catching up and keeping abreast was the price of any kind of national independence; states that could not, or would not, fell prey to imperialist penetration by the leading capitalist powers. Non-development came to mean underdevelopment and the incorporation of all such territories into the orbit of the dominant capitalist economies in ways that benefited those economies. The organisation of strong national state power in a given territory came to seem a necessary condition for ensuring an escape from underdevelopment and backwardness.[14]

The steady slide of the British economy, from a position of commanding superiority to a condition where some observers began to speculate whether Britain could be the first developed capitalist economy to become underdeveloped, prompts obvious questions. Why have the British been unable to organise a recovery? Why has there been no political reorganisation capable of enabling Britain, once it had fallen behind, to catch up? Why has the decline been so remorseless? Where is British nationalism? The decline has now been proceeding for a hundred years, half the period that industrial capitalism has existed in Britain. The panic that swept the British press and British ruling circles at the turn of the century about the rise of German and American industry, produced a stream of arguments and complaints very similar to those of the 1960s and 1970s.[15] British industry was technologically backward, uninterested in science, and staffed by mediocre managers; the scale of production was too small, and the amount of technical education inadequate. The British had become lazy, eager to consume, reluctant to work, and resistant to innovation. Fuelled by such books as E. M. Williams, *Made in Germany* (1896), A. Williamson, *British Industries and Foreign Competition* (1894) and F. A. Mackenzie, *American Invaders* (1902), as well as a vigorous campaign in the imperialist and protectionist press, widespread alarm about the penetration of foreign competition and its threat to British economic and ultimately political supremacy began to be voiced. A headline in the *Daily Mail* in 1900 summed up a characteristic theme: 'American Furniture in England. A further indictment of the trade unions'. Explanations for the growing British failure to match foreign competition began to dwell less on the supposed shoddiness of American and German goods and the subsidies that were held to make them cheap, and more on the short-comings in British social organisation. As the *Daily Mail* put it in 1901:

> At the risk of being thought unpatriotic this journal has persistently . . . called attention to the numberless blows administered to our commercial supremacy, chiefly by reason of the superior education methods and strenuous life of the American and the German.[16]

Such diagnoses of why Britain has fallen behind have prompted all manner of remedies. But the problem goes deeper than incorrect or insufficient policies. Whenever any particular feature of the British economy or British state is isolated and proclaimed to be the factor holding back the economy from performing more successfully, contrary evidence has never been long in coming to throw doubt on its importance.

Awareness of the nation's relative economic decline has come to dominate contemporary British politics. According to Martin Wiener 'the leading problem of modern British history is the explanation of economic decline'.[17] There is a growing realisation of the scale of the problem and the depth of the political failure to do anything about it. In his powerful polemic against the priorities of post-war economic policy Sidney Pollard writes:

> There is in operation . . . a law of the deterioration of British economic policies. Like the 'average' Russian harvest (worse than last year's, better than next year's) every government seems to have done more damage and to have succeeded in fewer things than the preceding one.[18]

The extent of the slide has been remarkable. From being the leading economy in western Europe in 1950 Britain had declined by 1980 to be one of the poorest. British output and productivity were little better than half the levels in comparable economies. The size of the gap that has opened in such a short time is astonishing. Pollard estimated in 1982 that if present trends continued, Britain would be overtaken by Greece, Portugal and Spain, and that the British economy would not reach the *present* level of national income enjoyed by the Federal Republic of Germany until 2051. The depreciation of sterling (against the dollar it has fallen from $4.03 after the war and stood at $1.56 in September 1989) reflects the relative impoverishment of the British economy.[19]

What is even more astonishing, however, is that a problem which received such sustained attention since the end of the 1950s and which produced so many new policies to remedy it should have proved so resistant to all the cures that were attempted. The problems appeared more intractable at the beginning of the 1980s than they were in the 1960s. Between 1979 and 1981 the economy was no longer merely in relative decline but actually began contracting. On some estimates unemployment reached 20 per cent of the labour force,[20] manufacturing output shrank to the levels of the mid-1960s and the public finances were under severe strain.

But has Britain actually declined? Is the decline real? Here there is an immediate paradox. The decline in Britain's world status and world power has been accompanied not by falling but by rising material wealth. The mass of British people were considerably better off in 1973 when Britain finally entered the EEC, as one of its poorer members, than they had been in 1900 when British power and economic superiority, though challenged, were still pre-eminent. Moreover, the performance of the British economy has steadily improved as the century has gone on. The annual rate of growth increased from 1 per cent between 1900 and 1913 to 2.3 per cent between 1922 and 1938 to 3.2 per cent between 1957 and 1965. The annual productivity increase in the same three periods was 0 per cent, 1.1 per cent and 2.4 per cent.[21] The period of loudest clamour about British decline actually turns out to be the period when the British economy has grown faster than at any time since 1870.

Is this decline? What has to be remembered are the different senses which are entangled in the word. Britain's decline can be most clearly perceived in the absolute decline of British dominance of the world economy – military, financial, and industrial. Britain's leading role was heavily qualified after the First World War. After the Second World War Britain, although still a world power, was no longer a major one, and its position dwindled still further as it shed its Empire and attempted to negotiate entry into the EEC. Decline as a process in British politics refers first to this loss of world power, the painful transition to a greatly reduced role and a greatly diminished capacity, and the corresponding alteration in national perspectives which had to result. This was an absolute decline because it involved an irreversible demotion to Britain from super-power status.

The second process involved in Britain's decline is not an absolute decline at all, but the relative economic decline that is apparent when British national economic performance is compared with that of its major industrial rivals, particularly the other states in the EEC, and Japan. Such a relative decline has been quite compatible with an absolute rise in production and productivity, whilst the world economy was growing and not stagnating. The idea of a relative decline is one of those notions which, like the rotation of the earth round the sun, appears to contradict common sense. As one of Shaw's practical men says of Copernicus: 'Can't the fellow use his eyes?'[22] The common experience has been not of declining but of rising living standards.

Certainly all measurements of decline must be treated with caution. There are great difficulties in measuring a national economy as though it were a single self-contained unit in the world economy. It is actually made up of a multitude of activities and relationships, many of them reaching beyond the arbitrary frontiers of the national territory. Within a national economy there is certain to be uneven development and an imbalance between different regions, different sectors, and different firms. Many individual companies and even whole regions can be prospering even whilst the economy as a whole is stagnating. Comparisons between national economies are notoriously difficult, since many indicators of performance, starting with GNP itself, can only be compared by assuming that the prevailing exchange rate between the two currencies is a reliable guide for measuring the size of one country's output in terms of the other. Similarly national income figures always leave out many things that are not traded on the market, so have no price, but can be decisive for living standards. One country might appear materially poorer but still be reckoned to enjoy a higher standard of living.[23]

But so long as the world economy contains within it separate territorial jurisdictions, comparisons between national economies will continue to be made. Despite all the qualifications, the relative decline of the British economy during the long boom, and the reason for its perilous condition after 1973 do stand out. The striking fact is not that there was no growth in the British economy, but that its rate of growth was less than that of the most technologically advanced economy, the United States. Whereas Germany, Japan and France all significantly closed the technological gap between themselves and the United States, Britain failed to do so. If anything the gap grew greater.[24]

The annual rate of growth of the British economy both in terms of output and output per head were significantly below all other major capitalist countries in the second decade of the long boom (see Table 1.1). Such a performance naturally had its effect upon the international growth league. In terms of Gross Domestic Product per head Britain slipped from ninth in 1961 to thirteenth in 1966 and fifteenth in 1971. By 1976 Britain was eighteenth, having fallen behind not just the

United States, Canada and Sweden, but Iceland, France, Finland, Austria, and Japan as well.[25]

Table 1.1   Rates of growth of GDP (Gross Domestic Product) 1962–72 (annual percentage rates)

	GDP	GDP *per capita*
France	4.7	5.7
West Germany	3.6	4.5
Italy	3.9	4.6
Japan	9.2	10.4
United States	3.0	4.2
United Kingdom	2.2	2.7

Source: OECD National Accounts 1961–72.

The most serious aspect of this relative decline which has often been highlighted is the erosion of the United Kingdom's position in wound manufacturing. The British share in world manufacturing output fell from 9.6 per cent in 1960 to 5.8 per cent in 1975.[26] Britain consistently failed to match the levels of productivity growth achieved in other countries (see Table 1.2). Gross Domestic Product per head in Germany in 1900 was 36 per cent below that in Britain. In 1973 it was 29 per cent higher. In Italy it was 63 per cent below Britain in 1900; by 1973 it was the same.[27] Many studies have confirmed this. The Central Policy Review Staff found that labour productivity on comparable vehicle models was 30 per cent below that in West Germany, France, and Italy.[28] Another study comparing labour productivity differences within international companies found that productivity levels in the United States and Canada were 50 per cent above those in Britain; West Germany was 27 per cent above, Italy 16 per cent above, and France 15 per cent above.[29] A major factor contributing to this has been the persistently low levels of investment in Britain, generally about half the levels of investment in manufacturing of Britain's major competitors. One study in 1978 estimated that the fixed assets per worker in manufacturing in the United Kingdom were only £7500, compared with £23 000 in West Germany and £30 000 in Japan.[30] Whereas in 1870 Britain enjoyed the highest

Table 1.2 Phases of productivity growth (GDP per man-hour), 1870–1976 (annual average compound growth rates)

	1870–1913	1913–50	1950–76
France	1.8	1.7	4.9
Germany	1.9	1.2	5.8
Italy	1.2	1.8	5.3
Japan	1.8	1.4	7.5
United States	2.1	2.5	2.3
United Kingdom	1.1	1.5	2.8

Source: A. Maddison, 'The Long Run Dynamics of Productivity Growth', in W. Beckerman (ed.), *Slow Growth in Britain* (Oxford University Press, 1979) p. 195.

Table 1.3 Shares in the value of world exports of manufactures, 1950–79 (percentages)

	1899	1929	1937	1950	1960	1970	1977	1979
United Kingdom	33.2	22.9	21.3	25.5	16.5	10.8	9.3	9.7
France	–	–	–	9.9	9.6	8.7	9.9	10.5
Germany	–	–	–	7.3	19.3	19.8	29.8	29.8
Japan	–	–	–	3.4	6.9	11.7	15.4	13.6
United States	–	–	–	27.3	21.6	18.5	15.9	15.9

Sources: London and Cambridge Economic Service, *The British Economy, Key Statistics* (London, 1970) and NIESR *Quarterly Bulletin*, May 1980.

productivity level amongst the major capitalist economies, by 1970 Britain had one of the lowest.

The failure to maintain superiority in productivity and in manufacturing has caused a steep fall in the importance of the British economy in the world economy and in its share of world trade (see Table 1.3). The significance of this table is not that the British share has declined, which might only be of arithmetical significance, but that the shares of Germany and Japan not only expanded greatly but were then maintained at a much higher level. The French share also remained constant. In terms of total trade (not just manufactures), West Germany became the second largest trading nation in the world in 1971,[31] and the first European nation to overtake Britain since trade statistics began to be collected.

The effects of all this on the British economy became increasingly sharp in the 1970s. Unemployment climbed steeply in Britain and inflation accelerated while industrial output stagnated. British performance was noticeably worse than most other major capitalist economies. Its level of unemployment was, until 1980, about average, but its record on prices and output was significantly below, as Tables 1.4, 1.5 and 1.6 show. Real take-home pay virtually stagnated also; in 1980 it had barely risen above the level it had reached by the beginning of 1974.[32]

1.4 The debates of the intellectuals

(i) The debate on policy

Decline re-emerged as a major problem for economic policy and as a major issue in political debate in the 1960s. During the past hundred years the perception of decline, both absolute decline in world power and relative economic decline, was politically important in the years before 1914 and again in the 1920s. But the context in which the problem re-emerged was very different. The displacement of Britain as

Table 1.4   Unemployment (% rate standardised according to international definitions)

	United States	Japan	France	West Germany	Italy	United Kingdom
1972	5.4	1.4	2.7	0.8	6.3	4.1
1973	4.7	1.3	2.6	0.9	6.3	3.0
1974	5.4	1.4	2.8	1.5	5.3	2.9
1975	8.3	1.9	4.1	3.6	5.8	3.9
1976	7.5	2.0	4.4	3.6	6.6	5.6
1977	6.9	2.0	4.9	3.6	7.1	6.3
1978	5.9	2.2	5.2	3.5	7.2	6.1
1979	5.7	2.1	5.9	3.1	7.7	5.8

Source: *National Institute Economic Review*, vol. 92, May 1980, table 18.

Table 1.5 Inflation (% annual changes in consumer prices for selected countries 1967–78)

	All OECD	United States	Japan	West Germany	France	United Kingdom
1967	3.1	2.8	4.0	1.4	2.7	2.5
1968	4.0	4.2	5.3	2.9	4.5	4.7
1969	4.8	5.4	5.2	1.9	6.4	5.4
1970	5.6	5.9	7.7	3.4	4.8	6.4
1971	5.3	4.3	6.1	5.3	5.5	9.4
1972	4.8	3.3	4.5	5.5	6.2	7.1
1973	7.9	6.2	11.7	6.9	7.3	9.2
1974	13.4	11.0	24.5	7.0	13.7	16.0
1975	11.4	9.1	11.8	6.0	11.8	24.2
1976	8.6	5.8	9.3	4.5	9.6	16.5
1977	8.7	6.5	8.1	3.9	9.4	15.9
1978	7.9	7.7	3.8	2.6	9.1	8.3

Source: OECD, *Economic Outlook*, July 1979.

Table 1.6 Industrial production (1975 = 100)

	OECD	EEC	United States	Japan	France	West Germany	Italy	United Kingdom
1969	88	89	94	80	85	90	87	97
1970	91	93	91	91	89	96	92	97
1971	93	95	93	94	93	97	92	97
1972	99	99	102	101	100	101	96	99
1973	109	107	110	116	107	108	105	108
1974	109	106	110	112	110	106	110	105
1975	100	100	100	100	100	100	100	100
1976	109	108	111	111	109	107	112	103
1977	113	110	117	116	110	110	112	108
1978	118	112	124	123	113	113	116	111
1979	124	117	129	133	117	119	123	115

Source: *National Institute Economic Review*, vol. 92, May 1980.

the leading world power had happened and Britain was no longer at the centre of the world economy resisting challenges to its industrial, financial and commercial leadership, but was now obliged to accommodate to the necessity of surviving within the new world economic order established by the United States.

Economic decline became an issue after the 1959 election because despite the successful reconstruction of the British economy after the war, despite the initial relative strength of the British economy compared with all other countries except the United States, Britain's economic growth was markedly slower than almost any other in Western Europe in the 1950s. This was so despite the overall buoyancy of the economy helped by the great surge of growth throughout the world economy. One of the many strange features of the most recent phase of British decline was that policy-makers first became concerned with the problem again after a decade when the British economy had performed better than at any time since before 1880. Living standards had risen, unemployment had rarely been above 1 per cent, and inflation was only 2–3 per cent per annum.[33]

The reasons for the concern about this performance (which in the inter-war years would have been hailed a remarkable success) was the much better performance that was achieved elsewhere, the awareness of the extra wealth that was being lost and the undermining of what remained of Britain's political and economic importance in the world. The anxiety about Britain's post-imperial future erupted in a flood of 'state of England' writing which investigated every British institution and ranged in attitude from bleak pessimism to enthusiastic social engineering.

The debate on economic policy was much narrower than this. There remained broad agreement on the framework and objectives of economic policy. The commitment to an open economy was the unquestioned assumption of foreign economic policy, the acceptance of the balance between public and private sectors and labour and capital shaped industrial policy, while the commitment to balance total effective demand with total resources defined the aims of stabilisation policy: full employment, stable prices, a surplus on the balance of payments, and economic growth.

The modernisation strategy of the 1960s did not question these broad commitments or the balance of power between labour and capital and the enlarged public sector on which they were founded. The policy debate centred on whether the right balance of policies was being struck. In foreign economic policy the major doubts concerned the importance given to maintaining a surplus on the balance of payments in order to fund overseas military spending and foreign investments. It was argued by a long line of critics that the financial burden of maintaining key aspects of Britain's former world role were out of all proportion to their benefits because they imposed deflation on the domestic economy and hindered expansion.[34] British policy in the 1950s and 1960s gave major priority not to maintaining full employment which would have been high regardless of what governments did[35] but to achieving a quite unnecessary balance of payments target.

Most of the economists who made this criticism of British policy argued that it would be best for this burden to be removed altogether and for Britain to give up its 'delusions of grandeur'. But many also argued that even if this were not possible it would still be preferable to devalue the pound, or float it, or borrow to finance temporary deficits, rather than deflate the domestic economy by cutting back investment in order to protect the pound. The main explanation they gave for the relatively slow growth of the British economy was the greater priority which policy-makers gave to the balance of payments rather than to economic growth.

The strength of this case has never been seriously dented. The importance which policy-makers attached to the defence of sterling and to achieving a satisfactory balance of payments is not in dispute, and it is clear from the crude trade statistics that without the massive deficit on capital account and on government account the British economy would not have suffered balance of payments problems in any of the years that sparked sterling crises in the 1950s and 1960s.[36]

Yet although this diagnosis formed so central a part of the modernisation strategy of the 1964 Labour government it was never acted upon. For many economists the failure to devalue in 1964 was the main reason for the eventual failure of the entire modernisation strategy. Other economists have pointed out that devaluation when it did come in 1967 was no panacea, nor did the removal of the balance of payments constraint in 1972 (when the pound was floated) propel the

economy into rapid and sustained growth. But the critics of
the bipartisan foreign economic policy argue that for the
twenty years during which world output, productivity, and
investment of the western capitalist economy grew more
rapidly than ever before, British governments persistently
pursued a policy which held back investment and destroyed
industrial confidence. By 1970 British productivity had fallen
behind its main rivals and British industry was seriously
under-equipped.

There were other features of the modernisation strategy,
linked very often to the overall critique of post-war foreign
economic policy. In stabilisation policy many economists
argued that the fine-tuning of demand practised by the
authorities had increased rather than moderated fluctuations
in output. There was strong condemnation of the restrictive
policies which the stop–go cycle involved and there was
considerable support for a policy of sustained expansion. The
main debate centred on whether the risk of higher inflation
which such a policy introduced was better dealt with by
creating more 'slack' in the economy or by attempting to plan
prices and incomes. In both cases the aim remained the same
– to produce a steady and sustainable expansion of demand
which would remain in balance with the growth of productive
potential. Such analyses implied that the central problem for
the British economy was its tendency to 'overheat'. This was a
direct consequence of the full employment objective and led to
continued inflationary pressure which was one factor in the
crises of financial confidence in sterling, which were only kept
in check by periodic deflation. This suggested that any policy
which could control inflation might help to avoid the necessity
of imposing deflationary measures to maintain financial
confidence. So the demand-pull/cost-push debate on inflation
and the different prescriptions associated with it became an
important subsidiary explanation of why Britain had declined,
and why sustained expansion was so difficult to achieve. If
inflation could be mastered either by an incomes policy or by
a slight increase in unemployment, then the obstacles in the
path of faster expansion would be greatly reduced.

Many economists also argued, however, that what was
wrong with post-war Keynesian stabilisation policy was that

its chief purpose was to manipulate demand, withdrawing from any attempt to plan or directly influence supply. Many advocates of modernisation in the 1960s favoured an active supplyside industrial policy. This included measures to raise investment both in new plant in particular sectors and in particular regions; measures to encourage mergers and industrial rationalisation; measures to improve the rate at which new technologies were designed, developed and introduced; and measures involving many major new public spending programmes to increase investment in the infrastructure of the economy, especially in transport, health, and education.

The argument behind such proposals was that Britain was failing to achieve faster growth because it lacked the close links between government and industry which all other successful economies had established. The French model of indicative planning was greatly favoured in the early 1960s, and it was one of the main inspirations for the National Plan with its 4 per cent per annum growth target.

The high hopes that were attached to modernisation were disappointed. The constraint of the balance of payments was not evaded, inflation was not held down either by incomes policy or higher employment, and the supply-side bottlenecks were not eliminated.[37] Wages were held down, however, public expenditure was increased faster than planned (because 4 per cent economic growth was expected) and taxation rose, while profits were severely squeezed. The main result of the various modernisation programmes appeared to be the creation of profitless prosperity; a continuing stagnation of investment, output and productivity, and increase in industrial militancy and inflationary expectations. All these consequences came to a head in the years of the Health government – the last attempt, as it proved, to achieve an expansion of the economy within the post-war framework of economic management.[38]

The inquests on the years of the successive attempts at modernisation between 1960 and 1973 took place against a background of the end of the boom and the re-emergence of world recession and much slower growth after 1973. Britain's weaknesses, accumulated but also partly disguised in the years of boom, were dramatically exposed. The debate on policy among economists became more complicated as wider divergences of opinion emerged among them.

One approach focused on foreign economic policy, arguing that it was the degree of openness of the national economy maintained by all British governments which was chiefly to blame for the failure to pursue a successful expansionist policy at home. It advocated controls on capital movements and either controls on trade or a very sizeable devaluation in order to create the external conditions necessary for internal reconstruction and growth.[39] Achieving internal growth in the economy was not regarded as a very difficult matter so long as the external constraint was removed. The openness of the British economy was regarded as the main problem not because the balance of payments or the pound still dominated domestic policy, but because twenty years of stop–go succeeded by world recession and international monetarism had left the British economy hopelessly uncompetitive – its manufacturing base threatened by rising levels of import penetration, its export of capital increasing, its level of investment and productivity well below international levels. The study has already been cited which estimated that Britain would need to spend £100 000 million to bring the level of capital equipment per worker up to the level of its main competitors.[40] On this kind of analysis the central problem was how to insulate the British economy for long enough to enable it to regain international competitiveness.

A very different approach came from those who emphasised stabilisation policy. Here the major new theory was monetarism which rejected Keynesianism as a framework for policy, particularly the idea that policy-makers should try to manipulate the total level of demand in the economy or try to strike a balance between inflation and unemployment, or the balance of payments and growth. Monetarism involved firstly a specific doctrine about the causes of inflation – it argued that there was a link between the growth of the stock of money and the rate of increase in prices in the medium term – and secondly a series of prescriptions about economic policy such as the injunction that control of inflation should be government's main policy priority, and that neither unemployment nor growth targets could be achieved by direct government action or traded for a particular inflation rate. Only when sound money had been restored could full employment and sustainable economic growth be achieved again.[41]

Monetarist economists blamed Britain's decline chiefly on the failure of governments to control inflation and the pursuit of targets for employment and growth by manipulating demand which had led periodically to unsustainable booms and accelerating inflation. The failure to control public spending was a subsidiary theme. On this reasoning it was always the acceleration of inflation in the past that made sustainable growth impossible to achieve and led to the cumulative weakening of industrial capacity and the unchecked growth of the public sector.[42] If macro-economic policy had been different and inflation controlled, the economy could have grown at a faster rate.

Despite the growing influence of monetarism in the 1970s there were still many Keynesians who argued that it was not demand management that was the problem, but the failure to sustain a permanent incomes policy. There was a sharp division of opinion among economists as to whether monetarism would work and whether any success it might have in reducing inflation was the result not of control of the money supply but of higher unemployment and the destruction of industrial capacity.[43] There was a similar debate on the effectiveness of incomes policy and whether all such policies would eventually break down.[44]

Both Keynesians and monetarists often pursued their differences into the debates within the third perspective, which gave primary emphasis to industrial policy and argued that the real shortcoming in British economic policy had been the lack of an effective supply-side policy. But there was no agreement on what an effective supply-side policy might be (particularly since those developed in the 1960s apparently yielded so little). Opinion ranged all the way from those who emphasised market rigidities and called for the curbing of union power to make labour markets work freely again, and for taxes and welfare benefits to be reduced to restore incentives to enterprise and work, to those who advocated much greater state involvement in industry to identify and encourage present and future leading secors.[45]

(ii) The historical debates

British decline has passed through several phases. It has never been a single uniform process, because the definition of the problem and the remedies for it have changed. Each phase is marked out by a particular debate about the nature of the decline. The crucial context for each debate is the world order and Britain's place within it. It is this that ties together Britain's absolute decline as a Great Power with Britain's relative decline in economic power.

There are three key debates on decline that can be identified in British politics in the last hundred years. They are best characterised by their main themes – National Efficiency, Modernisation, and Social Democracy.

National Efficiency The first debate, on national efficiency, developed between 1880 and 1914 in response to the growing challenge from Germany and the United States to the exceptional position of military and economic strength which Britain had built up during the nineteenth century. Britain seemed ill-prepared for a major military contest with its challengers. The blame was put on the shortcomings of British economic performance and the inertia of Britain's traditional liberal, *laissez-faire* policy regime. The lack of organisation and planning of British resources was cited by Social Imperialists, New Liberals, and Fabian Socialists as the basic problem that had to be remedied.[46]

The pace of advance of German and American companies in some sectors was taken as evidence that Britain was lagging behind in the development of new products and new industries, that its costs were often higher, and that its techniques of marketing and selling goods and services were backward. Recent research has indicated that British predominance was threatened directly only in a few spheres, but the spectre of Germany and the United States leapfrogging over Britain in industrial output and productivity fuelled a major political debate.

What worried the Social Imperialists were the consequences of the changing balance of economic power in the world economy for the political and military balance.

Britain was recognised to be particularly vulnerable because of its small land base and therefore limited physical and human resources of the British Isles itself compared to the much larger potential of the continental sized economies.

Britain ruled over a greater population and a greater land area than any other power in 1900, but the British Empire was a highly diverse and fragmented political entity. It compared unfavourably with the concentration of resources and territory enjoyed by both Germany and the United States. It was impossible for Britain to extend its immediate heartland, and indeed even part of that – Ireland – was seriously dis-affected.

The Social Imperialists advocated public programmes to remedy deficiencies in education, health, housing, and social security. They sought to weld the British Empire into a much more cohesive political and economic bloc. British industry would be partially safeguarded from competition by the imposition of a tariff, the proceeds of which would pay for the new spending programmes. The physical and human resources of the Empire would be much more consciously organised to promote increasing integration and common purpose. Britain's problem was that in the new era of organised capitalism only powers with access to vast physical and human resources could maintain their standing as Great Powers. If Britain could not mobilise such resources through its Empire, it seemed doomed to lose its preeminence.[47]

Modernisation The debate on modernisation emerged in the altered context of world politics that was created by the First World War and the entry of the United States on the side of Britain and France. England and Germany were severely weakened by the war while American power and influence were enormously enhanced. After 1917 it soom became clear that Britain's traditional naval predominance would never be restored, that her financial strength had been significantly undermined, and that it was no longer possible for Britain by herself to establish and maintain the conditions for a liberal world economic order. The attempt to restore the gold standard and with it pre-war prosperity proved illusory and collapsed in 1931.

What opened therefore in 1917 was a long period of ofte uneasy relationship between Britain and the United State during which British political opinion eventually becam reconciled to the United States assuming the roles whic Britain had once performed in establishing and sustaining liberal world order. Britain came to occupy a subordinat although still important place within this new order whic fully emerged in the 1940s.

The negotiated transfer of hegemony which took plac between these two Great Powers was unprecedented and b no means smooth. Britain at many points resisted America demands and fought for its own interests, and the preservatio of its Empire. The debate on Britain's relationship with th United States continued into the 1960s and the withdrawa from the last of Britain's colonies, but it was already clear b 1950 that a bipartisan consensus had emerged on th importance of the alliance with the United States as th cornerstone of British policy.[48]

Throughout this period a key theme of the domesti political debate was how Britain could modernise itself, t stay abreast of the economy that was increasingly perceived a the world leader, the United States. The need to modernis was accepted both by those who hoped to maintain Britis world status by retaining the Empire, and by those who cam to see Britain's future lying firmly within the America orbit.

The main thrust of the debate, building in part on th earlier arguments about national efficiency, was collectivis The objective was to modernise British industrial structur by changing the relationship between state and industry an the character and extent of state intervention. The deep seated social conflicts and tensions of the period between 188 and 1920 had given way to a period of greater stability. Th shape of a domestic compromise between capital and labou which laid the basis for the reforms of the 1940s had begun t emerge.[49]

The advocates of modernisation in all parties increasingl urged the adoption in Britain of the institutions and practice of Fordism, the political and industrial system pioneered i the United States, which was based on mass production an large production units and required the state to play an increased role in regulating and sustaining it.[50]

The extension of public responsibility, the growth of corporatist institutions for handling industrial relations, the acceptance of a Keynesian framework for managing the economy – none of these were accepted without considerable effort and political struggle. But the adoption of American methods of industrial relations and work organisation in many key industries proceeded quite rapidly during the 1930s. These were then consolidated by the political and legal changes of the 1940s. A full Fordist regime appeared to have emerged in Britain under the banners of collectivism, planning, and welfare.

Despite the apparent success of the British economy during the 1950s, however, evidence began to accumulate by the end of the decade that the British economy was growing much more slowly than other industrial economies. The debate on modernisation was renewed in the 1960s. The modernisation and reconstruction of the 1930s and 1940s had apparently failed to produce an economy that was internationally competitive in the new post-war international order.

This perception that Britain was still performing less well than comparable economies became a dominant issue in the 1960s and produced a great deal of diagnosis and many new policies and spending programmes aimed at remedying the deficiencies and closing the gap. But the issue was debated within the framework and assumptions that the leaderships of both main parties had accepted since at least 1945 and in some respects since the 1920s.[51]

Social Democracy The third debate, from the late 1960s up to the present, has focused on social democracy, its failures and limitations, its responsibility for decline. It too arose in a new altered context of world order, whose most important features were the challenges to American leadership of the world system, the end of the long boom in the world economy, the increasing pace of internationalisation, and the entry of Britain into the European Community.

The domestic compromise between labour and capital which had sustained the British polity for more than forty years broke down and its disappearance called into question the social democratic order that had been grafted on to Britain's old constitutional state.

The catalyst for the new debate on decline was the failure of successive governments to deliver the fruits of modernisation they had promised. The evident inability to arrest the relative economic decline did not at first harm living standards, which continued to rise, but had an increasingly severe impact on inflation and unemployment. Government authority was weakened, both main parties for a time lost support, and in the 1970s some thought democracy itself was at risk.

The debate on social democracy produced a polarisation of political argument, which included the revival of a socialist critique of British capitalism and its failings, the restatement of anti-collectivist arguments on the Right, and the emergence of a strong Centre critique of the impact of class-based politics on British economic performance.[52]

(iii) Four theses on decline

Underlying these debates on decline are four main theses: the imperial thesis, the cultural thesis, the supply-side thesis, and the democratic thesis. Each focuses on a different aspect of social structure – the world system, the cultural order, the economy, and the political system – in developing their explanation of decline. Each thesis has a number of variants corresponding to the three leading perspectives in political economy: market, state and class. The different explanations are summarised in Table 1.7.

These three perspectives provide not just explanations of decline but also assist the elaboration of programmes for reversing it. In this way they become a vital component of political strategies. Each perspective offers at least one version of each of the four central theses on decline.

Each thesis seeks to explain why the British economy has performed relatively poorly during the twentieth century. The imperial thesis lays the blame on Britain's world role, which led to an overextension of British power and the undermining of domestic economic performance. It sees decline as a result of the slowness with which Britain adjusted to its changed

Table 1.7 Theories of decline

	MARKET	STATE	CLASS
WORLD SYSTEM the imperial thesis: Britain's world role under- mined the domestic eco- nomy	legacies of empire i. lack of exposure to internatio- nal competition ii. protectionism, subsidy iii. abandonment of gold stan- dard	overextension of British state i. military ii. financial iii. foreign investment iv. misguided foreign economic policy	character of British capi- talism i. divided capitalism city/industry split ii. global capitalism
ECONOMY the supply-side thesis: state/economy relations weakened the manufactur- ing sector	economic management i. wrong macro-economic policy – Keynesianism ii. public spending public sector too large; taxes too high iii. too interventionist industrial strategy iv. trade union power	developmental state i. inadequacy of Keynesianism ii. lack of coordination between government, industry, and finance iii. poor industrial relations iv. no consistent industrial stra- tegy v. bias and size of spending on infrastructure	state/economy relations i. incomplete Fordism; unsuccessful corporat- ism; inadequate invest- ment coordination; poor industrial rela- tions ii. class stalemate
POLITY the state thesis: Britain's state was too weak to promote moderni- sation	weak state i. deficiencies of political mar- ket ii. excessive expectations iii. distributional coalitions; institutional sclerosis iv. political business cycle	weak state i. overload ii. adversary politics – lack of effectiveness – inadequate representation	weak state i. ancien regime ii. dual crisis of the state iii. exhaustion of social democracy
CULTURE the cultural thesis: Britain's political culture held back modernisation	anti-enterprise, anti-capitalist culture i. welfare dependency ii. elite culture and attitudes iii. egalitarianism	anti-industrial culture i. institutions of British Estab- lishment ii. liberal ethos	anti-modernisation culture i. aristocratic ethos ii. Labourism

status in the world and shed the burdens and attitudes and policies which the world role had left behind.

The supply-side thesis concentrates on the relative backwardness of British manufacturing, which it ascribes either to an inadequate relationship between the state and the economy or to a balance of power between the classes that has produced stalemate. Britain acquired Fordism but it was flawed and incomplete.

The state thesis shifts the focus to the institutions of the British state and why the organisation of this state makes it very difficult for British governments to carry through programmes of long-term modernisation. The state appears weak because it has proved neither effective nor representative.

Finally the cultural thesis sees the main cause of British decline in the existence of a deep-rooted anti-industrial political culture, which has created powerful resistance to modernisation and change, and perpetuated many traditionalist aspects of British society.

The Market Perspective (1) *imperial thesis*: The market version of the imperial thesis emphasises the distortions which empire and a world political role introduced into the workings of the British economy. The specific costs are seen as the retreat from free trade into imperial protection in the 1930s, the abandonment of the gold standard, and the growth of subsidy and other forms of internal protectionism, which gradually sealed off the domestic economy from international competition. A further burden was provided by the level of overseas government spending, much of it military spending, which helped to unbalance the British balance of payments, and contributed to the sterling crises and stop–go cycles of the 1950s and 1960s.[53]

(2) *supply-side thesis*: From the market perspective the failure of British governments to develop a successful supply-side policy is closely linked to the adoption of a mistaken macro-economic policy – Keynesian demand management – which raised the goals of full employment and economic growth to the same status as stable prices.

The market version of the supply-side thesis therefore starts from the monetarist and Austrian critiques of Keynesianism. The restoration of sound money is vital so that attention can be directed to the supply-side factors which affect output and productivity. Restoring sound money requires not just the replacement of Keynesian by monetarist macro-economic policies, but also a substantial reduction in public expenditure. The public sector is regarded as much too large, both in terms of spending programmes and of the size of the public enterprise sector. The number and level of programmes need reducing, to curtail government involvement in the economy and to make possible a substantial reduction in taxation.[54]

Keynesianism is linked in the market perspective with high public spending and interventionist industrial policies, which prevent markets from clearing and reduce competition by imposing controls and providing subsidies. The result is to produce a fettered market economy which performs poorly because the price mechanism is prevented from guiding economic activity. The relationship between state and economy is responsible for decline because the state is too interventionist and does not confine itself to guaranteeing and policing the market order.[55]

The market is fettered in a further way. Another version of the supply-side thesis identifies the problem at the heart of British decline in the relationship between capital and labour. From the market perspective the problem is that the trade unions are too powerful, and use their power to distort prices and to uphold restrictive practices which reduce the efficiency of production and create overmanning.[56]

(3) *state thesis*: The extension of the state beyond its proper limits has made it weak and ineffective. The stability and longevity of Britain's political institutions have produced institutional sclerosis as special interests have multiplied.[57] The way the political market works has led to continuous interference in the economic market. Some market theorists have suggested that a political business cycle has developed, through which politicians attempt to ensure re-election by manipulating the economy to create prosperity just before elections. Others have emphasised the damage to the market order caused by the generation of excessive expectations about

what governments can deliver, as a result of the competitive overbidding by the political parties.[58]

The political market is regarded as much more imperfect than economic markets. Voters lack a budget constraint and this makes them irresponsible in the way they cast their votes, since they can opt for the programme which offers them the greatest benefits without having to bear all or sometimes any of the costs. This process leads to a persistent bias towards the growth of government and interference in the workings of free markets. The state is too weak to assert a public interest, which from the market perspective is the enforcing of a market order in which general rules govern all individual exchanges, and arbitrary interventions by public bodies are minimised.

(4) *cultural thesis*: Cultural hostility to capitalism and enterprise are regarded as important factors in the decline. The source of this hostility is traced to the dominance of anti-market and collectivist ideas in key sections of the intellectual and political élite. A political culture developed which put a ·lower priority on production, incentives and enterprise, than on egalitarian redistribution, collective welfare and social solidarity. It was diffused through key institutions such as the civil service, the universities, the schools, the media, and the Labour movement. The low cultural value placed on risk-taking and profit-making acted as a persistent obstacle to creating a more dynamic economy, and perpetuated instead the development of a culture in which large numbers of individuals were encouraged to become dependent on collective provision.[59]

The State Perspective The state perspective views the process of historical change through the structures and institutions of the state.

(1)*imperial thesis*: British decline is here attributed to the overextension of British power. One version argues that there is a trade-off between economic growth, domestic consumption, and military security. States rise to be great powers by maintaining a balance between all three, but once they have achieved a position of dominance and leadership, they steadily lose the ability to maintain that balance. Most often they give greater priority to military security and domestic consumption than to economic growth, and fall victim to rising states which can afford to be more single-minded in their pursuit of economic success.[60]

There have been many explanations of Britain's relative economic decline as a consequence of the effort devoted to maintaining Britain's global role, both as a military and imperial power, and as the world's leading financial power. A higher priority was placed on keeping sterling strong and maintaining overseas military spending and foreign investment than on domestic economic reconstruction and modernisation.[61]

(2) *supply-side thesis*: A development state has failed to emerge in Britain. The contrast here is with the success of many other economies in moving beyond either a regulatory form of state or a central planning regime to an active interventionist state which promotes continual modernisation and economic growth. What has been stressed in numerous studies is the poor co-ordination between government, industry and finance in Britain compared with many other countries. British governments as a result have failed to develop either a consistent or an effective industrial strategy.[62]

They have also failed to remedy persistent British shortcomings in strategic spending on infrastructure, research and development, and training to promote modernisation and economic development. In industrial relations the lack of a developmental state has meant a persistent failure to incorporate the trade-union movement fully into national and industrial decision-making with damaging consequences in terms of macro-economic management, strikes and restrictive practices.

(3) *state thesis*: The lack of a developmental state is reflected in the character of the state in Britain, which makes it both ineffective and unrepresentative. It is ineffective because it has become overloaded through the multiplication of tasks and functions beyond its capacity to discharge them. It is unrepresentative both because the incorporation of major interests into national decision-making has never been complete, and because the simple plurality electoral system has encouraged the development of an adversary style of two-

party politics, which has created discontinuity in economic policy and frustrated the achievement of consensus.[63]

(4) *cultural thesis*: The anti-industrial political culture arises from the nature of the British Establishment, and the ethos of its institutions, particularly the public schools, the old universities, the civil service, the Monarchy, and the aristocracy. There is an orientation towards commerce and finance but not towards industry. This is reflected in the low status accorded industry and engineering in comparison with the professions.

In sharp contrast to the market perspective the low value placed on economic growth and modernisation reflects the persistence of a liberal ethos which accords a limited role for the state in the management of industrial modernisation.[64] The ambivalence of the British political élite to economic growth meant that the preservation of the values, status, and lifestyle of the British Establishment tended to be given higher priority.[65]

The Class Perspective The class perspective makes class organisation of the economy and society the key factor in explaining historical and political development.

(1) *imperial thesis*: Class versions of the imperial thesis have emphasised how the character of British economic development imbued British capital with a strong international orientation. There has been dispute over whether this reflects the interests of all the leading sections of British capital or whether it reflects the long-term hegemony exercised by the financial sector in Britain over manufacturing industry.[66]

The degree of institutional autonomy enjoyed by the financial sector in Britain has always been exceptional and predates Britain's industrial predominance in the nineteenth century. It reflects a much older feature of the relationship of the British economy to the world economy, the British role as a financial and commercial intermediary in world trade. The priority given to this role by British governments made British imperialism predominantly a free-trade imperialism, and entailed the subordination of domestic interests or their incorporation into British external expansion.

(2) *supply-side thesis*: Britain's weak manufacturing sector is an aspect of Britain's failure to develop a successful Fordist regime of accumulation. Those countries that did, created a variety of institutional means, including a developmental state, to establish close relations between the state, industrial companies, the banks, and the trade unions. Britain had some aspects necessary for a successful Fordism, such as Keynesian demand management, but its supply-side policies were very inadequate, and showed in poor industrial performance and poor industrial relations.[67]

A different class version of the supply-side thesis focuses not on the regime of accumulation but on the balance of power between classes. The cause of decline is class stalemate. The working class in Britain has achieved sufficient defensive strength to frustrate the desire of management to modernise plants and reduce manning levels. This argument echoes the analysis from a market perspective of the effects of trade-union power, but the two perspectives diverge not only over the remedy for this situation but over who was to blame for it.[68]

(3) *state thesis*: The inability of the British state to carry through modernisation is traced to its historical origins, and to the absence from British history since the twentieth century of the thoroughgoing reconstruction of the state which all other major capitalist countries experienced either as a result of revolution or invasion. The British *ancien régime* perpetuated a set of institutions and a set of élites which left British governments without the organisational means to carry through modernisation. Instead there was a consensus throughout the British state against modernisation.[69]

Other class analyses of the British state have put less emphasis on its pre-modern character, but have focused rather on its development in the last hundred years. Between 1880 and 1930 the liberal state was engulfed by a series of major crises. The solutions and compromises that were worked out to these crises moved the state some way towards social democracy, but never led to a major reconstruction. Social democracy as a result remained incomplete; corporatism was not successfully established nor was a developmental state.[70] This led in due course to a dual crisis, a crisis of the representative institutions of the state – the parties and parliament – which no longer ensured representation; and a crisis of the corporatist institutions of the state, because the national economic policy was not achieving results.[71]

(4) *cultural thesis*: The character of British capitalism and the British state are reflected in the political culture. The aristocratic ethos of the British Establishment and the Labourist ethos of the working class combine to reinforce the consensus against modernisation. The weakness of manufacturing in relation to finance is reflected in the cultural subordination of the former, and its failure to articulate its own programme and values. Culture is not a prime mover in the class perspective, but it acts as a very effective cement of an order which is incapable of reforming itself.[72]

1.5 Conclusion

The intellectual debates on Britain's decline have produced no agreement on either causes or remedies. The problems are intractable and resistant to conventional policy-making. But the debates have succeeded in highlighting the special historical features which mark British capitalism out from more successful national capitalisms elsewhere. There is firstly the international role of the British state and the way in which the national economy is integrated into the world economy; secondly the nature of the British state and its institutional relationships with the economy and society; thirdly the formation of the British working class and the manner and extent of its incorporation into British society. These three problems form the subject matter of Chapters 2 and 3.

Numerous studies have shown how decline cannot be reduced to technical issues and remedies. There is considerable agreement that Britain's problems lie in what are known as 'supply-side factors'. The Brookings report on the British economy at the end of the 1970s, a follow-up to their earlier report some twelve years before, rejected all conventional technical explanations which point to shortcomings in policy, and concluded sorrowfully that 'Britain's economic malaise stems largely from its productivity problem whose origins lie deep in the social system'.[73] It is deep into that social system and particularly into its external relations that we must now go.

institutional relationships with the economy and society; thirdly the formation of the British working class and the manner and extent of its incorporation into British society. These three problems form the subject matter of Chapters 2 and 3.

Numerous studies have shown how decline cannot be reduced to technical issues and remedies. There is considerable agreement that Britain's problems lie in what are known as 'supply-side factors'. The Brookings report on the British economy at the end of the 1970s, a follow-up to their earlier report some twelve years before, rejected all conventional technical explanations which point to shortcomings in policy, and concluded sorrowfully that 'Britain's economic malaise stems largely from its productivity problem whose origins lie deep in the social system'.[73] It is deep into that social system and particularly into its external relations that we must now go.

PART II

HISTORY

2
The world island

We can with safety make one prophecy: whatever the outcome of this war, the British Empire is at an end. It has been mortally wounded. The future of the British people is to die of hunger and tuberculosis on their cursed island.

Adolf Hitler[1]

Britain's decline can only be understood, indeed only exists, in relation to the world economic system of which Britain is a part. This chapter considers the history of the expansion of the British state, and the consequences for Britain's subsequent progress of the relatively slender base of population and resources upon which its massive world empire was established. All understanding begins here, for this is the feature that most clearly marks Britain off from other states.

2.1 The expansion of England

The expansion of England was a twofold process. There was first the expansion within the territorial limits of the British Isles, which created a unified English state. This state eventually succeeded in extending its control over all parts of the British Isles by military conquest of Wales and Ireland and unification with Scotland. The English state became Great Britain in 1707 and the United Kingdom in 1801.[2] But even while this process was being completed it was overshadowed by the external expansion of this state, the creation of a Greater Britain beyond the British Isles in the New World. The ability to seize opportunities that the emerging world economy was creating was greatly improved by the organisation of a strong national state secure in its own territory.

What is so striking about the process of English expansion within the British isles is how a state was eventually formed which, though composed of several nations, came to enjoy exceptional internal unity and cohesion. The major divisions which have so undermined the legitimacy of other states, divisions between regions, between religious groups, between races and between nationalities, have not been absent in Britain but have certainly been less important. One major reason for this lies in the successful organisation of a strong and centralised public power by the Yorkist Kings, and subsequently by the Tudors in the sixteenth century, which helped to moderate and contain internal conflicts. The subordination of nobility and then church to the royal authority, following the Wars of the Roses and the English Reformation, removed two major obstacles to the authority of the state and to its ability to frame laws and enforce them throughout its territory. It also increased its capacity to defend and extend that territory. In the sixteenth century the English state strove to consolidate its hold on Wales and Ireland, principally because the territorial integrity of England was seen to require English control of all parts of the British Isles, to deny possible bases for internal or external challenges.

The same considerations governed the attitude of the English towards the Scots. Even after the Union of the Crowns in 1603 Scotland remained a separate state, potentially threatening to England, not only because of the possibility that the Scots might act independently and in conflict with English interests, but also because in any such conflict Scotland might well ally with a foreign power against England. This possibility was ended by the Act of Union in 1707, which united the two Parliaments. It allowed the Scots to retain many of their own institutions, including their legal system, their church and their schools, and restored complete free trade and access by the Scots to the developing English commercial Empire. Henceforward the expansion of the new state was to be directed from a single centre, and the Parliament at Westminster became the central symbol and institution for maintaining its legitimacy.

One factor which greatly aided the successful unification of Wales and Scotland with England was the dominance of the English nation, the absence of clear racial or ethnic differences, and the overwhelming dominance of Protestantism. In terms of population and resources the English far outweighed the other nations, and English institutions, English agriculture and English industry were generally more developed. The rapid expansion of the English state abroad after 1650, and the industrialisation of its economy at home, certainly aided the integration of the three nations into a cohesive multinational state, whose centre was in London. All three nations developed along similar lines in the nineteenth century. By 1900 all had major centres of industry, all had a similar distribution of their working population between industry and agriculture, and a similar balance between the cities and the country. All were integrated into the same unified national market and the extended world market. All had in consequence a similar level of income per head and a similar rate of economic growth.[3]

The great exception to this harmonious pattern of development was Ireland, which was never assimilated, never integrated, and which prevented the kingdom ever being truly united. The history of relations between Ireland and the rest of Britain highlights how accidental and fortunate the smooth integration of the rest of the United Kingdom actually was.[4] Ireland was treated as a colony from the beginning, its military conquest being completed under the Tudors. Determined efforts were made to establish settlers on the same lines as the settlements in the New World. The settlers were alien in culture and in religion, which helped intensify the division between Ireland and Britain. The seventeenth-century civil war and the settlement of 1688, while laying the foundations for the rise of Great Britain, also prepared the way for the eventual separation of Ireland. The backing given by the Catholic Irish for Charles I and James II led to the reconquest of the country first by Cromwell and then by William III. Huge confiscations of land were made and an Anglo-Irish Protestant land-owning class established to rule over the Catholic peasantry. Ireland was denied free trade with the rest of Britain and all competition from Irish industry and Irish agriculture was prevented. As a result Ireland never achieved the same kind of industrial and social development as the rest of the United Kingdom, except in the area around Belfast where Protestant settlers were particularly concentrated. The bulk of Ireland remained poor and backward, frequently devastated by famines and milked by the huge annual tribute in rents which flowed across the Irish Sea, while suffering enormous emigration both to Britain and the United States.[5] It is hardly surprising that Ireland was the country that saw the first sustained nationalist revolt against British imperial rule since the rebellion of the American colonists.

What was so significant about the Irish problem in the nineteenth century was the complete inability of the governing class in Britain to handle it. So explosive did the Home Rule issue become in British politics that it produced some major political realignments,[6] and so deep a split within the governing class that it almost ended in open defiance of the authority of the Westminster government by sections of the army and the Unionist party. Only the First World War averted what could have been a major rupture in British constitutional development.[7] The history of the Irish problem shows how great an advantage constitutional legitimacy gave the British state, because it placed the British state upon a foundation so much more secure than many others, and made internal politics so much more manageable. It was not a matter of the innate skill of the governing class that Britain had so tranquil a development. That was due far more to certain structural features of the British position which made possible the integration of Wales, Scotland and England and which were lacking in the case of Ireland. Most important of all was the opportunity of sharing and participating in the overseas expansion of the British state.

2.2 The drive to empire

The building of a state that was secure in its territory, internally unified, and whose constitution enjoyed legitimacy over the greater part of its territory, was assisted by the successful expansion overseas, and in turn aided it. This expansion, which began to accelerate after 1650, was by no means inevitable, and little in previous British history anticipated it. England had been an unimportant and distant colony of the Roman Empire and subsequently a minor medieval kingdom, always on the fringes of European politics, culture and trade, never at the centre. The transformation of this island kingdom, in the course of two centuries, into an imperial power of unprecedented dimensions, shaped British politics irrevocably and brought a fundamental shift in British perspectives and British preoccupations.

In the Middle Ages Britain was a continental power, its kings pursued dynastic ambitions in Europe, and the country was wholly contained within European culture and European horizons. It was the discovery of the New World which transformed its position. The overseas expansion of Europe was begun by the Portuguese and the Spaniards in the fifteenth century, and created a new transatlantic world economy based around protected colonies and protected trade. Once established it provided opportunities for many other states, particularly Holland, France and Britain, and encouraged a competitive struggle for territory and wealth from which Britain ultimately secured by far the greatest returns.[8]

One principal reason why the British were able to benefit was that the creation of a world economy which spanned oceans, rather than merely an inland sea like the Mediterranean, greatly favoured those states able to develop sea power. Two-thirds of the earth's surface is covered by sea, most of its states have coastlines, and every part of the ocean is accessible from every other part. Few other states had the security of an island base as large as the British Isles, or with such a relatively fertile and extensive lowland plain (stretching to the Pennines and Scottish Lowlands in the North and the Welsh mountains in the West), and capable of supporting a large population. Sea power, an island base, and a strong, unified state gave Britain a strategic mobility, a flexibility, and a security which land-based powers lacked. Britain could afford to develop an oceanic strategy aimed at domination of the world economy, whilst other states were forced into continental entanglements.[9]

From 1650 onwards the British state began to pursue an outward-looking policy designed to assist the efforts of its merchants and its settlers in the struggle for the New World. The policy was never formalised as a doctrine and was not always pursued consistently. It was particularly vulnerable to the shifting balance of power between interests and factions in the English Parliament. Nevertheless the new course marked out in the few short years of the English republic after the execution of the King endured. It was a policy which increasingly put British commercial interests first and subordinated other considerations to them. Under Cromwell the Navigation Acts were passed, and these created a single national monopoly for British trade, open to all British merchants to engage in. The majority of the old trading monopolies were abolished; all trade had henceforward to be carried in British ships, and all the existing colonies were brought directly under the control of Parliament. Trade wars were fought with the Dutch and the Spanish, the Dutch monopoly of trade was broken, Jamaica seized, and an important alliance concluded with Portugal gave access to the Portuguese colonial empire in return for British naval protection. This new aggressive policy was continued after the Restoration, although without much success at first. All the wars of the next 150 years had a commercial purpose.[10] Britain fought Holland, Spain and France for control of the world economy, the possession of the new territories and mastery of the sea.

The colonial system, practised by all states, treated colonies as foreign estates, tended by settlers or by slaves, and designed to add directly to the wealth and importance of the home country. Taxation of them was often heavy, and their trade was strictly controlled, while the emigration to them of surplus labour was encouraged. Each nation tried to insist that its own traders should enjoy a monopoly of trade in its own colonies. This was why wars were so frequent.

Britain eventually emerged as the overwhelming victor in this struggle, and acquired in the course of it a potent definition of its national interest and a coherent strategic doctrine. Enunciated most clearly by leaders like William Pitt, its basic principles were simple. Britain should concentrate on its navy, maintaining only small land forces. British governments should avoid entanglements on the continent of Europe, and where these proved unavoidable the British aim should be to aid its allies with money rather than with armies. The major British military effort was to be concentrated at sea, securing the safety of the British Isles and prosecuting war in the New World. Britain's allies in Europe frequently found themselves bearing the brunt of the European war, whilst Britain devoted her energies to securing yet more overseas territory and agreeing peace terms when the objectives had been secured. This caused some resentment; Frederick the Great denounced Britain as 'perfidious Albion'. British policy became known for its ruthlessness, its single-mindedness and its occasional treachery and hypocrisy. But there was no doubting its success. France, although a wealthier and more populous nation than Britain, was comprehensively defeated during the eighteenth century in the battle for the New World, losing both India and Canada, and was stalemated in Europe by the alliance of continental powers which Britain organised against her.

The Napoleonic wars were the last of the great colonial wars of the seventeenth and eighteenth centuries. The basic reason for Napoleon's defeat was that during the whole war France fought on two fronts – in Europe and throughout the world – whereas the British, until the final stages, fought only on one. Unable to break the stranglehold of British sea power, or to damage British trade with Europe, Napoleon finally succumbed to the coalition of absolute Monarchs which Britain had organised against him. Britain entered the war on the side of European Reaction and against the Revolution, because a Revolutionary France, no less than an Absolutist France, challenged the commercial and strategic interests of the British state. Napoleon's defeat spelt the end of the French challenge for European and world hegemony, leaving Britain with the bulk of the spoils.

The only great setback to this policy up to 1815 was the successful rebellion of the American colonies in 1783 – the most important of Britain's overseas possessions. The burden of taxes and controls the British attempted to maintain on the American states eventually drove the colonists into revolt. The loss was a major one, and the eventual consequences for Britain were momentous, but at the time it did not stop Britain's advance to world power. The system of colonies and protected commerce, the trade in slaves and sugar, the looting of India, which had so augmented British strength and wealth in the eighteenth century, were rapidly overtaken in the early nineteenth century by a new source of power – modern industry.

2.3   Industrialisation and free trade

The great spurt of British industrialisation, which took place after 1780 and continued during the Napoleonic wars, meant that by 1815 Britain no longer dominated the world economy only through its navy, its extensive colonies, and its protected trade, but also through the much greater productivity of its leading industries. A major change in British strategy and policy was to follow. The colonial and commercial imperialism of the previous 250 years was to take second place to a new imperialism of free trade. The debate which raged in Britain in the early nineteenth century was not about whether Britain should have an empire or not, nor whether Britain should aspire to world power or not, but whether that empire should be based primarily on a free trade open to all the world, or on a protected trade based on the colonies. The argument that was put forward by all the interests and groups supporting free trade was that free trade was the cheapest policy to secure Britain's continuing domination of the world economy. The lead in productivity and technology which British industries had established meant that if trade was open, British goods had a decisive competitive advantage. They could undersell any rivals in price and out-perform them in quality. As one supporter of free trade expressed it during the debate in Parliament on the bill to repeal the Corn Laws, free trade was the beneficent principle by which 'foreign nations would become valuable colonies to us, without imposing on us the responsibility of governing them'.[11]

The strategy that had generally predominated since 1650 was a shrewd commercial policy, which exploited the opportunities that came Britain's way and made full use of the geographical and political advantages Britain enjoyed. The dispute over whether to adopt a policy of complete free trade in the decades after 1815 was a sharp one, because the position of a major domestic interest – the landowners and their tenant farmers – had necessarily to be sacrificed if the protection of agriculture was to be ended. But repeal when it came was only the last stage in a lengthy process of adjustment. Successive administrations since the 1820s had been reducing duties and opening British markets, because commercial interest now dictated it so strongly. There was no domestic lobby arguing for complete protection – the whole of the property-owning class had benefited too much from trade and the colonial system. The substance of the debate was over the question of the balance between agriculture and commerce. Those political economists, like Malthus, who argued the landowners' case, claimed that it was folly to risk destroying the agricultural base of society to realise what might prove only a temporary advantage in commerce.

The supporters of the Corn Laws were defeated because the balance of social forces had already shifted decisively against them. The importance of commerce and expansion abroad and the extent of industrialisation at home ensured the isolation of the protectionists. The new and rapidly expanding urban working class supported the relaxing of the Corn Laws in the hope of cheaper food. Fear of social disorder was used by the free traders as the final circumstance to clinch the case for repeal, but the central argument for it lay in their overwhelming confidence that complete free trade was the best means of extending and consolidating Britain's wealth and power in the world economy.[12]

The relative ease with which the transition to free trade was made is what now seems remarkable. The extent of the shift that was occurring was not fully realised either then or for long afterwards, because it seemed so in line with the traditional principle of maximising commercial advantage that had guided British expansion. Yet the move to free trade proved one of the decisive events of modern British history, perhaps *the* decisive event. Britain had participated in the world economy and had profited greatly from its growing network of trade, but always from a position of self-sufficiency. It did not depend on the world economy for its survival. The industrial and technological lead which Britain had established by 1850, and the naval strength and colonial possessions which already made Britain the leading power in the world economy, persuaded Britain's leaders that the abandonment of self-sufficiency and protection was not reckless, but the way to preserve British power in the future. Britain became the first major state to become dependent for the regular supplies of food and raw materials necessary to sustain its population on a trading link with areas of the world economy, over which Britain could not necessarily exercise control.

Since 1850 Britain's position in the world economy has been precarious and vulnerable. This was disguised at first, partly because British power and wealth continued to increase, partly because British agriculture was not immediately affected in the way that had been feared. But the final result was not altered. Britain's future and very survival became tied to the world economy. Free trade assisted the tremendous growth of the population to a size far beyond any level that could be supported by food production in

Britain.[13] Imports of food and raw materials raised foreign incomes, encouraged economic development, and so expanded markets for British manufactured goods and services. A new world division of labour sprang up with Britain at its centre, specialising as the world's workshop and exchanging its manufactures, particularly cotton goods and iron and steel, for the primary products of the rest of the world.[14]

2.4 The beginnings of decline

It could not last. For a time it brought Britain unparalleled dominance and wealth. But the very success of British industrialisation and the policy of free trade created the first great world capitalist boom during the 1850s and 1860s. Aided by exports of capital and machine tools from Britain, several other states began to industrialise extremely rapidly. The communications, the financial network, the trading system of the world economy were all developed enormously and all came to centre on London. This further increased the importance and the influence of Britain and permitted the further expansion of the businesses of the City to service the whole of the world economy. They came to supply a great part of its financial, shipping and insurance needs.

The industrialisation of the world economy, and the resulting development of the accumulation of capital on a world scale, meant that the predominance of British naval and commercial power came under threat. Whilst Britain might still use its naval power in the traditional manner to force states like China to open themselves to the penetration of British capital and British goods,[15] and to safeguard the trade arteries of the world economy, there was no way of similarly compelling the new industrial states like Germany and the United States to maintain free trade. To protect themselves from British competition, every strong nation-state seeking to industrialise protected its industries with high tariffs, designed to shut out British goods, whilst denouncing free trade as a hypocritical policy designed to promote British industry at the expense of the rest of the world.[16]

By the 1880s a new balance of power was already emerging in the world economy, and Britain's capacity to remain its leading state and the guarantor of the conditions world-wide under which accumulation of capital could proceed became more and more precarious. British decline begins with the rise of modern industry on a truly world scale. The challenge posed to Britain by Germany and the United States was both commercial and military, and it brought forth a new debate about Britain's foreign economic policy and its role in the world, the first of many during the hundred years decline. The tariff reformers[17] began to question whether free trade was still in Britain's commercial and strategic interest. They argued that it was now involving such costs that, just as the protectionism of the old colonial system had been abandoned for free trade, so now a further shift in policy had become necessary if the fruits of British expansion were to be preserved. There developed the great controversy over free trade and tariff reform which dominated discussion of economic policy in the early years of the century. But it was never simply a narrow debate about the best commercial policy for Britain. It ranged far wider, to focus upon the nature of Britain's Empire and world leadership and how they could best be preserved and decline averted.

The imperialism of the tariff reformers was a new perspective and a new programme, because the loss of the American colonies, the steady advance of free trade, and the informal empire it had created, persuaded most political leaders by the middle of the nineteenth century that the colonies were no longer an asset but a drain on the metropolitan country. 'Millstones around our necks' was Disraeli's judgement, and it summed up a widely held view even amongst those (like Disraeli himself) who opposed repeal of the Corn Laws. The radical wing of Liberalism, which included Richard Cobden and John Bright, went much further in condemning colonies, not only as very costly in taxes, but also as a means of perpetuating national rivalries and wars between nations. Free trade was held to promote cosmopolitanism and mutual interdependence, so undermining nation-states and promoting world peace.[18]

Despite considerable anti-colonial settlement, no British government parted with any British colony, and by the last two decades of the nineteenth century the colonial empire was appearing in a new light. The drive to industrialise had reawakened national rivalry and competition among nation-states for control of the world economy that Britain policed and serviced. A scramble for control of what territory still lay outside European control began, particularly for the inland areas of Africa. Britain, still possessing superior naval power and an unrivalled network of military bases and client states, was in a position to take the greater part of the spoils, and did so. Free trade and imperialism were reconciled in a new aggressive policy. An age of imperial expansion began, which was accompanied by mounting imperialist frenzy in all the major capitalist states. Britain's new insecurity and growing militarism and Jingoism[19] arose because the world seemed suddenly filled with industrial powers, whose metropolitan bases in terms of resources and manpower and industrial production were potentially much more powerful than Britain's. Trade rivalry and military rivalry became fused into one. To the tariff reform movement it seemed obvious that Britain could only remain a world power in the changed circumstances of the world economy by organising its world empire more effectively and revitalising its industry. As the centre of an Empire that covered one-fifth of the earth's surface Britain could secure its vital interests, particularly the supplies of food and raw materials for its metropolitan population and industries. But the actual empire that existed was chaotic. Much of it had been inherited from the pre-industrial colonial system, including the major territory under British rule, India. Much of the rest, particularly the territories in Africa, had not been acquired because of any kind of plan or systematic economic logic, but as a response to initiatives taken independently to British settlers, traders, and adventurers, or to forestall involvement by foreign powers.[20]

The tariff reformers drew on earlier ideas for transforming the Empire into an Anglo-Saxon world empire. The overseas expansion of the Anglo-Saxon race offered an opportunity for the creation of a truly effective and united Empire.[21] Colonies that were merely administered and held down by the metropolitan power were costly, but colonies that were settled by British subjects could become communities linked directly to Britain and could add significantly to British strength. What the tariff reform movement wanted was to construct an Anglo-Saxon empire in which Anglo-Saxon culture, Anglo-Saxon institutions, and Anglo-Saxon capital would predominate. Where this was clearly impossible, as in India and some of the African territories, the ideology of the 'white man's burden' suggested a paternalistic administration of the territories to raise them to civilisation. But the real desire of the tariff reformers was to create an imperial federation, which could be as united as Britain itself.[22]

The policy did not ultimately succeed. The principal settler colonies – Canada, Australia, New Zealand, South Africa – made it plain that they wanted independence, not federation,[23] whilst at home the policy of tariff reform was consigned to ineffective though vocal opposition with the election of a Liberal government, unequivocally committed to free trade, in 1906, which stayed in office until after the outbreak of war in 1914.[24]

One of the most remarkable aspects of British policy in the last eighty years has been this dogged commitment to free trade. The rival economic programme of the tariff reformers was only seriously attempted twice – briefly during the First World War, and then after 1931 when the world trading and financial order had broken down. By the 1950s it was clear that the tariff reformers' dream was over. They had failed to shift British policy on to a new course and free trade again became dominant.

The dilemma that faced the British state was acute. As a result of the formal and informal empires which British expansion had created, Britain derived some economic benefit from its colonies, but still greater benefit from being the financial and commercial centre of the capitalist world economy.[25] British manufacturing industry might be challenged and overtaken in some areas, but the international monetary system was centred on sterling and the international trade system on London. Apart from the complex shipping, insurance and banking services which were now provided for the world economy from London, Britain benefited enormously from the free flow of goods and food. Since the agricultural interest had been defeated, the dumping of cheap food on British markets was welcomed on all sides. The fact that the programme of tariff reform would have raised food prices was one of the main reasons why working-class opinion swung against it. From the standpoint of British capital, a further advantage from the world economy was the scope for British investment abroad. Assets reached the enormous total of £4000 million in 1914, which meant a steady investment income of some £200 million a year for British rentiers.[26]

A decision to abandon the effort to maintain the free flow of goods and capital, and instead to launch a bid to establish a new protectionist and self-sufficient bloc within the world economy, risked the stability of the world economy and went against the principle of maximising commercial opportunities for its subjects, which had so long guided British policy. The British had long regarded themselves as the most enlightened nation in the world economy, because they were willing to bear some of the burdens of maintaining the conditions for a free movement of goods, capital, and labour in the world economy, which was so greatly improving the wealth and speeding the development of all the separate nation-states participating in it. The continued possession of a formal Empire by Britain was widely viewed as an unfortunate necessity, a means of ensuring British predominance and allowing Britain to discharge its traditional world role. As Halford Mackinder put it:

> Under a condition of universal free trade, the dream of the sixties of the last century, industrial life and empire might be dissociated, but when competing industries seek to monopolise markets by means of customs tariffs, even democracies are compelled to annexe empires. In the last two generations . . . the object of vast British annexations has been to support a trade open to all the world.[27]

Accompanying this traditional policy of free trade imperialism there had evolved a military doctrine, which was
distilled in the nineteenth century into the strategic
principles that the ocean highways must be kept open and
the continent of Europe must be kept divided. The first
meant the maintenance of a strong navy to a two power
standard;[28] the second meant that, at the very least, no
hostile power should be allowed to become so predominant
in Europe that it could control Belgium and Holland. Some
British strategists became obsessed with the duel for world
domination between sea power and land power, and argued
that it was a fundamental British interest that no power
should arise or win control of the heartland of the Eurasian
continent, where its base would be secure from attack by
sea, and from which it could put pressure on the world's
coasts and ports which Britain dominated, and ultimately
raise a naval force to challenge Britain.[29]

Britain fought major wars to prevent first France, then
Germany, rising to a position of supremacy within Europe
and threatening Britain's world empire and the security of
its island base. But whereas Britain emerged from the
Napoleonic wars as the undisputed power in the world
economy, and embarked on a century of world domination
and leadership, Britain emerged from the First World War
only nominally victorious. The price of defeating Germany
was the alliance with the United States. Britain was proved
to be no longer militarily or industrially strong enough to
maintain itself as the dominant world power. The rise of the
United States signalled the eclipse of Britain's traditional
role.[30]

2.5 Britain and the world economy

The course of the hundred years decline was shaped
decisively by two momentous choices. The first was the
continued adherence to free trade and to the institutions of
the liberal world order long after the conditions which had
originally recommended it had disappeared. The second
was the decision to fight Germany rather than the United

States. In two world wars the British helped destroy German ambitions to become the dominant world power. But instead of Britain's power being preserved, that of the United States was established.

Many historians and strategists have commented on the ferocity with which the British contested German claims, but the tameness with which they conceded American. One of Britain's main war aims in 1914 had been to preserve its naval superiority against that of Germany and all other states. At the Disarmament Conference after the war Britain was warned by America that maintaining such superiority would no longer be tolerated. Britain conceded.[31]

Such episodes underline how supinely the British governing class reacted to the rise of the United States. The British position was surrendered without a fight. The Germans always found this hard to understand. Although there were circles in both Germany and England before 1914, and again in the 1930s, that worked for an Anglo-German understanding and an Anglo-German alliance, it never happened, although its real possibility, even in 1940, has tended to be obscured.[32] Many reasons can be advanced for this. They do not detract from the central point – that Britain chose to fight Germany, and to ally with the United States, and furthermore that Britain sought a total victory over Germany rather than an early negotiated peace in either war. As a result Britain was itself an agent in liquidating its own power and surrendering its world role to the Americans.

One of the decisive factors in this outcome was a fundamental loss of will in British ruling circles. The strategic dilemma at the beginning of the century was certainly acute. It was summed up in the assessment made by the Admiralty in 1902: Britain could not simultaneously fight a war against Germany and America. America, potentially, was a greater oceanic power than Britain and either had to be crushed or had to be made an ally. British dependence on the world economy for the very survival of its metropolitan base meant that there was no alternative but to ensure (as a minimum) American neutrality. Such neutrality depended, however, on making concessions to American interests. So long as the preservation of the capitalist world economy was considered Britain's pre-eminent interest, the Americans appeared both as a power that had to be appeased and a power that was more likely than any other to contribute to preserving it. Germany had quite different strategic aims. The rulers of Germany wanted to consolidate a land empire, securing control of a continental market by establishing a customs union protected by a common tariff extending from the Baltic, through Austria and the Balkans, to the Middle East and Persia. This would ensure the dominance of Germany over France and give parity with England. At the same time Germany sought to expand in Africa and extend its colonial empire there.[33]

The Germans had less interest in the wider world economy than in securing exclusive markets. They used tariffs as a weapon in their commercial struggle with England, and so helped undermine the free flow of goods and capital on which British prosperity had been founded, and on which British survival depended. The tariff reformers greatly admired German organisation and their policy of industrial development in a unified continental market protected by high tariffs. Their failure to move British policy in that direction was closely linked to the failure to reach an understanding with Germany and the increasing recognition that it was necessary to ally with the United States. A protectionist Greater Britain Federation might conceivably have so reduced British dependence on the world economy, and so eased the constraints which that dependence imposed on British policy, as to prevent an armed clash with Germany. It would, however, have made eventual war with the United States much more likely as American capital sought to break into these protected spheres. The significance of the defeat of tariff reform was not just that Britain did not abandon free trade, but that out of its two main industrial rivals and challengers, Britain fought Germany rather than America.

Not that the tariff reformers were reluctant to fight

Germany. On the contrary, they were among the foremost prosecutors of the war – one of their most prominent adherents, Lord Milner, was a leading member of Lloyd George's War Cabinet. But one of the results was that the tariff reformers themselves came to realise the extent of Britain's strategic weakness and America's growing power.

This produced two different reactions. One wing of the tariff reformers continued to fight tenaciously for an independent British imperial strategy. The other concluded that Britain could neither organise its own wider federation nor match American power and resources, so the best course was to seek an Anglo-American alliance in which America would gradually take over the British role of dominant power in the world economy. This current was to merge with that sector of liberal opinion which was forced to accept in the 1920s and 1930s that Britain could not maintain the international monetary system alone, that sterling was no longer strong enough to be the leading world currency, and that American co-operation was indispensable if an open capitalist world economy was to survive.

Decisive strategic choices were thus made in the first two decades of this century affecting the future development of the British state. The result of the two wars disrupted a pattern that went back centuries. British weakness was exposed and the total British reliance on sea power suddenly became outmoded. Just as air power changed the strategic balance, so the failure to consolidate the British Empire as a world state brought the end of British world power. It was still not certain in 1918 but there was no question by 1945. Sea power, industrial power, financial power, passed decisively and irrevocably to the United States. Henceforward the British Empire, the pound sterling, and the very survival of Britain, depended on American sufferance. The tariff reformers had enjoyed a belated triumph in the 1930s when the world economy fragmented into currency and trading blocs following the Great Depression. But the opportunity was already gone of turning the Empire from a strategic and economic burden into a source of British strength. The British state now began to acquire a very different relationship to the world economy it had once dominated and done so much to develop.

The military underpinning of the British state's traditional commercial policy had been sea power. Sea power had permitted the commercial alliances, the trade wars, the seizure of territory, the protection of shipping, the flow of slaves, settlers, plunder, and commodities which made Britain the greatest commercial nation in the world by 1815 enjoying control over more colonies than any other state But even at the moment that this policy was being so triumphantly successful it was giving way to a new set of commercial opportunities, which relied much less on British naval power and protection and much more on the lead established by British industry. A new informal empire began to grow up alongside the formal one, an empire which prospered and grew through free trade and a more specialised division of labour. By exploiting commercial advantages to the full, Britain abandoned first self-sufficiency, and then protection, for the unprecedented wealth created by modern industry. As Alexis de Tocqueville wrote of Manchester in the 1840s:

> From this foul drain the greatest stream of human industry flows out to fertilise the whole world. From this filthy sewer pure gold flows. Here humanity attains its most complete development and its most brutish; here civilisation works its miracles, and civilised man is turned back almost into a savage.[34]

The spread of industry in the world economy created new commercial and military rivals by the 1880s, and made formal empire valuable once more as security against the designs of the rising powers. But in the struggle that opened between rival imperialisms it became clear that much of the British Empire was a burden rather than an asset. To become effective it needed to be organised and co-ordinated in the manner of the great land empires of the United States, Germany, and Russia. The British state became caught between two strategies – securing its future by attempting to transform its loose and far-flung empire into a disciplined protectionist bloc in the world market, the equal of both Germany and the United States; and accepting the wider responsibilities for maintaining a liberal world economy that the success of commercial expansion and the adoption of free trade had imposed on Britain. What slowly became clear was that Britain was losing the strength and the capacity to fulfil these responsibilities. But the dependence on the continued existence of this liberal world economy did not diminish.

3

The unfinished revolution

In the course of the nineteenth century England adopted peacefully and without violent shocks almost all the basic civil and political reforms that France paid so heavily to achieve through the great Revolution. Undeniably, the great advantage of England lay in the greater energy, the greater practical wisdom, the better political training, that her ruling class possessed down to the very end of the past century.

Gaetano Mosca[1]

Sitting at your ease on the corpse of Ireland . . . be good enough to tell us: did your revolution of interests not cost more blood than our revolution of ideas?

Jules Michelet

The success of the policy of expansion was greatly aided by the organisation of a centralised and efficient public power controlling the whole of the land area of the British Isles. But it was also made possible by the English revolution in the seventeenth century, which cut short the development of royal absolutism in England and converted the central-ised bureaucratic military and legal apparatus, which the English kings had created, into an instrument for the security and progress of the civil society which developed alongside it. The interrelation between successful overseas expansion, the creation of a strong centralised multinational state in the British Isles, and the subordination of the state power to the interests and needs of a dynamic and assertive civil society, are the necessary historical ground for exploring the next major problem that arises from a study of Britain's hundred years' decline: why has Britain alone amongst major states experienced such an exceptional degree of institutional continuity, such a gradual evolution in its political arrangements?

3.1 The state and civil society

The British state has not suffered a major break in the pattern of its development since the civil war in the seventeenth century, which ended in the execution of the King and the establishment of a republican government. Changes there certainly have been. The basis of representation has several times been widened to embrace new social groups and interests; the major institutions of the state have frequently been remodelled and the pattern of recruitment to them altered. But all this has been done within the same constitutional framework. The central role of Parliament and its executive, and the supporting role of the Crown, have been preserved throughout.

All this has occurred during three centuries in which Britain has experienced not calm and stability, but profound social, economic and cultural change, the crossing of the watershed from an agricultural to an industrial society, the rise of an urban civilisation. Such changes elsewhere have been accompanied by major political upheavals and social revolutions. Political continuity has generally been the first thing to snap. Industrialisation has been accompanied by revolutions, counter revolutions, civil wars, military coups, new republics, new empires – the form of political regimes has been regularly shifting. When compared with the political history of France or Germany, Italy or Spain, China or Japan, the degree to which continuity has been preserved in Britain is remarkable. The early organisation of a strong state commanding the whole territory of the British Isles, and the consequent ability to resist foreign invasion and occupation, go a long way to explain it. External military defeats have so often accelerated internal revolution. Nevertheless, by itself the external success of the British state would not have been sufficient to preserve it from internal overthrow, had it not been for the relationship that was early established between the state and civil society.

This relationship was the lasting result of the English civil war, the Great Rebellion as it was known to contemporaries. It was fought between two sections of the landed gentry with varying degrees of popular support enlisted on each side. The major issues were what powers and prerogatives the King could rightfully claim, particularly in relation to taxation, the liberties of the subject, the toleration of religious belief, and the organisation of the church. Protestantism with its radical, individualist doctrines was a major driving force in enlisting support for the Parliament and against the King. There was no direct conflict of economic interests, although the forces ranged against royal power, and most anxious to repudiate royal authority, were strongest in the commercial centres and the more prosperous and advanced agricultural regions. The King's strongholds lay in the more backward North and West.[2]

The war was won by the New Model Army which Cromwell and Ireton created, but the demands which then ensued for much more radical social and political change were resisted and eventually contained. The programmes of Levellers, Diggers, and militant puritans were all defeated. This prepared the way for the Restoration of the monarchy after Cromwell's death, a move that by then commanded the support of the great majority of the landowners. The dispossessed royalists received back their lands, the Anglican state church was re-established, and Parliament reverted to its former composition. Little seemed to have changed. Cromwell's Commonwealth appeared a brief interlude, a short suspension of traditional political arrangements.

Nevertheless a fundamental breach had occurred; the British state had been set on a new course. The importance of the civil war was not so much in what it achieved as in what it prevented. It reduced royal power permanently. Charles II chafed under restrictions that never troubled his cousin, Louis XIV, and although he managed to regain some of the initiative, his brother James was swiftly deposed when he appeared to threaten one of the crucial aspects of the Restoration settlement – that England should remain a Protestant country.

James II's deposition in 1688 was proclaimed the Glorious Revolution, and though long regarded as more important than the Great Rebellion forty years before, in fact consolidated the gains of that period by demonstrating that the balance between King and Parliament had permanently shifted. The direction of the state and the centre of its authority had passed to Parliament. For the first time a state had been created whose policies and activities were shaped in response to the needs and movement of civil society. The state of the Tudor and Stuart Kings had been strong enough and legitimate enough to maintain social order, enforce its laws, protect property and guarantee a medium of exchange, and under it considerable progress was made towards the creation of a national market, as well as the establishment of a growing commerce in simple manufactures and primary products. This emerging network of economic relations was decisively strengthened by the political upheavals of the seventeenth century, for from that time onward it became inconceivable that the central public power would be used against the system of free exchange, against the vital interests of the civil society. On the contrary, its task became the active removal of obstacles to the widening of the sphere of exchange and the accumulation of wealth, both internally and abroad.

The idea that state policy should be governed by the private interests individuals acquired as members of civil society was a novel one, but it became the essence of the English way. What it specifically ruled out was the attempt made by many of the absolutist regimes in Europe in the eighteenth century to reimpose or reinforce the system of legal privileges for different estates of the realm as the basis of their authority. The legal codes they promulgated attempted to freeze these patterns of social relationships in

their societies by ensuring a permanently privileged position for the aristocracy and for landed property. Such codes
helped multiply the obstacles to the development of an
independent civil society and an economic system based on
equality, mobility and free exchange.

In England the position was different and increasingly
came to be recognised as different during the eighteenth
century when England first received wide acknowledgement
as the 'land of liberty'. From the seventeeth century
onwards the principle and the idea of legal equality, so
essential to a market economy, was gaining ground.
England remained laden with social privileges, yet these
were not in general buttressed by legal privileges and
English civil society, for all its inequalities of wealth and
property and for all its accumulation of ranks and titles, was
more flexible and open to change, and its property-owning
class more unified than any other society in Europe.[3]

A civil society emerged in England whose property
owners were generally more concerned with enlarging their
wealth than with preserving their status, and with preserving their liberties than with increasing the power of the
state. All wealth, however diverse its forms, came to be
viewed as having a common origin in human labour, whilst
the source of its expansion was found to lie in the widening
of exchange. For Adam Smith, in a society conducted on
correct economic principles 'every man ... lives by
exchanging or becomes in some measure a merchant, and
the society itself grows to be what is properly a commercial
society'.[4] The importance the English attached to trade and
exchange became notorious. England became widely
regarded as a new Carthage, a great commercial power,
preying parasitically on the great land empires of the
continent. 'A nation of shopkeepers', Napolean scornfully
remarked, whilst the German economist Friedrich List
fulminated against the English assumption that the world
was an 'indivisible republic of merchants'. The English
appetite for commercial opportunities, buying cheap and
selling dear, and the evident aim of their state to promote
the commercial interests of its subjects were widely noted.
Yet despite the expansion overseas and the beginnings of

industry at home in the eighteenth century, the property-owning class in England particularly that section with most influence over the state, belonged overwhelmingly to the landed interest. What made the difference between the landed aristocracy in Britain, and the landed aristocracy in many other states, was that in Britain the rapidly developing network of exchange in British civil society, and the growing hold of British interests over the world economy, provided a range of opportunities for property owners to consolidate and extend their wealth in agriculture, in trade, in colonies; and by the end of the eighteenth century another avenue for the creation and appropriation of wealth was emerging – industry.

The most important long-term result of the English civil war was the clear separation between the state and an independent sphere of private interests and private exchange, and the subordination of the former to the latter. This independence and importance of a realm of private individuals was proclaimed by numerous political writers, and became expressed in practical terms by doctrines of political and civil liberties, which defined the rights of all individuals, not just property owners, against the arbitrary exercise of state power. It was not just freedom of economic interests but freedom of private interests, including a degree of freedom of religious belief and worship.

English liberties and freedom from arbitrary government were sufficiently unusual to attract considerable attention, and became the basis for the Whig interpretation of history.[5] This laid great emphasis upon the uniqueness of English history, which becomes the unfolding of liberty, the story of liberties once held, then lost, then gradually regained. It is a history of progress and enlightenment, of the genius of the island race. The liberties once enjoyed by the Anglo-Saxons were taken away after the Norman Conquest, which brought a time of suffering only relieved by victories such as Magna Carta, the first step in challenging royal power and reasserting traditional liberties and throwing off the Norman yoke. The growing resistance of the people to tyranny and absolute power eventually erupted during the civil war, which only succeeded however in replacing one tyranny with another. It required the settlement of 1688 to inaugurate the new age of English liberty. It created a constitution which balanced the powers of the monarchy (the Crown), the titled aristocracy (the Lords), and the landed gentry (the Commons), so safe-guarding many vital rights and providing important checks to arbitrary government. It provided the stable framework within which progress was possible. New interests could be accommodated, new social forces represented, new rights recognised. The forum for the balancing and harmonising of interests was the British Parliament, whose legitimacy was paramount and whose independence was unques-tioned. Broadening the basis of representation, acknow-ledging and creating the rights of citizens to equal opportu-nities and certain standards of provision, all could proceed within the framework established in 1688.

Like all interpretations of history the Whig interpretation contains much myth. But it remains the most potent of all the interpretations of Britain's internal political evolution. What was real was the sphere of liberty that did emerge during the eighteenth century.[6] The idea that every Englishman was 'born free', and enjoyed certain inherited liberties as rights, was important. It meant widespread suspicion of government power and constant pressures to limit it. It encouraged the principles that the power to levy taxes should reside in the hands of Parliament, not the Crown or the executive, that the standing army should be as small as possible, that the judiciary should be independent of the government. The English claimed the right to revolt against tyranny, the right to freedom from arbitrary arrest and arbitrary search, the principle of equality before the law and the right to trial by jury. When to these were added a limited degree of freedom of publication, speech, and conscience, and a much wider freedom to travel and to trade, there was a body of rights which, although often abused and infringed, provided a distinct sphere of legal equality, the basis of a bourgeois order.

These rights were justified as the traditional liberties once enjoyed by Englishmen, rather than asserted as the natural and inherent rights of man. But they were no less real for that.

3.2 The English governing class

What emerged from the civil war and the consolidation of its gains in the eighteenth century was a relationship between state and economy which influenced the whole subsequent history of industrialisation. The extent of legal equality and personal liberty that were established tended to unify the different sections of property owners by making all forms of property commensurable. An aristocracy of wealth was more evident in Britain than in any other country in Europe. This made the constant widening of the ruling social bloc much easier to accomplish. Social privileges and distinctions were numerous, but they did not create insuperable obstacles to the assimilation of new groups. Most important of all was the accommodation reached in the 1830s and 1840s between the representatives of landed property and the representatives of industry.[7]

The ease with which new interests were accommodated, new groups absorbed, and the continuity and ethos of British institutions preserved, was in marked contrast to the often bitter struggles and political upheavals that accompanied similar changes in other states. The evident skill and flexibility of the British governing class was much admired. Joseph Schumpeter spoke of:

the unrivalled integrity of the English politician and the presence of a ruling class that is uniquely able and civilised make many things easy that would be impossible elsewhere. In particular this ruling group unites in the most workable proportions adherence to formal tradition with extreme adaptability to new principles, situations and persons. It wants to rule but it is quite ready to rule on behalf of changing interests. It manages industrial England as well as it managed agrarian England, protectionist England as well as free trade England. And it possesses an altogether unrivalled talent for appropriating not only the programmes of oppositions but also their brains.[8]

This skill and adaptability was not very evident in the seventeenth century, nor has it been in the years since 1945. If the British governing class and its politicians were really so able, why has the halting of Britain's economic decline proved so difficult? Why did its capacity begin to fail so visibly and so dramatically, so that even the central institutional symbol of legitimacy, Parliament itself, came under increasing attack?

One answer lies in the dominant pattern of relationships between the state and the economy, which have been modified but never fundamentally altered.[9] The early development of a market order, and the redefining of public interest to mean the safeguarding of private interests and the liberation of private energies, all meant that the efforts of the agencies of the British state were concentrated to a high degree on enlarging commercial opportunities for its citizens. This strategy proved successful, not because of any innate qualities enjoyed by the English aristocracy, but because it aided colonial expansion abroad, and first agrarian and then industrial expansion at home. The wealth and power which the policy brought to Britain was so enormous that a policy of conceding to the demands of new interests and then absorbing them was not too painful. The Whig perspective triumphed. If the object of the state was to preserve liberty and promote the conditions in which civil society would flourish, then the private realm had to be respected and its major interests, whatever they were, had to be recognised as the legitimate interest of the state.

Every particular concession was the occasion for sharp conflicts within the ruling groups, and those advocating flexibility did not always win immediately. The sphere of private liberties was exceedingly frail and always in danger of being encroached upon. The corruption of the eighteenth-century state was notorious. Yet the growing strength of a bourgeois civil society, a market order based upon the legal equality of all who participated in it, ensured that the state, despite its deformations, continued to respond to the movements and interests and pressures of civil society rather than seeking to lead it or dominate it.

The relations between state and economy in Britain were shaped by this pattern. Manufacturing, like overseas trade and agriculture production for the market before it, was seen primarily as another branch of commercial opportunity, another avenue to the creation of wealth and the enlargement of fortunes. The aristocracy were active in promoting it from the start. There was no fundamental issue of principle at stake. There were conflicts, but they were far from being irreconcilable.[10] The interests and the new classes that industrial capitalism created, and the wholesale transformation of British society that it necessitated, were accommodated within the existing state system. The price of admitting the industrialists into the groups that ruled England was reform of all the major state institutions, and acceptance (in 1832) of the principle of Members of Parliament representing individual voters rather than corporate interests. But although the state became more efficient and less corrupt in the course of the nineteenth century, as a result of the indefatigable efforts of utilitarian reformers and the pressure of a bourgeois public opinion and a bourgeois electorate, the guiding principle of its actions and its interventions remained the preservation and safeguarding of the system of free exchange. The success of this state depended on the continuing dynamism and expansion of the civil society which it served. It proved much less capable of intervening successfully to remedy some of the deficiencies of that civil society, which began to appear once other nations began to industrialise and to compete with Britain. The permissive orientation of the state to the market order, the tradition of suspicion towards the government and its initiatives, have constantly hampered the development of an interventionist state in the past hundred years. They have not prevented it from arising, but they have prevented it from being as successful as its protagonists hoped.

The greatest success and the greatest failure of all has been the attempt to incorporate the working class. The owners and agents of industrial capital themselves posed few problems.[11] They accepted the aristocratic panoply of the landowners' state with its titles and traditional flummery. They abandoned dreams of a republic and an egalitarian social order; they sent their sons to be educated in the new public schools which sprang up to provide an education for gentlemen and a training for service in the empire and the state;[12] they accepted the dense and secretive web of the British governing class and its internal rituals, whilst pressing successfully for the reform of its more obvious abuses, such as the sale of army commissions. But this accommodation within the ranks of property, which was worked out in the course of the nineteenth century and which was to give the British governing class so formidable and so impenetrable an appearance, and give the culture and outlook of the upper middle class such coherence and strength, had its costs. The most important was that the other great class which industrial capitalism had created was never fully incorporated as a constitutent part of British society. The working class in Britain has always remained to some extent outside – in it but not of it.

3.3   The resistance of the working class

The success of the traditional governing class in avoiding overthrow during the period of industrialisation, either by a radical industrial bourgeoisie or by a revolutionary working class, permanently shaped civil society and state in Britain. The degree of social conservatism amongst all classes, the tenacity of antiquated institutions, the secrecy surrounding central processes in government and the major institutions of civil society, the enduring liberal perception of the state's role in the market order – all these are easily recognised features of twentieth-century Britain, and they stem directly from the exceptional continuity which British institutions have enjoyed.[13]

The most important legacy of all which the bourgeois order of Britain's ascendancy bequeathed to a Britain in decline was the problem of the working class. From the outset it was a class of which much was expected and much feared, a class which came relatively early to occupy an important position in British society and which developed a unified and expanding trade-union movement and only one major political party. Yet despite all its advantages and all its social and political weight, it seemed to lose its early radicalism and be progressively incorporated within the British state as one more element of its constitution.

The result is often hailed as a triumph of Whig politics. If the bourgeois order could absorb and integrate a class as powerful and as alien as this, then it must be invulnerable. But as with the much simpler integration of the owners of the new industries themselves, the relatively smooth integration of the working class was only achieved at the cost of an accumulation of institutional and social weaknesses. In the hundred years' decline, weaknesses stemming from the international orientation of British policy and the external dependence of the economy have reinforced weaknesses stemming from the obstacles to more rapid capitalist rationalisation and reorganisation. These were sustained most obviously by the liberal bias of the state, the social conservatism and inertia of so many British institutions, and the organised political and industrial resistance of the Labour movement.

Industrialisation began in England in the eighteenth century. The overseas explorations and conquests had brought into the country significant hoards of capital, available for any profitable investment;[14] more important, they had permitted the organisation of wide markets and trading networks which could supply raw materials like cotton to the new industries. In the domestic economy, agricultural production for the market was flourishing, and the population was abundant and beginning to expand. The enclosing of the common land did not force an exodus of labour from the land, but it did mean that in many areas the choice of employment came to be between wage labour on the land or wage labour in the new industries. The scope for economic independence, whether as smallholder or artisan, steadily narrowed as capital accumulation got under way. A class of labourers began to be created who were free to sell their labour power on the market, but were also free from ownership of means of production that alone could ensure their independence.

From its beginnings the process of industrialisation was marked by repeated conflict between the owners of capital and the owners of labour power. Its history reveals little of the continuity, the harmony, and the gradualism so often paraded as the moving spirit of British development. Industries have risen and declined, traditional skills and whole communities have been displaced, culture and patterns of living have been radically transformed, and the economy has developed in spurts punctuated by major crises, heavy unemployment and widespread distress. The working class were both agents and victims of this most productive and destructive of all economic systems, and around their experiences of it resistance began to organise and to grow.

The struggle against capital centred on the process of production itself: the determination of the length of the working day and the intensity of work during it; and the conditions under which new machines were introduced to raise productivity.[15] The state which had emerged from the upheavals of the seventeenth century was concerned with the sanctity of contracts and the security of property. This meant the placing of its armed power at the disposal of the industrialists in any conflict with their workers. The early class struggles often took the form of machine breaking and riots.[16] So frequently did such conflicts occur, and on so large a scale, that the state gradually had to become involved in regulating not just the system of market exchange and the circulation of money, but also the production process itself. Governments were forced to acknowledge by their interventions that however free, equal, and unforced the contract between employer and worker might be, the antagonism between labour and capital in the production process made necessary external regulation of hours and conditions of work in the factories if social disorder and industrial conflict were to be kept within tolerable bounds. The early factory legislation and the Ten Hours Bill of 1847 were major working-class victories, which forced the public power to take note of the new interests and demands of the industrial proletariat.[17]

Working-class resistance to the conditions of work and the new labour discipline of the factories challenged the freedom of capital and its agents to control the labour process, and was broadened into a general attack on the existing basis of the state. Political agitation to extend civil and political rights to workers, particularly the right to form trade unions and the right to vote, grew rapidly. The struggle for socialism and the struggle for democracy were closely intertwined, not least in the minds of many of the representatives of the new bloc of property interests, who viewed with horror the rise of political movements like Chartism in the 1840s[18] and the growing numbers of the industrial proletariat in the vast new urban centres. If full citizenship rights were extended to the whole nation, the passing of power from the propertied to the propertyless, and an open attack upon property, seemed inevitable. How could democratic governments avoid plundering the rich and redistributing wealth? If state power remained securely in the hands of representatives of property, then challenges to the rights of property could be suppressed, as they had been so forcibly during the wars against revolutionary France. If, however, the franchise were to be broadened and an attempt made to give the working class full citizenship, what guarantee was there that the state power would any longer be used for the defence of property? Karl Marx expressed the fears of many in the British ruling class when he wrote:

> Universal suffrage is the equivalent of political power for the working classes of England, where the proletariat forms the large majority of the population, where, in a long, though underground civil war, it has gained a clear consciousness of itself as a class, and where even the rural districts know no longer any peasants, but only landlords, industrial capitalists [farmers] and hired labourers. The carrying of Universal Suffrage in England would, therefore, be a far more socialistic measure than anything which has been honoured with that name on the Continent. Its inevitable result here is the political supremacy of the working class.[19]

3.4   The response to the working class

The franchise was widened during the nineteenth century, if only slowly. In 1832 the grosser abuses of the old system were removed by the Reform Bill, and the basis of parliamentary representation broadened to include all the property-owning classes.[20] This reform was bitterly resisted by a section of the landowners and it almost precipitated revolution; its passing allowed the institutional order to survive but it also meant that further extensions were ultimately necessary. The state was already deeply involved as a constituent element of the market order by maintaining a framework of law in which free and equal individuals could make exchanges and pursue their interests. The equal rights under the law guaranteed by every bourgeois legal order were always in sharp contrast to the actual social and economic inequalities that resulted from market exchange. Maintaining the legitimacy of the market order has always been difficult, since the equal legal status of all individuals implies that all should have an equal voice in determining the national interest, yet the inequality of their social condition implies that the majority may vote for measures which will infringe the principles of the market order on which the security of a private realm depends.

The problem was particularly acute in England because of the great numbers and the urban concentration of its proletariat.[21] All capitalist states have had eventually to face the tension between the economic liberty of the capitalist market order and the popular sovereignty of the democratic political order, but none faced it so early as Britain, for nowhere else was the working class so quickly in a majority. No class of peasants, no smallholders, no backward regions existed in Britain to provide the social basis for a democracy organised against the interest of the working class. The franchise was extended in 1867 and again in 1885 when male manual workers first constituted a majority of the electorate. Full universal suffrage came in 1928.[22] The preponderance of the working class in the electorate has since that time been overwhelming; the urban character of Britain has become more, not less marked, and several generations have now experienced working-class life in an urban industrial society.[23]

From the standpoint of industrial capital there were two main ways in which working-class demands for greater control over the production process, and greater participation in the state, might have been met. The power and strength of the workers' movement could have been harnessed in an alliance to fight for a fundamental reconstruction of the state and the civil society aimed at the abolition of social privilege and exclusiveness and the inauguration of a genuine democratic republic of equal citizens, a more egalitarian bourgeois order, a more energetic and mobile civil society. The six points of the Charter were a programme for such a democratic republic.[24] It called for universal male suffrage, equal electoral districts, annual parliaments, the payment of members, a secret ballot and no property qualifications for MPs. These demands could not have been met in the 1840s when they were made, except by breaking the still powerful hold of the landed interest on the state and on civil society, and unleasing a much wider process of social change.

The danger of such an alliance lay in the radicalisation inherent in any revolutionary upheaval, with consequences witnessed in France after 1789 and 1848. So long as those sections of the bourgeoisie still outside the British governing class were not forced into revolution, it was almost certain that it would prefer a different path, the path of accommodation with landed property and its political arm, gradual reform of the state to make it more effective in protecting the market order and aiding capital accumulation within it, and gradual concessions to working-class demands. A radical break in British institutions might have placed property itself at risk. As it was, once the landed interest had divided and given way first in 1832 and then in 1846, the industrialists and the bourgeois radicals found they could achieve all they wanted.

What they gave up, apart from a democratic republic free of the aristocratic ethos and rituals which continued to shroud most national institutions, was the chance to forestall the working class organising itself industrially and politically as a class. Only the creation of a new order in which all individual workers could participate as full members – free sellers of labour power, sovereign consumers, and potential capitalists – might have prevented the independent political organisation of the working class as a class conscious of its common interests against capital. Liberalism offered instead the opportunity to rise as compensation for the inequalities of the market. As Napoleon put it, 'Every French soldier carries in his cartridge-pouch the baton of a Marshal of France.'

The bourgeois radicals did not believe in the existence of a working *class*; a market order contained only individuals – individuals who worked, individuals who consumed, individuals who competed equally under a common framework of rules, which provided benefits for everyone, though in differing proportions. The bourgeois radicals correctly recognised that their ideal of a classless individualist market order required resistance to trade unions and all associations that sought to interfere with the workings of the free market, and resistance also to any state interventions in relations between individual workers and individual employers. No one has expressed such ideas better than Richard Cobden:

> I yield to no man in the world (be he ever so stout an advocate of the Ten Hours' Bill) in a hearty goodwill towards the great body of the working class; but my sympathy is not of the morbid kind which would lead me to despond over their future prospects. Nor do I partake of the spurious humanity which would indulge in an unreasonable kind of philanthropy at the expense of the great bulk of the community. Mine is that masculine species of charity which would lead me to instil in the minds of the labouring classes the love of independence, the privilege of self-respect, the disdain of being patronised or petted, the desire to accumulate and the ambition to rise.[25]

The second strategy for dealing with the problem of the working class, which gradually became dominant, also sought on occasion to attempt to stifle the class as a class. But it did not in general seek to do so by trying to win the consent of workers to the rule of capital through their participation as individual citizens and producers in an expanding bourgeois order, although this element was never absent. Instead, occasional repression was combined with a gradual recognition of the right of the working class to exist as a class and to organise as a class. The working class came to be treated as an estate of the realm, a privileged caste, a corporate body which required exceptional privileges and dispensations. Working-class demands and pressures were met by making concessions which eased the pressures, at the same time disturbing as little as possible the overarching order of the British state. The effect of this strategy was to preserve the social privileges, the wealth and the aristocratic culture of the upper classes, while greatly increasing the corporate power of the working class and blunting any tendency for it to develop in the direction of revolution.[26] A place was found for it in the British state.

Every specific concession, whether over political rights, or trade-union rights, or social rights, still had to be fought for by the working class and often created sharp divisions in the British ruling class. There was never a single coherent strategy for handling the Labour movement. Nevertheless, out of the balance of forces in the British state and its priorities arose a pattern of response to Labour and its demands which helped establish the Labour movement as a powerful and privileged estate by 1914, a world of Labour with its own culture, its own organisations, its own ideology and preoccupations.

So although the rise of Labour was bitterly resisted, ways were gradually found of accommodating this unwelcome class. The development of British capitalism was as a result significantly unlike either the United States or Germany. Britain lacked the egalitarian, open, and mobile bourgeois society of the United States, where the 'desire to accumulate' and the 'ambition to rise' did not encounter so many social obstacles. But it also lacked the nationalist drive to political modernisation, the building of national strength and national organisation, which in Germany established a very close partnership between government and business. Britain failed to move strongly in either direction and it was this failure which was a prime cause of the relative economic decline.

It follows that it was not Britain's early start that was the cause of the failure to keep up with later competitors, but the very social relations that made that early start possible, and which remained intact and strengthened by the success of that start. British dominance and British industrialisation belonged to an earlier phase in the development of the world economy. The domination of that world economy by industrial capitalism and the new assertive nation-states it helped create only started to come about in the 1870s and 1880s with the beginnings of industrialisation in Germany and the United States. From the standpoint of world economy, what went before was a preliminary – the creation of the conditions for 'full capitalism', for capital accumulation on a world scale.

Such a view is reinforced when the character of industrialisation in Britain is examined. The superiority of British industry over all competitors in the first half of the nineteenth century, and the huge wealth it created for the propertied classes, was due less to an overwhelming lead in technology, or to the mechanisation of the production process, but rather to a fuller development of production for the market in all spheres. Even the most mechanised sectors of British industry in the middle of the nineteenth century still relied upon a vast array of manual skills and sweated labour. Labour power was in abundant supply and most production methods remained highly labour-intensive and often highly skilled.[27] Capital accumulation was able to proceed at such a rapid pace because a vast labour force was available to be drawn into employment when demand was booming, and expelled when it slackened. The existence on one side of a large surplus population which could find no employment or tenure on the land, and the possibility of feeding such a population by imports of cheap food through the established network of trade and colonies, created the particular character of Victorian capitalism – an unparalleled accumulation of capital and an enormous industrial proletariat.

Britain's subsequent failure to maintain its lead reflected the slowness with which British ruling opinion grasped that industrialisation as it unfolded had created new conditions for successful accumulation, in particular the continual raising of productivity not by individual skill, or by numbers, but through the constant revolutionising of techniques and the reorganisation of production. In Britain, the security of Empire, and the stability of its domestic institutions, prevented changes occurring rapidly enough, which alone could have met the long-term peril. The response to competition that did occur – the retreat into trade and finance, the preference for traditional methods and traditional technologies – has been well documented.[28] The very success of the market order in Britain, and its extension overseas, geared commerce and industry and government to the maximisation of short-term profits, the exploitation of every existing opportunity to the full. The more difficult task, the planning for future growth and the anticipation of the long-term needs of capital accumulation, was provided for neither by British civil society, whose social conservatism continued to grow in line with its wealth, nor by the British state, which remained wedded to the liberal conception of its role in the national economy.

3.5 Mass democracy and the imperial state

The 1880s are a decisive watershed in the development of a world capitalist economy, not only as the period which saw industrialisation accelerating in several major states, but also because, as the scale of capital accumulation grew, so the conditions for maintaining it became increasingly onerous and the resistance to it more organised. The interventionist role of every national state expanded to promote the conditions, both in production and circulation, that would sustain accumulation and offset the tendency for profitability to decline; and also to meet and incorporate all those political pressures from nation-states, from the working class, and from oppressed national groups, which threatened the survival of the state and the viability of national capital. The result was a considerable expansion of both the administrative and the military agencies of the state and their links with the leading business sectors; at the same time the basis of representation was broadened, and national assemblies and parliaments gradually became institutions not for the direct representation of property interests, but for the conferring of national legitimacy upon the executive which now presided over the enlarged and expanding permanent apparatus of the state. This was accompanied by rising public expenditure and a broadening of the tax base until it embraced the whole community.[29]

Such developments were common to all the major states, although the exact pace of development and the eventual balance established varied according to local circumstances. Every major capitalist state saw a steady expansion of military and police expenditures and of welfare expenditures, as well as more overt intervention at many levels of the economy. In Britain the political system, through which the new pressures and problems of mass democracy were channelled, still centred upon Parliament. This had been reformed but very gradually. The franchise had been widened, and after 1885 the manual working class for the first time was in a majority. The ballot had also become secret. But the procedures of Parliament, the hereditary basis of the House of Lords, and the bizarre and arbitrary electoral system with its random relationship between votes cast and seats won, still remained.[30]

The rise and containment of the Labour movement has dominated the hundred years of British mass democracy. That this has coincided with the hundred years of British decline is not thought coincidental by many on the Right. Yet it is parties of the Right which have dominated British government since the advent of mass democracy, particularly before 1945. Whilst the Right emphasises the *rise* of Labour and the spread of collectivism throughout British society, the Left laments the containment of Labour and the blunting of its socialist purpose.

The parties that initially contested the space which mass

democracy created, the Liberals and Conservatives, were both developed out of the fairly loose factional groupings and personal cliques that dominated the unreformed Parliament. As the franchise was extended, so the party leaders began to perceive new realities that faced them, and the urgent need to create a party organisation outside Parliament if they were to compete effectively. The Liberals led the way, the Conservatives followed.[31] What each leadership also came to recognise was that the effect of mass democracy, and the expansion of the state administrative and military machine to cope with the new responsibilities and range of interventions that were required, brought a sharp separation between the roles politicians traditionally had to perform – organising support and exercising power. The task of managing the new electorate, the mass parties, and the party in parliament, became tasks which were related to, but by no means identical with, the tasks of directing the government and presiding over the permanent agencies of the state. Each group of party leaders became involved in an elaborate balancing act, because the open debate on policies, ideologies and values which took place in the political arena produced a conception of national interest which then had to be reconciled with the national interest as it was perceived by its more permanent guardians, those who staffed the agencies of the state.

The party debate conferred legitimacy on the executive through the idea that the party winning the election could employ the sovereign power to carry through its policies. But such an arrangement, such open competition between parties, the 'parts' of the political nation, was only stable so long as certain conventions were observed. In some states these were enshrined in formal constitutions. In Britain they were understood as unwritten rules and conventions. They included the notions that no party should implement a policy to which another was fundamentally opposed, that election defeats should be accepted, and that a new government should not attempt to reverse measures passed by its predecessor. Most important of all, however, was the idea that governments should attempt to govern according to realities and circumstances, which generally meant as these were perceived and interpreted by their military, financial and administrative advisers. They had to pursue policies which, by falling within a range accepted as politically practicable, would not create such opposition that they could not be implemented.

Democracy in capitalist states has always been marked by the open and pluralist nature of its electoral arena, and the narrow bounds of the consensus within which state policy moves. The harnessing of the two is performed by politicians, often imperfectly. For such a feat to be possible, the party system has continually to uphold the constitutional legitimacy of the government and the social organisation of the economy. Parties which seriously question either have to be excluded from government, or the political system will be in danger of collapse.

The history of British democracy reveals these problems well. In the period up to 1916 the competition for votes was dominated by the Liberals and the Conservatives. Both parties had established party caucuses, but although fears were expressed that Parliament might come to be dominated by the party caucuses, what actually happened was that both the party caucus and the parliamentary parties came to be dominated by the party leaderships. The competition between the parties centred upon foreign policy, education and church reform. Both parties in government accepted a policy consensus which covered the Empire, the gold standard, free trade, and the principles of sound finance, as well as taking for granted the capitalist organisation of the economy. A major conflict developed over free trade and tariff reform but the determination of the Conservatives to implement the latter was not tested before 1914. The other major conflict which came closest of all to a breakdown of the political system was over Home Rule for Ireland, but this was averted.

The undercurrent throughout this first period of mass democracy was the steadily growing influence of the working class. In electoral terms they were now dominant. The exceptional uniformity of the social structure in Britain gave little scope for regional ethnic or religious parties, and forced all parties to present themselves as national parties appealing on a national base, putting forward programmes and policies in the national interest, claiming to speak for the whole national community. It also forced them to compete for the votes of the working class, and gradually made the concerns of the working class the central concerns of domestic politics. Every party seeking to be a party of government in Britain has been obliged to be a working-class party – in electoral terms at least.

3.6 The Labour party and the Constitution

When the Labour party first appeared, in 1906, it was from the start a very different party from the two principal established parties. First, it did not originate in Parliament but out of an alliance between the trade unions and three socialist societies. Its mass organisation preceded its entry into Parliament. Second, it had no need to make a national appeal since it aspired to be the party of the working class. It was the only party which could afford to be openly sectional in its appeal to the electorate. Third, its aims at first were decidedly limited. It did not aspire to form governments. The aim of the Labour Representation Committee was 'to organise and maintain in Parliament and the country a political Labour party'. Its purpose was not to supplant either the Liberals or the Conservatives but to help defend trade-union rights. These had been seriously undermined by the legal judgement in the Taff Vale case in 1901, and this had persuaded the unions to modify their electoral alliance with the Liberals by sponsoring a party directly under their control which could put their case in the Imperial Parliament.[32]

The formation of the Labour party at first made little impact, but the situation was transformed by the First World War, which was the occasion for the first of the two major and lasting shifts that have so far occurred in the hundred years of mass democracy (the other was the Second World War). The disintegration of the Liberals, the considerable strengthening of the trade unions, and the shockwaves of the Russian Revolution all helped catapult

Labour from the modest 30 seats it had won in 1906 to being the major opposition party after 1918.[33] Once that happened, a central question of domestic politics came to be how Labour was to be handled. How was the governing class to adjust to the prospect of Labour becoming the second party in the two-party system, and therefore the alternative party of government? Labour was no longer the voice of a sectional interest but a party which had adopted in 1918 a new constitution whose goals included public ownership and industrial democracy, and proclaimed its readiness to make those goals the basis for a government programme.[34]

The task of handling Labour devolved upon the Conservative party, which had emerged after 1918 as the undisputed party both of property and of the state machine. Formerly it had been the party of landed interests and sections of industry, as well as the party of the Establishment. It was the party of the established Church, the Law, the Crown, the Universities, the Armed Forces. It was the party more mindful of England's institutional continuity than any other. It had become before 1914 the party of the Union, the party of the Empire, and the party of Tariff Reform.

In 1918 this party entered the period of its greatest electoral dominance. Between 1916 and 1945 the Conservatives were out of office for only three years. Yet throughout this period the party remained on the defensive. Although overwhelmingly dominant in Parliament, it entered coalitions on three occasions (on two the Prime Minister came from another party). Although committed on paper to overturning free trade, the party continued throughout the 1920s to pursue the orthodoxy of free trade and sound finance.[35] Only in 1931 when the gold standard had to be abandoned did the party partially implement its protectionist programme. Similarly, and despite the existence of contrary views within the party, the Conservatives moved cautiously in confronting Labour.[36] Conservative tactics helped to contain and delay Labour's advance but they did not prevent it, and they helped to prepare the ground for Labour's electoral triumph in the 1940s.

The party was divided in the 1920s between the advocates of three strategies. There were those who wanted to treat the Labour party as the advance guard of Bolshevism, and to use every opportunity to smash the Labour movement both politically and industrially. There were those who believed class war was the greatest danger facing the country, and that the way to avert it was to implement the programme of Social Imperialism which Joseph Chamberlain and Lord Milner had evolved before 1914, and create a national movement that transcended class divisions.[37] Finally there were those who believed that the primary task must be to incorporate the Labour movement within the state by winning its leaders both in Parliament and in the trade unions to constitutional methods, to an acceptance of the existing state and the need to govern within its constraints.[38]

All three strategies involved risks and costs, but the third was most in accord with the past pattern of British development. Its triumph is most visible, perhaps paradoxically, during the General Strike – the most serious confrontation between organised Labour and the state this century. This was a strike deliberately provoked by the government, which had made meticulous preparations and calculated the balance of forces with precision.[39] The more serious period of unrest immediately after the war had been ended by a slump and rising unemployment after 1920. By 1926 trade-union membership and industrial militancy were already falling. The government had no need openly to confront the industrial power of the working class. In 1919 Lloyd George had pledged that the National government was 'determined to fight Prussianism in the industrial world as they have fought it on the Continent of Europe, with the whole might of the nation'. But there was no longer anything very Prussian about the stance of organised labour in 1926.

The reason the government provoked the strike was that it needed to force through a general reduction of wage costs in British industry, following the decision to return to the gold standard in 1925 at the pre-war parity of \$4.86. Otherwise British exports would be uncompetitive. As

Baldwin expressed it, 'all the workers in this country have got to take reductions to help put industry on its feet'. The coal industry was a leading exporter and began making heavy losses following the return to gold, and so the mineowners demanded a lengthening of hours and a cut in pay, to make exporting profitable again. The miners' refusal was backed by the TUC which threatened a general strike in their support. The government postponed the strike for six months, during which it made its preparations, then it precipitated it, arbitrarily breaking off negotiations with the TUC.

On the government side there were many who wanted to use the strike as the opportunity to deal a mortal blow to the Labour movement. The *Daily Mail* articulated such views with its customary vigour. It denounced the TUC as a 'barely disguised Soviet' and it declared 'Two Governments cannot exist in the same capital. One must destroy the other or surrender to the other.' In an editorial on 5 May, the day before the strike began, the *Daily Mail* told its readers:

> In Italy . . . the Government, which had been placed in power by lawful and constitutional means, failed to do its duty. It did not organise the essential services. It did not protect the nation against a truculent and lawless minority and the immediate consequence was that, after a period of intense suffering, society in Italy organised itself in the Fascist Movement to defend its existence.

Several government ministers, including Churchill, and Joynson Hicks, the Home Secretary, were closely associated with this perspective. Churchill, placed in charge of the *British Gazette*, the Government newspaper, was responsible for many of its inflammatory statements[40] and was reportedly in favour of sending troops and tanks into working-class districts.

The other face of government strategy was represented by Baldwin. He had no illusions as to the nature of the TUC challenge. From the start the TUC defined the strike as a large sympathy stoppage with limited aims, to bring pressure to bear on the government and the mineowners to prevent the cuts in the miners' standard of living. There was no thought of seeking the overthrow of the government. Baldwin also knew that many of the Labour party leaders feared a victory for the strikers far more than they feared a victory for the government. As Jimmy Thomas put it so memorably in the House of Commons: 'I have never disguised that in a challenge to the Constitution God help us unless the Government won'. The government, by defining the strike from the outset as a challenge to the Constitution and therefore refusing to negotiate on any of the strikers' demands, ensured that the leaders of the Labour movement would quickly be faced by the alternative of either challenging the Constitution and organising to overthrow the government, or surrendering. After nine days they surrendered, leaving the miners to fight on alone to eventual defeat.[41]

The complete victory won by the government helped consolidate the strategy of ensuring that the TUC and the Labour leadership would always act within the existing Constitution, and would not seek to use industrial power to obtain political ends. Subsequent political developments, notably the collapse of the Labour government in 1931, and the muted resistance of organised labour to the slump and the depression, fully justified Baldwin's decision against arresting the TUC leaders in 1926 and attempting to crush the strike militarily. He recognised that an important factor in containing and blocking the advance of Labour was the nature of its leaders and their political perspectives. In this sense the General Strike and its outcome represented an important stage in the accommodation of Labour's interests and the incorporation of its leadership.

Yet the policy had its drawbacks. For although the Conservatives remained overwhelmingly dominant electorally, they were now compelled to fight on a different terrain. By helping to define the basic party division in Britain as between Conservative and Labour, they helped make class the basis of party politics. Class identity became for fifty years the most important factor in electoral choice. This placed the Conservatives in a highly vulnerable position, since it threatened to place them in a permanent minority, should a high proportion of the working-class electorate ever identify with the party of the working class. Since the 1920s the Conservatives have been obliged to compete in a class-based two-party system by maintaining an appeal to working-class voters across the class divide.

Conservatives were confident that they could do so because of their deep understanding of the nature of class in Britain. They saw that much class voting was a passive affirmation of a particular status rather than a class interest, and that that particular status was not a universal experience or aspiration throughout the working class; many workers could be detached and won for Conservatism by identifying the party with the authority and hierarchy of the traditional state, and by appealing to the patriotism of the working class, and to the desire of many workers for social mobility or for economic independence. This electoral perspective proved highly successful. The national issues the Conservatives have espoused have kept the Labour party from the position of natural dominance of the electoral system, which a class-based politics would appear to ensure for it.[42]

But for such a class-based party system to function smoothly both party leaderships had tacitly to agree to govern within the constraints of the Constitution and the state. The price of ensuring that the Labour movement would observe those constraints was confirmation of the special role and privileges of its organisations. This helps account for the strange aftermath of the General Strike. Before the strike began the *Financial Times* wrote:

> The strike will be the biggest bull point that the Stock Exchange has had for years if it should be settled in favour of authority. For investment and speculation alike have been overcast these many years by Labour threats, fears, strikes. Victory of the Government in this greatest strike of all would mean the loss by the trade unions of so much prestige and money as would cause wholesale defections from their ranks amongst the men of whom great numbers are none too loyal Trade Unionists as it is.

It would also have the moral effect of showing the nation is strong enough to defeat the poisonous doctrines chewed by foreign-bred firebrands. Once a permanent peace becomes assured, finance will find its feet firmly fixed upon a basis more secure than it has obtained this century.[43]

The strike was indeed settled in favour of authority but the British economy remained stagnant and unemployment high. Part of this was due to the difficulties in the world economy, but part was because an employers' offensive did not materialise. There were many sackings and victimisation of strikers in some industries in 1926 but there was no general reduction of wages. The government, urged on by its backbenchers, passed a Trades Dispute Act in 1927 which limited trade-union privileges, but it did not remove those that had been granted in 1906.[44] The Conservatives failed to press home either their victory over the Labour movement in 1926 or the political victory in 1931, and this was not because of the great strength of trade unionism, which was declining, but because of the paramount importance attached by the Conservative leadership to encouraging the emergence of a responsible leadership in control of the Labour party.

The story has often been told of how the British Labour movement lost its revolutionary will after the collapse of Chartism and became increasingly integrated within British capitalism; how a defensive trade-union movement, organised initially around skilled craftsmen, fought for extremely limited material gains and the defence of trade-union rights; how the close involvement of the trade unions with the Labour party committed that party to the defensive and corporate perspectives of the unions, and nourished the growth of a leadership that was prepared to meet basic trade-union interests whilst managing the state in a traditional and orthodox manner. But the other side of that process is just as important. The party never succeeded in being entirely a party of managers, nor in severing completely its links with the union leaders, and socialist activists in the constituencies.[45]

The two-party system where parties are expected to alternate in government depends much more than do multi-party systems upon a consensus on fundamentals. The Labour party's adherence to that consensus has been real but it has also been insecure. The insecurity derives from the way the party is organised, and has periodically threatened the ability of the party leadership to assert its control not only in the parliamentary party but over the party organisation outside Parliament. The ability of the leadership to dominate the party has always rested heavily on the support of major trade-union leaders whose block votes can dwarf constituency party votes. Whenever that support has been lost or split the party leadership has been in trouble. The party originated as the political arm of the Labour movement, a mass organisation outside Parliament. Its internal structure has been more democratic than other parties for that reason, and its debates have been less about how support can be organised for the government policies that are deemed to be necessary for the state, than about which policies will most advance the interest of organised labour and the construction of socialism. Given the political goals and ideologies of the Labour rank and file and the close links with organised labour, the Labour party despite all the efforts of its leaders has never succeeded in ridding itself of its class character. Although it became an alternative party of government, particularly between 1940 and 1980, it never entirely lost its identity as a political movement. The constitutional question posed by the rise of Labour was not fully settled in that period because the Labour party never completely accepted capitalism ideologically and never severed its connection with the trade unions.

The way in which the working class was eventually incorporated preserved property and preserved the existing state; it averted social revolution but it also put major obstacles in the path of a successful capitalism. It prevented a consensus ever being extended to include the overriding importance of a successful and competitive industrial economy. Instead, the economy became the main battleground between the parties, with continued disputes over the rival merits of private and public enterprise and over the system of taxation. The consensus on foreign policy, on Britain's relations with the world economy and alliance with the United States, as well as the consensus on the formal constitution of the state, was complete. What was lacking was a consensus on the means for industrial modernisation.

PART III

STRATEGY

4

Managing social democracy

The question is whether we are prepared to move out of the nineteenth century *laissez-faire* into an era of liberal socialism, by which I mean a system where we can act as an organised community for common purposes . . . while respecting and protecting the individual – his freedom of choice, his faith, his mind and its expression, his enterprise and his property.

J. M. Keynes[1]

When we came in we were told that there weren't sufficient inducements to invest. So we provided the inducements. Then we were told people were scared of balance of payments difficulties leading to stop–go. So we floated the pound. Then we were told of fears of inflation: and now we're dealing with that. And still you aren't investing enough!

Edward Heath (speech to the Institute of Directors, 1973)

The history of external expansion and internal compromise examined in Chapters 2 and 3 left important legacies and allowed the accumulation of specific internal weaknesses. The legacies were the patterns of external dependence of the British economy and the international orientation of the British state and British business. The weaknesses were the institutional organisation of the principal classes and interests, and their relations to the state. In the social democratic era that opened in 1940 the interaction of these two elements established the constraints within which government operated.

Britain's dilemmas in the post-war world stemmed from an inability of its leaders to make clear strategic choices about the relative importance of the traditional world role, as against the modernisation of the society and the economy. The fatal persistence in the belief that no choice was necessary gravely undermined the modernisation strategy of the 1960s and wrecked many of the reforms which it launched. This chapter considers the background to that modernisation strategy and outlines its main features.

4.1 The triumph of social democracy

1940 was a major watershed in British politics. It also opened a new phase in the hundred years' decline. The war emergency meant not only the organisation of a war economy but the establishment of a national coalition between the Conservative government, now led by Churchill, and the Labour party. Participation in the National government completed the incorporation of the parliamentary and trade-union leadership of the Labour party into the service of the state. As a result the second war against Germany was fought, to a greater extent than in 1914–18, in the name of goals that commanded popular support: the defeat of Fascism, the defence of democracy, and the promise of reforms after the war that would eliminate unemployment and create a more egalitarian society. The military struggle and the plans for reconstruction were closely related in the overall war effort.

The war established social democracy in Britain. The patient strategy of containment of the Labour movement pursued by the Conservatives finally broke down as German tanks poured into France. Labour's leaders henceforward were to be generally accepted into the policy-making élites, and major concessions were made to the long-standing demands and interests of the Labour movement. But important though this internal accommodation was, both for the degree of resilience and unity with which Britain fought and for the development of British politics after the war, it was greatly overshadowed by the effect of the war on the world balance of power and the organisation of the world economy.

Britain's decision to fight Germany a second time brought a sudden end to Britain's world dominance. Between 1939 and 1945 Britain was not only forced to liquidate a great part of the foreign assets accumulated before 1914 and then rebuilt after 1918; it also amassed sizeable debts. Sterling liabilities were now three times as great as British gold and foreign currency reserves, whereas before 1939 they had been roughly in balance.[2] This was seriously to undermine the continued operation of sterling as an international currency. In order to prosecute the war against Germany and Japan, and still more to win, Britain was forced to rely on United States aid.

In military terms the war not only established the ascendancy of the United States and the Soviet Union; it also exposed the weakness of the British Empire. British naval power was clearly no longer sufficient to protect it, and parts of the Empire, particularly India, could not be retained for very long against the wishes of the two leading world powers and rising nationalist opposition. The course and outcome of the war made eventual withdrawal from the Empire certain. It ended for ever the traditional military strategy which had aided British expansion and secured British dominance.

The war also brought about what years of peace had not accomplished, a new world economic order. Its basis was the now immense productive and military power of the United States. Britain's forlorn attempt in the 1920s to rebuild a stable international system and free trade had finally foundered in 1931, when the gathering Depression forced even Britain off the gold standard and into adoption of protectionist policies. There was to be no repeat attempt after 1945. British financial and industrial weakness, in relation to the United States, had become such that Britain was quite unable to continue to play the leading role in maintaining the institutional order of world capitalism.

The rebuilding of the world economy around the United States, which at first was intended to embrace but later excluded the Soviet bloc, formed the framework in which Britain's experiment in social democracy went forward. The political basis of the British war effort substantially increased the support of the Labour party so that it became an equal contender with the Conservatives, and it also weakened the resolve of the Conservative leadership to resist the consolidation and extension of new state functions and responsibilities which had been developing since the beginning of the century.[3]

Labour's victory in 1945 was decisive in parliamentary terms (a majority of 146), although this was still less than half of the poll.[4] The new government began carrying through the plans for reconstruction which had been agreed by the Coalition. The war marked a sudden alteration in Britain's world status and the balance of its internal politics, but there was no similar discontinuity in the formal organisation of the state itself. The general character of British institutions was little changed. Whereas some of the defeated powers had their institutions entirely remodelled, few such changes occurred in Britain or were proposed by the Labour party. The fundamentals of the education system, the electoral system, the House of Lords, and the civil service all remained – although all had been major targets for reform in the past.[5]

The changes Labour did introduce, and which became the basis for the internal policy consensus of the post-war years, owed a great deal to the ideas and plans of Keynes and Beveridge. Their acceptance was most clearly signalled during the war with the publication of the White Paper on Full Employment (1944), which committed governments to maintain a high level of activity and employment in the economy; and by the Beveridge Report (1942), which laid out plans for a comprehensive scheme of social security. To these were added Labour's plans for a national health service and the nationalisation of major public utilities including gas and electricity, as well as the railways and the mines.[6]

The implementation of all these plans meant a permanent enlargement of the public sector, more detailed public regulation of the economy, and a higher level of public spending.[7] This required a further major extension of the tax base; direct taxes on the whole working population were to be the major source of revenue for the social democratic state.[8] Apart from the measures of nationalisation, which were mostly confined to loss-making industries and public utilities,[9] the status and organisation of private business were not questioned, but confirmed. What had changed was the relative weight of the Labour movement. The trade unions recovered the privileges they had lost in 1927 and won the commitment to full employment, concessions which were expected to increase their membership and improve their bargaining position.[10] The working class as a whole now exerted more pressure on government, because the new levels of public expenditure that were established made issues of collective consumption, as well as economic prosperity, central to the competition between the parties.[11]

4.2   Reconstruction

The economic policy of the Labour government was naturally dominated by the problems of reconstruction. The loss of exports and of overseas investment income during the war meant a huge structural deficit on the balance of payments.[12] Essential imports could not be financed. The difficulty of quickly switching the economy back to peacetime production, the backlog of demand built up during the war, and the continuance of public spending at a high level, mainly because of the new welfare plans, all added to the pressure of demand and the risk of a very rapid inflation. These difficulties, however, were overcome with assistance from the United States, exports were expanded enormously and the export gap closed.[13] Manufacturing output recovered.[14] Strikes remained illegal under wartime regulations, rationing and many physical controls stayed in force to restrain consumption and direct investment, interest rates were kept at 2 per cent, the trade unions accepted wage restraint and the electorate accepted austerity.[15] Inflation was not entirely avoided but fairly successfully suppressed, until the decision to rearm in 1951.[16]

A measure of the success of reconstruction was the fact that Britain still accounted for 25 per cent of exports of world manufactures in 1951. At the beginning of that decade the British economy looked strong. The slump in the world economy which had been widely expected after the post-war reconstruction boom had not occurred and Britain seemed certain to benefit from any expansion in the world economy that now took place. Britain's industrial structure had been substantially transformed in the inter-war period, particularly during the 1930s when both domestic and imperial markets were protected by tariffs. The new high technology and mass production industries – electrical engineering, cars, chemicals – which had been so slow to develop in Britain before 1914, were all now well established.[17] Britain still possessed a powerful financial sector with unrivalled and long-established banking, commercial, insurance and shipping businesses. The Americans, who had always been one of the most protectionist nations in the world economy, were now eager to reduce trade barriers. Britain had also emerged once more from a major conflict still formally undefeated, still free from invasion, its institutions still intact, and having apparently increased its cohesion and its unity by completing the successful incorporation of the Labour movement within the state, and establishing a new social democratic consensus, guaranteeing civil, political, and now social rights to every citizen.[18]

How could such a state fail? Yet fail it did. It was during the decades of the long boom, as the tables in Chapter 1 clearly indicate, that Britain's decline began in earnest. For Britain to fall behind the leading world powers with their continent-sized economies was unsurprising; it had been inevitable from the time Britain committed itself to remain inside the liberal world order and decisively cast aside any attempt to develop its empire as a protected sphere. What is more surprising is why despite all the initial advantages it appeared to enjoy in 1945, Britain has consistently performed worse than other states with similar populations, resources, and industrial, and social structures.

The obstinate refusal of the economy to respond to the national consensus for growth and modernisation has produced sweeping searches for sinister sectional interests which have dared frustrate the national will. Gladstone once remarked, 'The interests are always awake, while the country often slumbers and sleeps.' Scapegoats for Britain's ills have included the civil service, the trade unions, the City of London, the managers of industry and, more generally, Britain's 'anti-enterprise' or 'anti-business' culture.[19]

Certainly Britain had accumulated many internal weaknesses during the years of power and success, affecting the performance of all sections of society. But, in themselves, these weaknesses could have been identified and might have been overcome. What preserved them and made their effect ultimately so damaging was the world role of the British state in the post-war period.

4.3 The American connection

The real linchpin of the post-war consensus is the one least often discussed – the alliance with the United States. It was the policy which all governments maintained and, though occasionally questioned, it never looked remotely like being overthrown or seriously challenged. That was because it was no ordinary alliance. It was a 'special relationship', more special for the British than for the Americans, because it was the means by which the British world role was preserved – by being transferred to the Americans. Britain accepted American leadership in the new world economic and political order and became prepared to act as a junior partner of the Americans, subordinating its interests to the United States, but maintaining those roles and commitments which the Americans found useful. Britain reduced its commitment to police this world economy and no longer provided its principal medium of exchange, but still maintained extensive military commitments in certain parts of the world – including Greece, Palestine and the Middle East, Singapore and Malaysia; and sterling was restored as an international currency, not as powerful or important as the dollar, or as eagerly sought, but an international medium of exchange none the less.[20]

Why were the British prepared to undertake such heavy commitments to assist the Americans in the new global role as the dominant capitalist power? Two interlinked considerations were crucial: first, the dependence of the British economy on an open liberal trading network; and second, the need to ensure the security of the capitalist world against the Soviet Union.

The terms of the special relationship after 1945 meant the prolongation, not the termination, of Britain's traditional world role. The Americans came to appreciate the advantages of sharing the burdens of leadership in the world economy, so long as Britain remained subordinate to overall American interests and strategy. Earlier antagonism between the two powers had been much more intense. The Americans were strongly opposed to the British Empire, particularly in the 1930s, when it formed a protectionist bloc which discriminated against American goods.[21] As American productivity rose so the Americans became articulate advocates of the need for free trade and open national economies, and American industries emerged from behind the protectionist walls that had nurtured their early development.

American hostility to Britain was still marked at the end of the Second World War. One American General objected to weapons purchased under Lend–Lease being used to recapture Hong Kong and so restore part of the Empire to British control. As one Congressman attacking further loans for Britain put it, aid would merely promote 'too much damned socialism at home, and too much damned Imperialism abroad'.[22] The existence of the British Empire and the colonial empires of other European states was viewed as inimical to American interests, and Britain was still regarded as a major commercial rival. As soon as the war was over the United States dismayed its principal ally by abruptly ending Lend–Lease. The American view was that British imperialism only deserved aid when it was fighting on behalf of the United States. This ruthless decision reflected how much the British war effort had depended on American aid and the British naturally felt they were being treated as one of the defeated powers. They were forced to apply to the Americans for a new loan to pay for the imports they desperately needed while the economy was reconstructed.

The loan that was finally negotiated – the Washington Loan Agreements (1946) – spelled out fairly clearly the new balance between Britain and America. The conditions of the loan were that Britain should not seek to reintroduce imperial preference and discriminate against American goods in Empire markets; and that sterling should be made convertible at the earliest opportunity.[23]

Strong opposition was mounted in Britain to the terms of the loan by the imperialist wing of the Conservative party and by the Left of the Labour party. The former stressed the loss of British independence of action, the latter argued that a 'socialist' Britain should not ally with a capitalist America. Many in America likewise questioned whether a capitalist America should grant loans to countries that were planning to nationalise industries and take other steps hostile to capitalism. That the terms of the loan had to be accepted, however, was never in doubt in Britain, partly because of the serious consequences if the loan were withheld, partly because the makers of British foreign policy were anxious that nothing should be done to jeopardise the willingness of the United States to use its dominant military and industrial power to create a new world political and economic order. The shape of such an order was already appearing with the Bretton Woods Agreement of 1944, which resulted in decisions to set up the IMF (the International Monetary Fund), and a World Bank; to establish the dollar as the leading world currency; and to work for more open and unrestricted trade in the hope of avoiding any return to the protectionist and fragmented world economy of the 1930s.[24]

The bitterness over the terms of the Washington Loan Agreements was soon forgotten once the Cold War began. As soon as the other capitalist powers – former allies like Britain, or occupied enemies like Germany – were no longer seen primarily as potential or actual industrial and military rivals, but as territories that might be penetrated and incorporated into an expanding Soviet Empire, American attitudes to loans for its allies abruptly changed. The plan to dismantle German factories and plough over their sites was shelved. The Marshall Aid programme poured in funds to help rebuild the economies of the capitalist world, both to provide long-term markets and investments for American companies and to stave off either internal social revolution or external Russian intervention.[25]

The British played a major part in this change of direction of American policy. A crucial moment in the evolution of the new strategy was the speech by Churchill at Fulton, Missouri, in 1946 when he declared that an Iron Curtain had descended across Europe. Churchill's speech continued the policy over which he had presided when Prime Minister, and reflected the Foreign Office view of the Soviet Union and its intentions. In the latter stages of the war British strategic thinking became preoccupied with containment of Soviet power. In this perspective the utter defeat of Germany would make Russia the supreme continental power in Europe, a power which not only strove to be autarkic like Germany, but had also abolished capitalist relations of production, and proclaimed an ideology of world revolution which disguised the pursuit of its national interests.

It was a major triumph for British policy after 1945 when the Americans endorsed the idea that the Russians must be contained and isolated at all costs, for the security of the world order. The moral and crusading bent of American foreign policy soon made the Cold War assume extravagant dimensions.[26] Its lasting result was to launch the Americans irrevocably on their career of world power and responsibility. The British loyally supported them. The role of principal ally proved more rewarding than the role of principal commercial rival.

The change in direction in American policy was a fundamental one. Their hostility to colonial empires remained, but pressure on Britain to withdraw immediately from its colonies was eased. Similarly the failure of the attempt to restore convertibility for sterling in 1947 was accepted calmly. Sterling did not in fact become fully convertible until 1958. More important to the Americans became the fact that the British were active and willing members of all the military alliances the Americans set up – NATO, SEATO and CENTO; that they were prepared to rearm, and to maintain armed forces in Germany and in a network of bases around the world; that they fully accepted the new economic and financial institutions, in particular the IMF and GATT (General Agreement on Trade and Tariffs) and the programme of financial stability and more open trade.

In return the Americans were prepared to underwrite aspects of the British world role. Sterling was allowed to remain an international currency. Britain was allowed to retain a colonial Empire that was still sizeable, even after the granting of independence to India and Pakistan in 1947. It was not simply an illusion after 1945 that Britain still had a world role and could still act in part as a world power. The special relationship with America permitted it. The Foreign Office view of Britain's place in the world prevailed.

4.4 The burden of the world role

An influential school of writing on British decline has long argued that the effort to sustain a world role helped cripple Britain in the post-war world.[27] It postponed the acknowledgement that British world power was finally at an end; at the same time it imposed quite exceptional burdens on the British economy. Britain emerged as one of the two states bearing the costs of maintaining an international economic and political order, yet it no longer had the industrial base to support such costs. Military spending was higher in Britain than in any country of the western alliance other than the United States itself.[28] More important, overseas

military spending was high,[29] much higher in real terms
than it had been in the heyday of the Empire, when British
forces had been kept to a minimum and the cost of forces
stationed overseas had largely been met by local taxation.
Government policy placed a heavy extra burden on the
British balance of payments.

This meant that Britain had a very different relationship
with the reorganised world economy from that of Germany,
Japan or even France. The level of military spending and
overseas military involvement, the special status of sterling,
and the scope for the international expansion of British
business, all marked out Britain from the others. It helps to
account for one of the great paradoxes of British decline –
why an economy performing so poorly should nevertheless
have produced more transnational companies than any
country apart from the United States. The opportunities
that Britain's imperial trading and financial connections
provided led to the development after 1950 of some large
and very successful international businesses. In 1970,
although Britain was considerably poorer than Germany,
eleven of the world's one hundred largest businesses were
British, compared with eighteen for the rest of the EEC.
Among the 200 largest non-American companies, fifty-three
were British, forty-three Japanese, twenty-five German and
twenty-three French. Throughout the period of the long
boom foreign investment and overseas sales were both
much greater by British companies than by German,
Japanese or French. By 1971 the value of foreign production
by British business was more than double the value of
visible export trade, whereas it was less than 40 per cent for
Germany and Japan. The number of British firms operating
six or more foreign subsidiaries had expanded from one-
fifth in 1950 to one-half in 1970, and all the top hundred
British manufacturing companies had become multinational by 1970. Furthermore, investment overseas as a percentage of investment in domestic manufacturing was never
less than 17 per cent in the 1970s and in some years was
above 30 per cent.[30]

As a result, Britain's relationship to the world economy
after 1945 was more like that of the United States than like

that of France, Germany and Japan. Britain achieved a growth rate similar to that of the United States, but the productivity gap between the two economies remained immense. The result of the renewal of Britain's traditional liberal orientation to the world economy was that a serious conflict began to develop between the international priorities of British policy and the needs of the domestic economy. This was sometimes presented as a new clash between manufacturing industry and the financial sector. But the real clash was between the new and often combined international operations of British industry and British finance, and the requirements of domestic expansion.[31]

The conflict was expressed in the repeated balance of payments crises of the 1950s and 1960s. The margin of failure was always small. British trade had improved dramatically compared with the position before 1939. After 1945 exports of goods were seldom less than 95 per cent of imports in value. Before 1939 they had generally covered only 75 per cent. The 5 per cent shortfall was more than made up by the regular surplus on invisible trade. Therefore, taken on its own, the British balance of *trade* would have ensured balance of payments surpluses in every year up to 1973, with the possible exception of 1964.[32] The immediate cause of the sterling crises in 1947, 1949, 1951, 1955, 1957, 1961, and between 1963 and 1967 was generally, though not invariably, a deficit on the balance of payments. These occurred not because exports were too low but because government spending overseas and private investment overseas were too high.

The argument of the Treasury, the traditional custodian of Britain's liberal external policy, was that such spending was essential to maintain political stability and an open world trading system, and to develop new supplies of food and raw materials. The Treasury calculated in the middle of the 1950s that an annual surplus of £200 to £300 million was required on the balance of payments to finance the level of overseas spending that was considered desirable.[33] If such a surplus however were not forthcoming there was rarely any suggestion that overseas spending should be cut or drastically restricted. The burden of adjustment was placed instead on the domestic economy. If demand were reduced sufficiently in the economy imports would fall and external balance would be restored.

The external balance had to be corrected because of the effect on sterling if it was not. Sterling was used as an international currency not because it was any longer the currency of the capitalist economy which enjoyed the highest productivity in the world economy, but partly because it was the international medium of exchange for the sterling area, and partly because of its use in international trade.[34] This latter function was closely linked to the financial, shipping, and insurance services provided by the City. The willingness of foreign holders of sterling to continue to hold it and use it depended on them remaining confident that the value of sterling would be maintained at its fixed parity of $2.80. The surest trigger of a sterling crisis was the announcement of a heavy balance of payments deficit. Restoring confidence was achieved by raising interest rates, squeezing credit and increasing taxes, in order to lower the level of demand in the economy. Such measures caused a stop–go cycle, and alternating periods of expansion and stagnation, and this cycle can be identified as a leading cause of Britain's slower rate of growth of productivity and output, especially since the periods of 'go' got shorter, whilst the periods of 'stop' got longer.[35]

The fluctuations in demand appear to have been of relatively little importance in themselves. Other countries suffered as great fluctuations without any apparent adverse effects on investment.[36] One reason was that their industrial structure was different. Japanese and German firms were nationally based and nationally directed. In Britain a significant section of its leading businesses was already internationally oriented. Erratic growth of demand in Britain appears to have accelerated the tendency for firms to diversify and expand abroad. The virtuous circle between high growth of output, high investment and high productivity was not realised within Britain, in part because of the opportunities many British firms already had, and others sought to acquire, of expanding outside the British economy. The result was that the leading sector of British capital retained its competitiveness and its strength by operating internationally, rather than by building outwards from its base in the domestic economy, and this was an important reason why exports, productivity and investment were all lower than in the more successful economies.

4.5 The growing awareness of decline

The return to Britain's traditional liberal, outward-looking policy after 1945 was revealed principally in the priority given to sterling and also by the relatively few restrictions placed on the export of capital. These policies were not the only cause of Britain's slow growth rate, but they made it much more difficult to tackle the internal weaknesses of the economy, and with each successive sterling crisis the prospect for escape from the straitjacket grew smaller. After the special circumstances of reconstruction, government energies were never so concentrated again on renewing and reorganising domestic industry for the industrial challenge that now faced it.

The difficulties the British economy encountered during the long boom were not those of an underdeveloped economy lacking in successful businesses. On the contrary it had a very successful business sector. The problem was that this sector often found it easier to accumulate capital by expanding abroad than by investing in the domestic economy. This had been true of the City before 1914 when the greatest outflow of capital of all took place. But that movement reflected the fact that the absolute level of British productivity was still considerably higher than productivity in most other countries, and that the rate of return on loans, even at 5 per cent, was generally higher than could be obtained by investing in Britain, where technological advance was only proceeding slowly. British industry was not starved of funds by the City – it was merely that domestic investment did not appear profitable enough.

The situation was apparently very different during the long boom. The technological lead established by American industry was now colossal, and America was far better organised than Britain had ever been to develop new technologies. The overseas expansion of American goods and American capital now became a flood, as American companies strove to expand their markets and their overseas production by exploiting their technological and organisational advantages over their competitors in the rest of the world. International companies became the major agent of capital accumulation and an ever-extending division of labour. The older pattern of foreign investment of capital loans raised in one country and employed by local entrepreneurs in another was superseded. Britain had been the centre of the old kind of *rentier* investment, but its assets had been severely depleted by the cost of the two world wars. What was surprising was that British companies should be second only to American in expanding overseas after 1945, when British productivity lagged so far behind. What might have been expected was that the 'best-practice' techniques developed by the Americans would have spread to British industry, either through direct American investment by American companies, or through the sales of patents and licences and the reorganisation of British industry by its own efforts. In this way innovations would have been diffused and absorbed, investment and productivity raised throughout the world economy, and the technological lead of the Americans steadily reduced.

This kind of process is precisely what did happen to many developed economies during the long boom, and was a major factor in the economic 'miracles' and the exceptional rates of growth that some countries achieved. It was certainly a factor in the improved rate of growth of output and productivity that Britain experienced. But by the end of the boom the gap between British and American productivity was still virtually as wide as at the beginning.

The problem that began to preoccupy policy-makers was why this should be so; why countries like Germany and Japan were able to grow continuously at such higher rates than Britain and to adjust to new industries and new techniques so much more rapidly. One major factor that was isolated was the growing division between the profitable and expanding international businesses of the City and the leading manufacturing companies in Britain on one side, and the rest of British industry on the other. It was argued that much of British industry had been uncompetitive for far too long, shielded by first informal and then formal protection in Empire markets, and protection in the 1930s in the home market. With government encouragement aimed at reducing the numbers of closures and bankruptcies during the Depression, the formation of cartels, price-fixing and production-sharing agreements had grown apace in the 1930s.[37] Allied to the social conservatism of British institutions, the comparatively low status of industry in relation to the professions and public service, the lack of technical and business education, the proliferation of small family businesses, and the resulting poor quality of many British managers, what British industry clearly required after 1945 was a wholesale clear-out and reorganisation, and the patient building of new practices in technology and organisation that the most successful industrial capitalism in the world was employing.

No such new beginning was made. The pace of adjustment to the demands of competition in the world economy was leisurely, and this was partly because of two major factors from Britain's past development – the liberal ethos of the state which had always characterised government – industry relations, and the relations between the state and the working class. The first was most clearly evident in the general reluctance governments had long displayed in enforcing greater competition in the domestic economy except through the external sanction of free trade. This reluctance showed itself most clearly in the unwillingness to tackle the uncompetitive, status-ridden institutions of British society, which helped maintain the cohesion of the ruling class but also diverted energies into the service of the Empire, and the state, and encouraged conservative attitudes which impeded industrial rationalisation. A traditional British lament was that expressed by the *Westminster Gazette* in 1900:

The problem if we are considering civilised life and not merely what is called commercial supremacy, is to find

the mean between this American disease and the complacency which is fully convinced that old ways are best
because they are old.[38]

That mean was not easily found, that complacency not
easily dispelled.

Alongside the failure of the state to create greater
competition in the past and to ensure a more dynamic and
expanding civil society, growing dissatisfaction began to be
voiced at the inadequacies of the traditional non-
interventionist role of the state in the economy. As with so
many other things the Attlee government had left much of
this untouched. The state was spending more in the 1950s
and was involved more in ensuring the success and viability
of the economy. Governments were expected to find
remedies for economic problems rather than declaring in
the traditional manner that it was nothing to do with them.
They organised their economic policy around the achievement of full employment, stable prices, a surplus on the
balance of payments and economic growth.

What is remarkable in retrospect is the scale of the goals
governments sought to achieve, and the paucity of the
means with which they equipped themselves for achieving
them. The bulk of industry was still in private hands and
industry retained its traditional suspicion of the state.[39]
The far-reaching controls of the war economy were all
dismantled and nothing was put in their place. No effort
was made to forge the close institutional links between
government, industry, and the banks that existed in many
other countries and formed the basis for their national
industrial and commercial strategies. The Keynesian
'revolution' in Britain, although it marked a stage in the
extension of government involvement in the economy, was
also fully in accord with the liberal tradition of economic
policy. As understood and practised by the Treasury,
Keynesianism meant a policy of manipulating the total level
of demand to correct the tendency that markets had, if left
to themselves, to produce unemployment and stagnation.
Beyond such 'fine tuning' no interference with individual
decisions on investment, prices or output was contempla-

ted. So long as the government maintained through its monetary and fiscal policies a correct balance between effective demand and the productive potential of the economy, the market could be allowed to work freely to create prosperity and rising output and living standards.[40]

The failure of such indirect manipulations of the economy to produce a rate of growth or a level of investment that matched Germany and Japan created great pressure in favour of more active government involvement in the economy, more planning, more spending on infrastructure and on research, more attention to the questions of supply rather than the questions of demand which dominated government policy in the 1950s. It was all to bear fruit of a sort in the 1960s.

The other great problem which began to receive attention in the search for explanations of Britain's poor growth performance was the working class. The very high levels of employment that were achieved in the 1950s were taken as a sign of a shortage of labour and as a factor in increasing the bargaining power of organised labour. Other countries during the boom were able to draw on supplies of labour from their undeveloped countryside or from abroad. In Britain reserves of labour were small, although the employment of women began to expand greatly. Immigration from the New Commonwealth provided extra workers, but increasing restrictions were placed upon it after 1961 because of internal political pressures.[41] The only other source of labour was from industry itself, and this could only be realised by drastically reducing manning levels and eliminating restrictive practices. Any such programme needed the co-operation of the trade unions, whose legal position had never been stronger, but who remained split in a variety of craft, industrial, and general unions. The defensive strength and conservatism of the unions meshed with the conservatism and international orientation of large sections of British capital, and greatly reduced the scope for increasing productivity.

The unions were undoubtedly partly responsible for the low rate of increase in productivity, for as shown in Chapter 1, not just the quantity of investment but its efficiency was much lower than in many other countries. Low investment was however the key problem, and it was the failure of British companies and British governments to create the kind of climate for large-scale investment and rapid increases in productivity that was most striking. Few British industries adopted the kind of organisational practices which were developed by their competitors to overcome restrictive practices on the shop floor and make investment pay. The failure was more a failure of management than of the work-force. By the end of the 1950s it was apparent that any successful strategy for growth had to find a way of winning and keeping the co-operation of organised labour. But it was not to prove an easy task.

4.6   The attempt at modernisation

On the surface, the 1950s were a period of great prosperity in Britain. The pace and duration of the long boom brought the end of austerity and all controls on consumption. With only minor exceptions, all four targets of government economic policy – full employment, sustained growth, low inflation, and a balance of payments surplus – were broadly met.[42] The Conservative government elected in 1951, and its successors, proved quite ready to govern within the constraints of the new political consensus established in the 1940s. Projecting itself as the party that could best ensure prosperity while maintaining welfare provision, the Conservative party succeeded in winning three elections in a row in the 1950s. The Conservatives went on to govern for thirteen years, a longer period on their own than any other party had managed this century before the election of the Thatcher Government.

Yet the 1950s for all their outward success were also the years when the decisive slide in Britain's relative economic position began. Much of the British governing class was more concerned with the rather more precipitate decline in Britain's status as a great power, of which the events at Suez in 1956 were a painful reminder, and with the task of organising an orderly withdrawal from the Empire. But many were becoming aware that despite its success the British economy was being outperformed by its European rivals and still more so by Japan. This realisation and the anxiety it caused erupted in a flood of self-criticism spiced with denigration of the British Establishment in the early 1960s,[43] and helped to prepare the way for a major change in the direction of policy after the 1959 election victory.

The change did not disturb the fundamentals of the consensus that had been established after the war. What was now agreed was that the rate of growth was too low, and that demand management policies were no longer enough. Government needed to intervene more actively to create a general climate for growth and to remedy deficiencies on the supply side of the economy. The new policies were initiated by the Conservatives but taken up and continued enthusiastically by the Labour party. The 1964 election was fought on the question of which party was more likely to modernise Britain faster, and enable the British economy to break out of the cycle of stop–go and emulate the rates of growth of the most successful national capitalisms. The Labour administration it brought to office, headed by Harold Wilson, promised the creation of a New Britain.[44]

The new policies intended to create the British economic miracle were diverse. There was a more effective competition policy initiated in 1956 with the Restrictive Practices Act and continued with the abolition of Resale Price Maintenance in 1964 and the Monopoly and Mergers Act of 1965. There were concerted attempts made to revive the co-operation between labour and capital that had existed during the war, by creating the kind of institutionalised, tripartite links between government, industry and unions which many other countries had developed so successfully, and to experiment with the planning of incomes and output. The National Economic Development Council (NEDC) and the National Incomes Commission (NIC) were followed after 1964 by an attempt to draw up a National Plan, and by the establishment of a Prices and Incomes board to oversee a permanent incomes policy. In addition Labour established new ministries, the Department of Economic Affairs (DEA) and the Ministry of Technology, which were intended to represent the interests of the national economy. From them flowed programmes of subsidies, investment incentives, and rationalisation. The Industrial Reorganisation Corporation (IRC) was established to assist in the rationalisation of British industry and the creation of industrial enterprises that could compete successfully in world markets. Finally, public expenditure was greatly increased with the intention of modernising the infrastructure of the British economy, its communications network, its educational system and its health service, so as to assist in the task of creating a dynamic and fully adaptable industrial economy.[45]

Such an array of virtuous policies, accepted by both parties and implemented with such vigour, could surely not fail. But in general they did. The judgement of Francis Cripps writing at the end of the 1970s has been echoed by many others:

> After two decades at least of government attempts to improve the non-price competitiveness of UK exports none of the policy instruments tried so far seems to have had any measurable effect.[46]

The explanations from Right and Left as to why it failed are examined in the next two chapters. The failure greatly undermined the consensus and brought a new political turbulence and the rise of new political forces. The immediate reason for the failure is not hard to grasp. Neither the Labour government between 1964 and 1970, nor the Conservative government before it, was either able or willing to defy the international orientation of British economic policy and break the stop–go cycle. The whole strategy of expansion and modernisation depended upon financing increased public expenditure from growth, and winning the co-operation of the trade unions to temporary pay restraint in exchange for the prospect of faster growth in living standards. But both policies depended in the short term on governments finding some way to expand the economy that would not lead straight to a balance of payments crisis and a sterling crisis, or if it did, on finding a way to handle them without resorting to the deflation of home demand. This entailed decisions on the exchange rate, on the future of sterling as an international currency, on the scale of British commitments abroad, and on the freedom of its leading firms to expand abroad. Without such decisions, expanding the economy meant certain balance of payments and sterling crises followed by the familiar deflationary package to restore confidence. Yet for all their intellectual recognition of this dilemma successive governments proved quite incapable of escaping it in practice – the Wilson government least of all.[47] But the spending programme of modernisation was not curtailed, and this meant a rapid increase in public expenditure and in taxation against a background of a stagnant economy and collapsing profits. Much of the burden of adjustment was thrown upon the working class through heavy increases in taxes and increasingly draconian pay restraint. Since inflation was accelerating, such measures led eventually to a pay explosion.[48]

4.7 The Heath government

The Conservatives won the general election in 1970 against a sombre background: the industrial and social turmoil of the late 1960s, the evident failure of the strategy of modernisation on which such hopes had been placed to reverse decline, and growing difficulties both in financing public expenditure and in containing the pressure for pay increases to match the rate of inflation. Although the Conservatives had initiated the modernisation strategy, dissatisfaction with Labour policies had grown, and the Conservative leadership had been subject to intense pressures from its own supporters to promise a major change of direction in economic policy. The Heath government saw its own election as marking a major break with the consensus, both in the nature of its policies and in the vigour with which it attempted to implement them. But in the context of the record of the government as a whole, the Heath government's 'quiet revolution' to 'change the course of history of this nation' not only turned out to be an extremely noisy one, but also a final attempt to create an expanding economy within the limits of the social democratic state. The highest priority was given to the achievement of sustained economic growth; at first free market policies were attempted, but when these failed to work quickly they were replaced or supplemented by interventionist policies which went beyond anything tried in the previous decade.

The strategy of the Heath government was the most radical attempted by any government since the war. It had been planned in much greater detail than was usual for Oppositions. It attempted to break out of the vicious circle of low investment, low productivity and higher costs by seeking to reduce the short-term constraints on government economic management.[49]

The setting of the Heath strategy was the determination to make Britain a member of the EC, a decision which involved a major reassessment of British policy and Britain's role in the world. The first application to join the EC made in 1961 was already a tacit recognition that the history of external expansion was over, and that British economic security was best served by joining a regional economic bloc within the wider world economy.[50] The costs, including the abandonment of cheap food, were to be weighed against the benefits of free access to the European market. Many supporters of the decision to enter the EC, which had been so strongly resisted after 1945 and in 1956, hoped that the community would evolve into a federal or a unitary state capable of protecting European economic interests, and bargaining on equal terms with the United States and Japan.

The European policy that was launched in the 1960s therefore implied a fundamental re-evaluation of the American connection and the long subordination of British interests to American. It implied that Britain was ready to shed the last vestiges of its world role – the pretence of an independent nuclear deterrent, the overseas military bases, the international currency role of sterling – and to approach world political and economic problems from a European rather than an Atlantic perspective. It was because he seriously doubted whether such a change in outlook had genuinely occurred that de Gaulle vetoed Britain's application twice during the 1960s, fearing that Britain would be merely a Trojan horse for the United States inside the Community.

Heath's success in securing entry in the 1970s depended upon convincing the French that Britain now had a political leadership which was firmly European in its outlook, and which accepted that Europe was to be the focus of British energies and political ambitions; that the independent world role was over, that British interests could no longer be protected by the British state alone, and that a strong Europe was more likely to protect them than was America. But there was a further problem remaining. For Britain to play a leading role in the EC, British economic decline had to be reversed and a strong national economy built, able to compete on equal terms with Germany and France.

The Heath government hoped to create such an economy by attempting to remove some of the major constraints on economic management. Its competition policy, for example, aimed to eliminate subsidies and incentives which had proliferated under Labour, axeing all the agencies of detailed intervention, and reducing public expenditure and taxation. The intention was to force industry to solve its own problems and become more efficient and competitive, so restoring profitability, boosting investment, and preparing the way for a rapid expansion of output and productivity. The trade-union policy was aimed at reducing obstacles in the labour market and in the labour movement to expansion and modernisation. The government reformed trade-union law with its Industrial Relations Act[51] and renounced a formal incomes policy, hoping that between them the new laws and the more competitive climate in industry would restrain wage costs.

The aim of both sets of policies was to prepare the way for a new experiment in sustained expansion. In its first two years in office the Heath government inherited the huge balance of payments surplus which was the main fruit of Labour's economic policies over the previous six years.[52] In 1971, with the disintegration of the Bretton Woods interna-

tional monetary system the government seized its opportunity and in 1972 floated the pound.[53] It was determined
that once the economy began expanding again the expansion would not be cut short by a balance of payments crisis.

The priority which the government gave to achieving
growth was shown by the lengths it was prepared to go to
ensure it. All its free market policies had run into difficulty
by 1972. The Industrial Relations Act which had been
intended as an extension of the successful Restrictive
Practices legislation of 1956 and 1964 suffered from a fatal
ambiguity of purpose, and still more from the intense
opposition it aroused from the trade-union movement. The
attempt partially to withdraw from pay determination led to
a series of major strikes and courts of enquiry, some
victories and some defeats for the government, but little
noticeable reduction in the level of pay increases and an
explosion, not a diminution, of industrial militancy.[54]
Government efforts to reduce public expenditure were
singularly unsuccessful although it did carry through some
major tax reforms including the introduction of VAT.
Unsuccessful also were attempts to create a more competitive climate in industry. Aid to a few major firms like Upper
Clyde shipbuilders was cut off, causing still more industrial
unrest, but most state funding of industry continued and in
the case of firms like Rolls-Royce, which suddenly became
bankrupt in 1971, it had to be extended.

The failure of pay settlements to come down, the high
rate of inflation, the high unemployment in 1971, and above
all the slowness of industry to begin investing on an
appropriate scale, prompted a major revision of policies
during 1972. The level of industrial unrest which the
policies had created and the growing electoral unpopularity
of the government were also important in persuading the
government to seek alternative means of reaching its
objectives.[55] Membership of the EC was now within its
grasp, and it appeared anxious that the British economy
should be in a condition to prosper in the Community as
soon as entry was formally achieved at the beginning of
1973. It had been an axiom of Conservative electoral
strategy since the war that the party could not afford to be

identified with a negative and restrictionist policy, but should be ready to encourage more rapid rates of growth, if necessary by using public agencies to prod capital to invest more and to produce more.

In 1972 the Conservative Chancellor of the Exchequer, Anthony Barber, collected what became known as the Barber boom. In some respects it was a continuation of the Maudling plan of 1963–4. Maudling, appointed Chancellor of the Exchequer by Harold Macmillan in 1962, had believed that Britain could break out of the stop–go cycle and achieve its own 'economic miracle' so long as overseas borrowing could be arranged to cover any temporary deficit that arose on the balance of payments. In this way there would be no interruption to the expansion of demand. If the policy of expansion was persevered with, then in time investment would start rising, so would productivity, and so would output.

This plan was never tested because the deficit did not arise until after the general election: Labour having inherited the deficit proceeded to precipitate the crisis and gave first priority to defending the exchange rate. In 1972–3 the Heath government, urged on by most commentators at the time, showed that it was quite prepared to risk inflation in order to boost growth. Public spending was greatly increased, and the money supply was allowed to soar so as to raise the level of demand in the economy. The government reversed its industrial policy and with the passage of the new Industry Act appeared prepared to intervene on a considerable scale.[56] Major new prestige projects like the Channel Tunnel and Maplin airport were announced, and at the end of 1972, having failed narrowly to reach agreement with the TUC and the CBI, the government introduced the most comprehensive statutory prices and incomes policy since the war.

For a short period it looked as thought the policy might succeed. The entire capitalist world economy began to expand strongly in 1973 and for once the British economy was expanding as fast as its rivals. Its rate of growth in 1973 was 5 per cent which equalled Germany's.[57] The counter-inflation policy proved very successful in its first two stages,

and looked like moderating the upward movement of prices
and pay.[58]

The whole strategy suffered a spectacular shipwreck at
the end of 1973, partly because of the internal crisis over
pay caused by the miners' overtime ban and subsequent
strike, partly by the loss of control of monetary policy, but
mainly because of the abrupt termination of the world boom
by the quadrupling of oil prices by OPEC, which was the
trigger for the commencement of a generalised recession
and plunged Britain into a balance of payments deficit
which dwarfed all previous experience. Once again the
attempt to break out of the constraints which for so long
had governed British economic management had failed, and
the economy was left in an extremely weak position to face
the full force of the recession. It was to become clear that
the old priorities of the social democratic consensus could
be maintained no longer and that a new political terrain and
new political possibilities were emerging. This was reflected
in increasing polarisation between elements of the two
major parties, and the canvassing of much more radical
political solutions to Britain's problems than had appeared
for a long time. But the key strategic question of the
continuing debate about how to reverse the decline of
British capitalism in the new context of world recession
remained in keeping with Britain's past: not the issue of
internal organisation, of individualism versus collectivism,
or the free market versus planning, but the relationship
Britain should have to the world economy and to the other
capitalist powers, now that the long boom had ended and
the recession had begun.

5

The sovereign market

The visible signs of Britain's unique course – as it slides from the affluent Western World towards the threadbare economies of the communist bloc – are obvious enough. We have a demotivating tax system, increasing nationalisation, compressed differentials, low and stagnant productivity, high unemployment, many failing public services and inexorably growing central government expenditure; an obsession with equality and with pay, price and dividend controls; a unique set of legal privileges and immunities for trade unions; and finally, since 1974, top of the Western league for inflation, bottom of the league for growth.

Sir Keith Joseph (1979)[1]

Two new strategies emerged in the 1970s to challenge the priorities of the established social democratic consensus: the free economy strategy of the New Right and the alternative economic strategy of the Labour Left. Both arose because of the apparent inability of either major party to secure the full co-operation of the organised working class and of business, in modernising the economy. The failure to secure and extend social democracy gave the opportunity for unravelling the post-war settlement and exploring new ways of ordering British capitalism and making it legitimate. This opportunity was seized in the great revival of economic liberalism which started at the end of the 1960s and began to make powerful inroads into the Conservative party. The ideological and political roots

of this strategy, which so strongly influenced the policies of
the Thatcher government, is the subject of this chapter.

5.1   Free trade and sound finance

Of the many possible standpoints within political economy
from which the problems of capitalist development and
economic policy can be assessed and analysed, two have
been particularly important in the economic policy debates
on British decline. They are liberal political economy, the
standpoint of the market, and national political economy,
the standpoint of the national economy. Both take for
granted the existence of the modern state, and its separation as a public realm from the economy, but they clash over
the principles for regulating and managing modern economies and determining the boundaries of state activities.

Liberal political economy has always been the stronger
ideological tradition in Britain, and its ascendancy became
firmly established in Britain during the movement to free
trade in the first half of the nineteenth century. It was
always associated with Liberals, Radicals and Utilitarians
and the analytical refinements undertaken by Ricardo gave
it a solidity and a certainty as a doctrine which made it a
formidable weapon in ideological debate. By the middle of
the nineteenth century liberal political economy had
become orthodoxy for British governments, because it
seemed to express so well the national interest of the British
state, and the logic of its commercial policy, clothing both
with the dignity of universal principles.

The virtues of liberal political economy as an ideological
doctrine would not have given it such ascendancy, however,
had it not also found continual reinforcement in some
important features of the organisation of the British state
and the British economy. British economic policy and
British business have long been dominated by perspectives
originating in banking and trade rather than in industry.[2]
This has given both an international orientation, which
liberal political economy with its emphasis on the world

market perfectly expresses. It has been strengthened in numerous institutional ways. The wide-spread use of sterling as an international currency, and the importance of London in the operation of the gold standard in the nineteenth century, encouraged expansion of the banking, insurance and shipping services provided by businesses in the City. The size and importance of the financial sector was enhanced because the British government depended on it to fund the National Debt and to control the money supply. The Bank of England, established in 1694 expressly for this purpose, grew to be the main channel for articulating the City's view of the national interest in economic policy.[3] Within the government two of the oldest Departments, the Treasury and the Board of Trade, have always tended to share this perspective on British national problems and therefore have endorsed the assumptions of liberal political economy. But the most important factor has been the external dependence of the British economy on the world economy, which the policy of free trade helped create in the first place. This basic reality of Britain's position has enormously reinforced the tendency to view Britain's economic problems from the standpoint of the world market. The external links of the British economy with the world economy have generally been presumed to be beyond dispute; any attempt to reduce them or limit them has been condemned as wrong in principle and damaging in practice; and national policy has been conceived as finding ways to adjust the national economy as smoothly as possible to world economic conditions, so uniting external and internal economic management.

In the nineteenth century this unity was achieved in the programme of free trade, sound finance, and *laissez-faire*. All three principles supported one another. The ideal state was a minimal state, which was parsimonious in its expenditures and undertook only those functions that were necessary to permit the widest possible sphere for free association and free exchange. The extravagance of the military establishment, and the expenses of administering colonies were prime targets for attack, because such state expenditures supported an idle and unproductive aristocracy and were financed by taxes on those directing the creation of wealth. A policy of sound finance meant subordinating government policy to the overriding need to maintain a stable medium of exchange, while the policy of *laissez-faire* meant that the budget should be balanced at the lowest level of expenditure that was compatible with maintaining the conditions for free and expanding markets. Stable money was also assured not only by governments concentrating on those functions that the market could not perform, but by the severe discipline of the gold standard. By tying domestic currency to gold reserves, limits were placed on domestic currency expansion, since all issue of paper money had to be backed by gold. At the same time deficits on trade had to be paid in gold, so any persistent imbalance in trade resulted in a loss of gold reserves which required automatically a contraction of the amount of money in domestic circulation, hence a fall in prices and a general deflation, until costs had been lowered and balance restored.

Before the nineteenth century economic doctrines played only a small part in shaping economic policies and economic strategies, but since that time they have become much more important. No system of political economy has ever been applied in isolation. Intellectual strategies have always had to wrestle with the multitude of immediate pressures arising from the interplay of institutions, interests, and circumstances. But the different systems of political economy have been increasingly employed to isolate causes, define goals, and suggest ways of reaching them.

So firmly embedded, however, did liberal political economy become that it has rarely appeared a crusading doctrine in England, but generally as an orthodoxy emanating from the bowels of the state. Only in the early nineteenth century and in the 1960s has it appeared as an outsider creed. Its rise to orthodoxy was consolidated during the struggle over the Corn Laws, the final bastion held against free trade. Their repeal in 1846 signalled the complete triumph of the free trade cause. The landowners who opposed repeal were defeated mainly because so substantial a measure of free trade had already been conceded that by the 1840s the balance of the economy decisively favoured the new financial, commercial, and industrial interests. If the final move to complete free trade had been blocked, not only would it have meant a decisive turn from the established commercial policy of expansion, but it would have directly threatened political stability, and might have led to the violent overthrow of the landowners' state. Cheap food was needed to sustain both the standard of living of the urban proletariat and the profits of the manufacturers.

Repeal in 1846 signalled that the state policy would conform to the new interests and new classes that had become dominant within the market order. The course Britain pursued after 1846 was consistent with the policy of the past 200 years, a hard-headed assessment and exploitation of commercial opportunities. Nevertheless it was to be a course without historical parallel. The balance between industry and agriculture was deliberately allowed to disappear as the law of comparative advantage suggested it should. The law stated that if all nations specialised in producing for the world market those things they could provide more cheaply than anyone else and relied on exchange to obtain whatever other goods they needed, then all nations would be better off. Yet even in states devoted to free trade principles, agriculture has normally been excepted from this remorseless logic and protected against foreign competition, because of its importance to the existence and independence of a national economy. The lack of protection afforded British agriculture between 1846 and 1916 is a major exception.[4] But the policy worked. It aided the expansion of the cities as well as an urban proletariat and contributed to an enormous enrichment of the whole British propertied class.

What made such boldness conceivable was not just the doctrine of free trade and the faith it inspired in the law of comparative advantage, but the fact that comparative advantage in producing manufactures was reinforced by a comparative advantage in naval and colonial possessions. These gave the British state the effective power to take on state functions for the world economy it dominated – policing the free movement of goods and capital and labour along the major trade routes, coercing recalcitrant and militarily inferior states into opening their markets to western trade, and increasingly guaranteeing a stable medium of exchange throughout the world economy.

A great challenge to free trade imperialism arose once the expansion of the world economy had brought the beginnings of industrialisation in states too strong to be coerced by Britain militarily. Once the world economy moved into a period of depression after 1873 and markets contracted, these states, Germany and the United States in particular, protected their industries against British competition by extremely high tariffs, and built up their productive capacity behind them. From the 1890s onwards when markets began to revive, many British industries began to face increasing competition both in the British domestic market and in world markets, yet still found themselves effectively shut out from the German and American markets by high tariffs. Such tariffs were increasingly used as weapons for waging trade war, since they maintained domestic producers' control of their own home market, and enabled them to sell their surplus production on world markets at prices that competitors could not match. In the face of the rising commercial and naval challenge of Germany and, to a lesser extent, of the United States, Britain's adherence to unilateral free trade brought the first major domestic clash over the priorities and direction of British economic policy since the struggle over the Corn Laws.

By the end of the century the landed interest as such had become relatively insignificant in domestic politics,[5] so the battleground over tariff reform was drawn within urban and industrial Britain, and expressed divisions among the leaders of industry and finance and their political representatives and allies. Both sides actively sought the support of the working class, whose electoral weight had become much greater since 1885. Apart from Irish Home Rule no other issue proved so divisive before 1914. The programme of Social Imperialism which the tariff reformers advanced is discussed in the next chapter. What is remarkable is that, despite all its apparent advantages, it was successfully resisted until 1916. Only total war forced the British government to abandon free trade.

The ascendancy of the Liberal party before 1914 preserved free trade. It was based on a number of factors. The bulk of British capital appears to have continued to favour free trade. No bankers are known to have supported or been associated with the campaign for tariff reform, and although industries like iron and steel, chemicals, glass and building wanted protection, all the leading export industries, including coal, cotton and shipbuilding, remained tied to free trade. The years of the tariff reform campaign were also years of booming world trade and a recovery by the old established industries of their former prosperity. The concrete advantages of the network of trade and finance which Britain had established, which the British state guaranteed, and which liberal political economy had consecrated as embodying not just a national and sectional advantage but the advantage of all nations, remained more attractive than the more speculative benefits of an imperial policy. Even when it came under challenge the informal commercial empire which Britain maintained over the whole world was still thought superior to a formal political empire over only one-quarter of it.

Tariff reform might still have triumphed, however, had not the Liberals preserved their electoral dominance. They did so partly through their parliamentary alliance with the Irish Nationalists after 1910, but mainly because they won the battle for working-class support. They constantly emphasised that tariff reform would mean dearer food, and that large sections of the working class were employed in industries which had grown to their present size because of free trade.[6] The Conservatives had hoped to prise the working class from its alliance with Liberalism by presenting tariff reform as a programme that would guarantee high employment and fair wages, and would provide revenues for social reforms and higher welfare spending.

The Liberals, however, now showed themselves quite prepared to legislate to give the trade unions crucial immunities from certain provisions in Common Law.[7] The Liberals proved more skilful in adapting to the pressures of the new working-class electorate, and recognised the more general need for the state to expand its role and assume new tasks. They sacrificed and compromised important principles of the traditional individualist doctrine of liberal political economy, to take account of the emerging needs of a developed industrial economy and the demands of an already overwhelming working-class electorate. Social Imperialism could not be rooted in the working class on a scale sufficient to tip the electoral balance. A large reservoir of peasants and smallholders would have been needed to provide the necessary political support; but if that had existed, the policy of free trade might never have been established in the first place.

The Great War of 1914–18 marks the beginning of the collapse of British military, financial and industrial power. Though the British ruling class was divided over free trade before 1914, and over whether Ireland should be allowed its own Parliament, it was much more united over the need to prevent Germany establishing a mastery over Europe, which could overshadow and undermine Britain's world interests. The war was fought with strategic and political and economic objectives that were closely intertwined. One major British interest was to force Germany to abandon its policy of capturing world markets from a protected home base and to accept the disciplines of the liberal free trade order Britain had constructed.

Yet from the outset British leaders knew how much Britain stood to lose from a protracted war, and serious attempts were made to limit the disruption as much as possible. Only later when the struggle became prolonged did Britain's leaders accept the need to abandon hopes of maintaining the international credit and trading system intact, and to wage total war. The war economies that were established after 1916 and after 1940 brought lasting changes to the British economy. They expanded the role of the state more successfully than in any time of peace.[8] They are major landmarks in the progress of collectivism in Britain. They inspired policies to plan investment, to direct labour, to channel consumption, to fix interest rates, to increase direct taxation, to control prices, wages and rents, to improve education, to stimulate research and to mobilise all unused resources.

After neither war did the state revert to its former size or former role. The war economies helped to move internal economic policy away from the individualist principles and *laissez-faire* principles of nineteenth-century liberalism.

They had much smaller impact, however, in relation to external policy. In 1918 and in 1945 the British state emerged quite determined to restore a liberal world trading and financial order as quickly as possible. After 1918 it was assumed that Britain would quickly resume its former role; in 1945 leadership and initiative had plainly passed to the Americans. Nevertheless on both occasions it was accepted almost without dissent that the reactivation of Britain's traditional international policy was a priority. The decision was particularly odd in 1918, since the difficulties in its path were enormous, and because the Conservatives, the bitter enemies of free trade, now dominated the government. The Liberals were losing ground as a major party, to Labour. Yet it was Conservative government in the 1920s who removed almost all the protective tariffs imposed during the war[9] and who took the major decision to restore Britain to the gold standard in 1925 at the pre-war parity of $4.86.[10] The main argument for the return was that only if the old trading and financial networks were reconstituted would prosperity return to the industries whose markets had been so disrupted and diminished during the war. Despite the deflation this policy imposed on the British economy, despite the evident inability of the British state to carry it through, and despite the industrial confrontation it directly created, the policy was little challenged either intellectually or politically. The Conservatives in government accepted without reservation the orthodox external policy. The political will to fashion something different had passed.

The only period apart from the two war economies when liberal orthodoxy has been overthrown was during the 1930s. But once again the abandonment of the gold standard and the turn to protection were policies forced on the National government by the severity of the world slump. The National government was explicitly formed in order to *prevent* the collapse of the gold standard. The organisation of the sterling area and imperial preference was a response to the fragmentation of the world economy, stagnant world trade and output, and the absence of any power strong enough to rebuild an international order. The new policies sank no lasting roots, and once a power appeared after 1945 ready and able to undertake the rebuilding of the capitalist world order, the traditional international policy of the British state re-emerged to flourish once again.

What stands out in British economic policy is not simply the dominance of liberal political economy, and the failure of any political party successfully to challenge free trade, the international status of sterling and the free movement of capital, but the precise nature of this dominance. British policy pursued open markets for British industries, but as important for Britain's rulers became the state functions the British state performed for the world economy. This became the heart of the liberal orthodoxy. At home the core of the policy was sound finance, which meant after 1918 continual attempts to retrench government expenditure and balance the budget at a level of taxes that was thought politically practicable. Persistence with this orthodoxy in the face of the slump after 1929 brought the financial crisis of 1931, because paying dole to the rapidly growing numbers of unemployed unbalanced the budget.[11] Rather than raise taxes, the leaders of the minority Labour government preferred to follow the advice of the May Committee and cut the dole. The government fell when nine members of the Cabinet refused to support such measures[12] and they had to be implemented by the National government which Ramsay Macdonald proceeded to form.

The policy of sound finance was tied remarkably closely to the policy of maintaining sterling on the gold standard. The chief reason why an unbalanced budget was so much feared was that it might cause a run on the pound. Sound finance always had both an internal and an external dimension. But strong as this liberal orthodoxy was, it was consistent with other internal policies that had long been undermining the basis of the individualist market order in Britain. The National government did not go back on retrenchment in the 1930s but it did permit a significant weakening of internal competition. Liberal political economy had always prescribed open markets as the best means for ensuring domestic competition, but in Britain this traditional external policy had not been accompanied by measures aimed at improving the workings of markets by creating the conditions for a more aggressive and dynamic capitalism. Instead the market order was allowed progressively to silt up. The wealth and power from long years of formal and informal Empire helped to ossify not just British industry but liberal orthodoxy as well. That was why the revival of liberal political economy in the 1960s was to have such impact.

5.2 The New Right

After 1945 the principles and perspectives of liberal political economy once more governed Britain's external policy, but internally Keynesianism triumphed. Nevertheless, although Keynesianism justified a much larger role for the state in the economy, and broke decisively with the orthodox notion that the government should not concern itself with the overall performance of the economy, it remained compatible with the goals of liberal political economy, because it proposed no interference with the detailed workings of markets and individual decision-making, only with aggregate demand, aggregate investment and *national* income. The automatic link between internal and external policy was dropped, but the priority given to sterling and to increasing the openness of the British economy meant the effective subordination of internal Keynesian demand management to the traditional liberal concerns of Britain's external policy.

Although Keynesianism originated as a variant of liberal political economy and many attempts were made to assimilate it theoretically to the main corpus of liberal economics,[13] in practice it took the standpoint of the state and the national economy, and so was particularly suited to social democracy because it justified interventionist policies.[14] The modernisation strategy of the 1960s did not flow directly from Keynesian principles, from which could be deduced only the indirect manipulation of demand, but it did fit with the general Keynesian presumption that if the market economy were not functioning satisfactorily, ways should be found through public agencies of correcting its outcomes. Keynesianism never shared the assumption of liberal political economy that if markets were not working there must be some obstacle which should be identified and removed.

During the 1960s a fierce onslaught on Keynesianism began which developed into a major revival of liberal political economy. The main thrust of the attack was over the policy of demand management and it crystallised in the doctrine of monetarism. The dispute between Keynesians and monetarists over the causes of inflation might have remained merely a technical dispute, a development of the earlier dispute between adherents of demand-pull and cost-push theories of inflation.[15] But monetarism proved to be only part of a much broader ideological and political attack upon government intervention and upon social democracy.

The political force behind the revival of liberal political economy was the rise of a New Right in the Conservative party. The promulgation of the doctrines of economic liberalism and the principles of a market order became linked by New Right Conservatives to positions on issues like immigration, law and order, strikes, social security abuse, and permissiveness. A general offensive was initiated upon many of the positions and values and assumptions of social democracy by a great variety of right-wing pressure groups, which from the late 1960s onwards began germinating like dragons' teeth.[16]

The main target of the New Right has been social democracy; not merely the party and trade unions of organised labour but also the willingness of Conservative governments since the war to accept social democratic policies and goals, and to work within social democratic constraints. A constant complaint was that since 1945 the Conservative leadership had constantly betrayed Conservative principles by acquiescing in the steady consolidation of the power of organised Labour and the social democratic state, and had never 'put the clock back a single second'. Collectivism had steadily increased, economic liberty had been undermined, the economy as a result had declined and political freedom itself placed in jeopardy.

After 1968, and still more after 1974, the refurbished doctrines of liberal political economy made rapid progress. Keynesianism was in considerable disarray; the monetarist doctrines on the control of inflation became increasingly influential; and state expenditure, state intervention, and state enterprise all came under considerable attack.

It might seem surprising that the agency in Britain of this world-wide swing back to liberal political economy should be the Conservative party. which had always distanced itself from economic liberalism. It had often chosen to present itself as the party of the national economy and the state, the party of the community rather than the market, the party of protection and social imperialism, intervention and paternalism rather than the party of free trade, cosmopolitanism, self-help, and *laissez-faire*.

It was not inconsistent with its traditions that this party with its instinct for changing realities of power should have accepted Keynesianism and social democracy after 1940. The party had always had an individualist wing, but in the era of mass democracy its collectivist paternalist wing was more often in the ascendancy. Party historians were able to show how hostile the party had been to the doctrines of economic liberalism and to the policy of *laissez-faire* and free trade, and how often in the past Conservatives had condemned economic liberalism as doctrinaire and inflexible.[17]

One major reason for earlier Conservative hostility to economic liberalism was that it promoted individualism, questioned the authority of established institutions, and encouraged selfishness and competition between individuals and social classes. The Conservatives tended to think that preserving the social order was more important than preserving a market order. This attitude survived the disintegration of the Liberal party after 1916 and the entry of numerous 'doctrinaire' Liberals into the party, whose presence was resented by its imperialist and protectionist wing. But although these elements may have helped dilute the enthusiasm of the party for abandoning free trade, throughout the 1920s the Conservative leadership showed hardly any signs of even attempting to move outside the traditional liberal consensus on the role of sterling and the importance to Britain of the liberal world trading order. In their domestic policies the Conservatives pursued financial retrenchment. Neither policy involved a crusading commitment to the principles of economic liberalism, merely the acceptance of policies that had become orthodoxies for the British state. The substantial erosion of competition which took place in the 1930s worried the Conservatives not at all. On the contrary they encouraged it.[18]

The steady growing ascendancy of the doctrines of economic liberalism within the Conservative party can be traced back to the 1950s, but it acquired much greater significance once it became joined in the late 1960s to the forces and spokesmen of the New Right. The calls for greater competition and more economic freedom, which both the Conservative Bow Group[19] and the Institute of Economic Affairs.[20] had begun making in the late 1950s, acquired quite a different meaning in the general groundswell of New Right opinion. By the late 1960s a substantial section of the Conservative party was openly critical of the social democratic state and much of the record of post-war Conservative governments. In this context liberal political economy was used to challenge the assumptions and the priorities of economic management that social democracy and Keynesian economics had established.

The considerable advance made by the New Right within the Conservative party and the increasing pressure it was able to exert on the leadership, particularly when the party was out of office, was the result of the linking of the principles of a free market with more congenial Conservative emphases on a stronger state in the fields of defence, and law and order, and a strengthened family. It made the liberal political economy of the New Right in the Conservative party very different from the liberal political economy of Cobden and Bright.

The growth of popular discontent with so many of the institutions and policies of social democracy created a major problem of internal political management for the Conservatives, whose leaders remained committed to governing within the limits of the social democratic consensus. If the Conservatives had been unable to contain these new ideological forces they might have spilled outside into new parties and organisations. The danger was all the greater since the Conservative party has no formal democratic structure, and the leadership is more effectively insulated than the Labour party from the demands and pressures of its members.[21] To some extent a movement outside the party did begin to arise, but it was limited by an important shift within the Conservative leadership itself towards acceptance of the programme of the New Right.

Enoch Powell prepared the ground for this, although it was Margaret Thatcher who ultimately benefited, and it was Thatcherism not Powellism that captured the party and gave its name to the new strategy. Powell's importance initially was that he became an articulate exponent of the principles of liberal political economy from the 1950s onwards, and was regarded as highly eccentric and old-fashioned for doing so. But then in the 1960s, as a response to the failures of the modernisation strategy and the increasing disarray of social democracy, he broadened the focus of his political concerns and began to denounce not merely inflationary economic policies and the evils of high government spending and intervention, but also the permanent settlement of West Indian and Asian immigrants in Britain. Combined with his later attacks upon the EC, and his defence of the Ulster Protestants and the need to maintain the Union, he developed a major new political programme in which economic liberalism and political nationalism were skilfully and explicitly combined.

Powell attracted considerable support, bursting through the log-jam of political alignments and interests.[22] Ejected from the Conservative Shadow Cabinet he nevertheless became a power within the party that the Conservative leadership could not ignore. He acted as a focus for New Right opinion, and he demonstrated the popularity of a political programme that declared itself against the state and openly expressed popular frustrations and grievances. Powell won a big following in the working class for his nationalist position on immigration, but he chose not to consolidate it by establishing a new party. He preferred to continue to remain inside the Conservative party, and there became an isolated and ineffective critic of the Heath government and of the last desperate bid to achieve expansion within the constraints of social democracy.[23]

Nevertheless, after the Heath government's strategy had collapsed and the Conservatives had once again lost office, the alternative strategy Powell had staked out in his criticisms of the policies of the government became a rallying point for many in the party. The dismay in the party at the government's defeat in 1974, and the retrospective gloom which that threw over the whole record of the Heath government allowed Margaret Thatcher to seize her chance and to win the leadership. Powell had disqualified himself from contention by refusing to fight as a Conservative in 1974, but more importantly because his positions on Europe and immigration were not policies the party leadership was prepared to accept. Nevertheless, with the election of Thatcher to the leadership, the New Right, although not dominant within the party, was stronger than ever before.[24] The leadership in particular was extremely divided, and this was reflected both in the balance of the Shadow Cabinet and in the character of the policy documents that were issued.[25]

Unlike Powellism, Thatcherism has not been an anti-state movement. Thatcher owed her elevation to the normal procedures of the Conservative party, not to any popular pressure; nor did she encourage any movement outside the institutions of the established political system. She always operated as an insider. Whereas Powell did attempt to change British politics by establishing a populist and nationalist platform from which he strongly attacked many Establishment institutions and policies, Thatcher's style was to translate the themes of the new economic liberalism into slogans and ideas that tapped popular discontent with many aspects of the existing state, such as the arbitrariness of bureaucracy, the inefficiency of nationalised industry, the burden of taxation, the 'privileges' enjoyed by immigrants, the damage caused by strikes, the lawlessness of demonstrations and the undermining of the independence and moral responsibility of families. The key to the translation was the posing of central questions of government policy as problems of individual responsibility and individual choice. This ideology of self-help preached the right to be unequal, the need for self-reliance, and the need for everyone to take full responsibility for themselves and their families. It was closely allied to the call for stronger measures to discipline and control all social elements and minorities that threatened social order.

After 1974 Thatcherism emerged as the leading ideological force within the party and helped to revitalise Conservatism. It sought the creation of a new national consensus, through the breaking of the chains of collectivism, the revival of a liberal economy and the liberal society, and the restoration of Britain's national economic fortunes. An end to decline was what the New Right promised, and an end also to social democracy. The core of the strategy was derived from liberal political economy, but its especial strength and its popular appeal rested on rather different foundations, an atavistic emphasis on nation and family of the kind that have always nourished political movements of the right.

5.3 The free economy

The development of a strategy based on the principles of liberal political economy for halting economic decline already began from a position of considerable strength. Throughout the long night of Keynesianism and social democracy the liberal orientation of British external policy and the openness of the British economy were not threatened, they were restored. In the 1950s sterling was made convertible again, the specialised commodity markets of the City of London were reopened, trade barriers began to come down, the export of capital was resumed. But internally Keynesian demand management policies were pursued, public spending and taxation were high, and the government attempted to reconcile stable prices with unemployment, economic growth and a surplus on the balance of payments.

The key to the free economy strategy as it emerged in the 1970s was that it attempted to bring the internal policy once more into line with the external. Such a correspondence existed under the gold standard, when the internal money supply and level of activity was directly affected by any change in the external balance, because the money supply was tied directly to the gold reserves, and the gold reserves were used to settle debts. Governments could not interfere with the mechanism of adjustment, whatever the short-term effects on prices and employment. Expansions and contractions of the money supply and domestic activity were determined by changes in the trading balance, and the shipments of gold which these made necessary. The ideal of an international monetary system that was 'politician-proof' inspired Montagu Norman, the Governor of the Bank of England, in his efforts to rebuild the international monetary system during the 1920s.[26] It is remarkable how strong the faith remained. Even in the 1950s, during the height of Keynesianism, a plan was drawn up, although never implemented, by the Treasury, 'Operation Robot', for reuniting internal and external management once more, making many key economic policy decisions automatic, and therefore binding on the Chancellor, rather than a matter for his discretion.[27]

The heart of the free economy strategy was a search for just such a robot which could be entrusted with the management of the economy. For economic liberals the modern economy is not truly an economy at all, in the sense of a household which is centrally controlled and planned because it seeks to balance income and expenditure. Rather, it is a market order, a complicated network of individual exchanges organised through many different markets. This network of markets is not controlled by anyone, and so long as its basic rules are guaranteed, offers unparalleled opportunities and freedom for individuals to choose how to make the most of their talents, how to satisfy their wants, and how to live in the way they choose. A market order is a fragile and artificial creation which is threatened both by anarchy and by tyranny. To avoid anarchy a public power must be instituted to keep the self-interest of individuals within bounds, to protect property and persons, to enforce contracts and to guarantee a medium of exchange. A market order is necessarily an order governed by general rules which apply equally to all. Such rules create a sphere of individual liberty – the market. But the difficulty arises as to how the public power that is instituted to maintain the market order can be prevented from going beyond the establishment and enforcement of general rules, and intervening in the detailed choices and outcomes of the market.

From the perspective of liberal political economy such interference must be arbitrary and discretionary. It has nothing to do with law, understood as a system of general rules. A liberal government would be one which confined itself to its primary functions and sought to keep its expenditure at the minimum required to do so effectively. The problem with which all modern liberal thought has wrestled is that the greatest threat to the market order, the greatest urge to expand discretionary intervention and bureaucratic administration, to plan and organise ever greater parts of society collectively, to increase public spending and the taxes that have to be levied to finance it, have all been associated with the rise of democracy. The assertion of equal political and social rights, alongside equal legal rights and the development of collective organisations and mass parties to press for them, has created a continual tension between the ideal of a market order and the ideal of a social democracy. It is hard for the modern state to be both, and it has become increasingly difficult to find a democratic basis for a market order. That is why most economic liberals put liberty first and democracy some way behind.[28]

From the standpoint of the new economic liberalism, the cause of Britain's economic decline and the steady withering of Britain's industrial base is the wholesale perversion of the market order that has occurred in Britain since the turn of the century. It involved the supplanting of individualism by collectivism and it led, so it is argued, to the proliferation of obstacles to the workings of free markets throughout British society, so that Britain was rather rapidly transformed from a country with some of the most sensible and efficient social and political arrangements from a liberal point of view, to a sink of collectivism, bureaucracy and inefficiency.[29]

In foreign economic policy there had been a partial retreat from the principles of free trade and openness to the world economy with the introduction of protectionist measures during the 1930s. Market liberals wanted a return to free trade principles and an end to all controls on capital movements and on trade.

There was disagreement over the best kind of international monetary system. The impossibility of maintaining sterling's traditional international role was acknowledged, but opinion tended to be split over whether floating exchange rates or a new gold standard were the best solution for creating the kind of international financial stability that international capitalism has lacked since 1971. The problem with floating exchange rates is that they impose no automatic constraint on the domestic expansion of the money supply in individual nation-states, and can therefore permit and even encourage accelerating inflation. They do not force countries to adjust to external price shocks. They leave them the option of inflating. On the other hand floating exchange rates do avoid the problems of fixed rates. There is no longer any need for periodic realignments of currencies, whilst the need for either international political agreement or the unchallenged dominance of one state in order to preserve international financial stability is reduced.

Another problem in Britain's external relations with the capitalist world was disagreement over the EC. Many economic liberals denounced the EC because one of its key programmes, the Common Agricultural Policy, was protectionist and inefficient. It subsidised the weakest producers. Those like Powell who were British nationalists opposed also any moves towards tighter federation and to economic and monetary union because they would have involved the loss of the freedom of each nation to determine its own taxes and expenditure and to be responsible for its own money supply and exchange rate.[30] Some economic liberals support the EC because of the progress it represents to freer and wider markets, but do not accept that Britain's sovereignty must eventually be merged in a wider European sovereignty.

But whatever the disagreements, the priority accorded to maintaining Britain's traditional liberal orientation was never questioned. No course other than complete integration in the world economy was contemplated. The thrust of the free economy strategy was aimed at identifying and removing those obstacles in Britain's internal policies and arrangements that prevented a more rapid and flexible adjustment of the British economy to the requirements of international capitalist competition.

5.4 Monetarism

Four areas were singled out by the free economy strategy for major changes. They were Keynesian economic management, the interventionist role of government in the economy, the power and privileges of the trade unions, and the demands for high public spending which arise in democracies. All created obstacles to the workings of free markets; and together they provided the core policies of social democracy.

The significance of monetarist doctrine for liberal political economy is that stable money is one of the indispensable conditions for a market order.[31] Inflation attacks the basis of the market order, since not only is it a tax that no one has voted for, but it threatens to disrupt the elaborate mechanism of exchange between individuals and therefore calls into question the legitimacy of the market order itself.

The starting point for all free market thinking was that the chief aim of government economic policy should be maintaining price stability by firmly controlling the money supply. Monetarism revived the traditional orthodoxy on monetary questions. Inflation is always and everywhere a monetary phenomenon; it can be halted if the growth of the money supply is curtailed; and control of the money supply is one of the few things that governments can control in a capitalist economy, provided they are determined enough.[32] They must aim to balance their budgets, or at least borrow in a way that does not increase money supply. This means they must either raise their taxes or reduce their spending. They must also set firm monetary targets, preferably several years ahead, in order to keep control of the volume of private credit. The recommendation for monetary targets appeared to have special force in a world of floating exchange rates, since only if internal monetary discipline is observed can internal inflation be mastered and external inflationary shocks, such as a sudden rise in the price of oil, be accommodated. In this way the policy of openness to the world economy was reconciled to domestic stability.

Monetarist doctrine made stable money and the control of inflation not just the main goal but the only legitimate goal of government policy. Money is an essential condition for a market order, so must be guaranteed by a central authority.[33] But while money can and must be an object of government policy, and general rules should be pursued in regulating its supply, monetarists argued that no such general rules can cover growth, employment and the balance of payments. From the monetarist standpoint this is not to compare like with like. Growth, employment and the balance of payments are all regarded as the outcomes of a multitude of individual decisions in which no government should be directly interfering. The delicate trade-offs of Keynesian economic management, the careful adjustment of the fine tuners, were to be no more. To trade unemployment against inflation was to sacrifice one of the fundamentals of a free market and opened the way to ever greater discretionary intervention in pursuit of a national economic interest.

Inflation had to be mastered if the market order was to be preserved, and demand policies that raised the rate of inflation only ensure that the cutback which would eventually be necessary to restore stable money would be more painful and involve higher unemployment and a deeper recession. Salvation either lay in the market or it did not exist at all.[34]

5.5 State intervention

Sound money is compatible with many different levels of government activity. In market doctrine, however, only a minimal state will ensure that sound money is maintained, and that it has the beneficial effects on the economy that are intended. The attacks made by nineteenth-century liberals on the expenses of the military establishment and the administration of the colonies as an unproductive burden upon industry have been refurbished; only this time the target is rarely the enormous defence establishment, but the social and welfare programmes of advanced capitalism when these are financed collectively through the state.

In Britain, this part of the public sector, which has been steadily expanding since the turn of the century, and was significantly enlarged after 1940, was treated by market strategists as a major obstacle to greater internal competition and a major unproductive burden on the 'wealth-creating' sector and on taxpayers. It was regarded as 'unproductive' because only individual producers could create 'wealth' by producing commodities and exchanging them on the market. The government was only a producer in its role as manager of the nationalised industries. In all its other roles it was necessarily a parasite dependent on raising taxes from individual commodity producers and property owners.[35]

Only the private sector can create wealth, only the public sector can guarantee the right framework for its operation. In so far as the state carries out those functions it is legitimate and has a duty to raise taxes because it is enforcing what is a true general interest – the preservation of the market order. But once it begins increasing its expenditures and interventions, then it undermines the workings of the market order by reducing the incentives for individuals to work and compete, and to take responsibility for themselves and their families. It also distorts the pattern of choices and activities that would have spontaneously emerged if state intervention had been absent.

Cutting back public expenditure from the levels it had attained in Britain was a central part of the free economy strategy for reversing decline, not just to assist in the control of inflation, but to inject greater dynamism and incentives into the economy by making market forces more effective and lowering taxation. The society would not only then be morally improved but more efficient too. If government spending is too high and the government is forced to borrow money, then either it borrows from the banks, which directly increases the money supply and eventually the rate of inflation, or it must raise the money from the financial markets, paying whatever rate of interest is required to elicit funds. Since the government has compulsory powers of taxation, it can normally afford whatever interest rates are needed, but in the process it 'crowds out' the borrowing of private individuals and companies who cannot afford credit at the going interest rate.[36]

Both sound money and a free, competitive market require major reductions in the size of the public sector, and the confinement of government to a 'neutral policy stance' eliminating detailed interference in markets. Again the principle is quite clear. Apart from the maintenance of the general conditions without which a market order could not exist at all, governments composed of fallible politicians and bureaucrats are regarded as quite unsuitable to be trusted with decisions which could be left to markets. This is because governments do not have to calculate risks in the same way as private individuals and companies, because they are protected from the consequences of failure. Their interventions lead necessarily to privileges being granted to particular individuals and interests in the market and denied to others. Subsidies, special incentives, special prohibitions have all to be financed out of general taxation. Instead of taxes being used only to provide 'public goods'[37] which cannot be provided by individuals, they are used to give some individuals special advantages over others.

The main targets were public spending on welfare, and subsidies to industry, including nationalised industries. Welfare spending came under such attack because most of the services, including health, education and housing, could be provided almost entirely through the market. Individuals would have to pay for all the services they used and to insure themselves; but the great reduction in public spending that would result would allow genuine reductions in taxation – not just a rearrangement of the balance but actual reduction of the burden. The immediate aim would be to cut back state spending sufficiently to reduce income tax by one-third to one-half. Ending all subsidies to industry and returning all nationalised industries to private ownership would force much more rapid contraction and reorganisation on industries like shipbuilding, steel and cars – all of which had previously been given government aid to ease their steady run-down. A free economy strategy could provide large redundancy payments (although even this would be to give the workers involved 'privileges'), but every firm would have to survive in the world market entirely on its own. Market forces alone would be relied upon to force restructuring of industry, the raising of productivity and the creation of conditions in which profitable enterprises could once more emerge.

5.6   Trade-union power

The major obstacle to the rule of the market once the state had been rolled back was the resistance of the trade unions. Britain had long been regarded as possessing an especially powerful trade-union movement. From a New Right point of view trade unions are voluntary associations which have a legitimate purpose in providing insurance and welfare for their members. When, however, they seek to interfere in contracts in the labour market, and to influence the attitudes and behaviour of employees at work, they cease to be voluntary associations and become coercive groups and private monopolies. As such they are by far the most important obstacle to the workings of a market order. Monopolies enjoyed by firms are regarded not only as rarer but as a much more minor problem. There are no suggestions amongst market theorists that existing concentrations of capital should be broken up, or that attempts should be made to create competitive markets made up of a multitude of small individual producers. From the social market standpoint the activities of even the most gigantic economic 'individual' like General Motors are still regulated by the world market and by international competition. Trade unions, however, stop markets from functioning at all.

Their ability to do this in Britain is regarded as resting upon three special privileges which they enjoy – Enoch Powell listed them in 1968 as 'the freedom to intimidate' (peaceful picketing), 'the freedom to impose costs on others with impunity', and 'the immunity of trade unions from action of tort'.[38] These three privileges do represent a major part of the concessions won by trade unions in their long battle for recognition and for greater bargaining power. They are the essential privileges protecting and making effective the right to strike. Granted in 1906, they were not revoked even in 1927, and had been confirmed or extended by parliamentary legislation whenever threatened by new legal interpretations based on the Common Law. It is these privileges that the free economy strategy would revoke in order to create a much more 'flexible' labour market and a much more co-operative work-force.

Trade unions were seen as the organisations which must either be destroyed or drastically reduced in their importance and power if a social market economy is to arise. This is because although they are absolved from direct responsibility for the rate of inflation, they are considered responsible for most of the other ills that afflict the economy. They are blamed for whatever level of unemployment exists, because by resisting cuts in real wages they prevent competitive downward bidding among the unemployed for the available jobs.[39] They are blamed also for stagnation and low productivity, by insisting on levels of manning, and rules covering the safety, the speed and the intensity of work, which impose significantly higher costs on firms and prevent more rapid rationalisation and modernisation. Instead of firms being co-operative ventures between management and workers, trade unions often make them a battleground for opposing interests and limit managerial authority.

Ways of tackling union power varied. The simple monetarist line was that once sound money is restored trade unions lose their power, because they can no longer influence government policy and because they cannot indefinitely resist market forces. They can create unemployment by pricing their members out of work, but they cannot cause inflation itself (since they cannot directly print money). Rising unemployment is expected eventually to break the militancy and weaken the organisation of the unions by reducing the numbers enrolled, as it did in the 1920s and 1930s. Other advocates of the strategy, however, argued that high unemployment in the past weakened but did not destroy or reform the trade unions. They feared the consequences of prolonged high unemployment on the electorate, on social order and on the finances of the state, so they called for more direct measures; not outright abolition of the right to strike, but certainly the organisation of powerful strike-breaking forces and the rescinding of the legal privileges trade unions had enjoyed. A minimal state does not mean a weak state. On the contrary the state had to be strong to ensure the conditions in which a free economy could work. That meant confronting and transforming all those institutions and interests which currently stood in the way.[40]

5.7 Democracy

The problem of trade unions merges into the problem of

democracy itself. Free economy strategists are acutely aware of the short span of time available between elections to introduce changes, and how much longer on average are the time spans of the policies themselves. They place more importance on the presence of a public power that is able to guarantee a market order and therefore a realm of individual liberty, than on how that public power is established and to whom it is answerable. It makes them unenthusiastic democrats. They have never accepted that temporary democratic majorities have the right to interfere with the workings of the market order or to threaten individual economic liberty. Since the fundamental principles and conditions of economic freedom are already known they may be endorsed but cannot be discovered through the democratic process. It has always seemed safer to economic liberals to devise ways in which economic policy can be placed above politics, and made a matter of expert administration within unalterable constraints.[41] Some states have experimented by writing certain precepts of economic liberalism into their constitutions, so taking a range of important economic decisions and options out of the hand of politicians. There has been some support for such constitutional devices in Britain.[42]

The chief problem with democracy for the social market strategy is that it tends to generate pressures and demands that are not compatible with a market order. In Britain the problem was regarded as especially serious, because the trade unions were not only a major obstacle to the working of the market order, but are also closely associated with one of the two leading political parties. The Labour party, in which the trade unions are a major force and the main source of funds, has been a vehicle both for the preservation and consolidation of trade union privileges, and also for the extension of bureaucratic intervention in the economy, for expanding public enterprise, and for expanding public expenditure and taxation. As a result of post-war electoral competition between the two main parties for the votes of the working class, free economy theorists argued that the balance of the economy had swung away from the market order towards collectivism. Governments had steadily

expanded universal welfare provision and adopted numerous policies, for example in housing, which enlarged the
scope for arbitrary administrative decision-making and
weakened the flexibility and the universality of the
market.[43] At the same time the electorate was encouraged
to expect that governments, using their new technical
ability to control the economy, could achieve goals like
prosperity, growth, and full employment. So anxious did
governments become to fulfil them that they expanded the
money supply and raised demand whenever there were
temporary setbacks to growth or slight rises in unemployment. In this way the sphere of bureaucracy expanded and
the sphere of law declined, and the economy became
riddled with distortions, inefficiencies and accelerating
inflation. Prosperity was maintained but at an increasing
cost.

The problem of how to prevent democratic electorates
voting for policies that damage the market order and lead to
economic ruin was one of the central problems for free
economy strategy. In Britain it appeared to require either
the destruction or the transformation of the Labour party,
or the severing of the links between organised labour and
any political party. Otherwise any revocation of legal
privileges might not endure. Some Conservatives as a result
became convinced of the need for a radical overhaul of the
British political system, including the introduction of
proportional representation.[44]

The free economy strategy was an ambitious attempt to
realign Britain's external and internal policies of economic
management, to recreate a free economy and to make the
state strong enough to establish and police it, and to attack
social democracy at its roots. It identified the main causes
of British decline as the abandonment of the domestic
commitment to sound money, the growth of state spending
and state intervention, and the power of trade unions. All
these have come about and consolidated one another as the
result of the workings of British democracy over the past
hundred years. As a result Britain has become progressively
enfeebled, less and less able to compete internationally.

Since Britain's integration in the capitalist world market

was taken as the starting point for the strategy, the whole burden of adjustment to the demands of international competition falls on internal institutions and practices. The strategy therefore envisaged a prolonged struggle to force through the necessary changes in attitudes and behaviour. Its advocates were always more adept at setting out the general principles of their doctrine than at specifying exactly how the political and social conditions necessary for its implementation could be created.

6

The enterprise state

The post-war consensus, built upon full employment and the welfare state, failed to command the support of people because they have seen first that it did not contain within it any element whatsoever of transformation, and secondly, that even by its own criteria it failed. That policy could not bring about growth, it could not extend freedom, it could not even maintain let alone develop welfare and it could not sustain full employment.

Tony Benn[1]

The second strategy to be discussed is the alternative economic strategy of the Left in the Labour movement. Like the free economy strategy this was not a single strategy. Many variants existed and many different groups on the Left contributed to it. There is considerable ambiguity surrounding the alternative economic strategy because it drew on two different traditions of political economy – national political economy and the socialist critique of political economy. The free economy strategy fits into a tradition of liberal political economy that stretches back through the nineteenth century. But the immediate precursors of the alternative economic strategy with its concern for the national economy and making the state an 'enterprise state', devoted to raising industrial output and social wealth, were the alternative strategies of Joseph Chamberlain and the Social Imperialists, and Oswald Mosley and the Fascists. Neither movement at the time attracted significant support from the organised Labour movement. But just as the programme of Margaret Thatcher is not that of Richard Cobden, so the alternative economic strategy is different from these predecessors. What they have in common is the perception that it is the external policy which must be challenged and the external relations which must be transformed to reverse decline, whereas liberal political economy has always started from the assumption that it is individual attitudes and behaviour within Britain that must be adjusted to world market forces.

Many socialists became supporters of the alternative economic strategy and argued that the objective of seeking to establish control over a national economy was a socialist objective, because the world economy had moved into a new phase. The rise of nation companies and economic interpenetration had destroyed the world of competitive national capitalisms of the period before 1914 and during the 1930s. The bourgeoisie had become international, and the appropriate response for every national working class was to seek to win control of each national economy and in this way lay the foundations for a socialist world economy. Such arguments, with their often explicit relationship to Marxist theory, shared many of the central preoccupations of national political economy.

6.1 Social Imperialism

Liberal political economy became a doctrine of compelling force in the nineteenth century but it did not go unchallenged. Standpoints other than the market arose for viewing and assessing the development of capitalism. One of the most important of these was national political economy. Its standpoint is not the market and the individual, but the national economy and the state, an approach rooted in the fragmentation of the capitalist world market into a large number of rival political authorities, the nation-states.

The distinctive doctrines of national political economy were never strong in England because national economic policy early embraced the doctrine of free trade and identified the British national interest with the furthest possible expansion of the world market. Those who argued for a different external policy and a more cautious development of industry were cast aside.[2] National political economy developed at first in other countries, notably Germany and the United States.

From the outset it was directed against some of the key doctrines of liberal political economy, particularly free trade. It never had the intellectual coherence of economic liberalism but it increasingly exercised great practical influence. This was because it offered explanations for the shortcomings of markets, and remedies, which did not involve submitting to the internal restorative powers of markets themselves. As capitalism developed so there were more and more things which liberal political economy seemed unable to explain: economic backwardness and the problems of industrialisation; economic power and military power; the rise of bureaucracy and large-scale enterprise; the increasingly collective basis of the industrialisation process and the need for greater state intervention; the independent industrial and political organisations of labour movements; crises of overproduction and the collapse of investment and demand; and amidst all this growing difficulties in maintaining the legitimacy of the market order on which capitalist relations and capitalist production depended. All these trends which accompanied the development of capitalism as the first world system of production and accumulation continually created the need for national economic policies that protected nations and groups within the nation, against the effects of markets.

National political economy as a rather disparate collection of doctrines draws its fundamental strength from viewing capitalism as more than a series of markets connecting the economic activities of individuals. It places the emphasis instead on capitalism as a system of organised and increasingly collective and interdependent production. The aim of policy accordingly is not to give first priority to fostering commercial opportunity and the widest possible system of exchange, but to building up and safeguarding productive capacity and securing collaboration between the major classes and interests involved in industry.

Such an emphasis was already present when national political economy first took shape as a protest against Britain's industrial monopoly and the way in which free trade consolidated it. The most vociferous advocates of protection against British competition were in Germany and the United States, the two countries with the greatest prospects of effectively challenging it. Friedrich List[3] quite readily accepted the superiority of liberal economic theory but denied that the political conditions – a single world state – existed for a liberal order to be practicable. Rivalry between nation-states provided the framework within which all economic development had to proceed. To elevate the principles of liberal political economy from a distant goal into a set of maxims for policy favoured the interests of the strongest states against the weaker.

National political economy originated as a protest against the inequalities and injustices of free trade, and this has remained one of its central features. But as industrialisation developed and the character of the new processes of production became better understood, so national political economy became broadened into a concern with production rather than with the market and with the role of public agencies in making good deficiencies in markets. This rarely meant a wholesale rejection of markets but it did entail going beyond the liberal rationale for state involvement – creating the conditions for markets to function effectively. The basis of national political economy in all its forms has been to recognise not how smoothly the market economy adjusts to shocks and disturbances, but how discontinuities and crises and instability are inherent in the working of the capitalist production process. The remedy as far as national political economy is concerned is not the removal of obstacles to the workings of markets but the removal of obstacles to the development of production.

Viewing capitalism as primarily a system of production rather than a system of markets flows naturally from the assumption that it is not individuals who compete in the world market, but nation-states. Economic policy must have the aim not merely of realising the interest of individual producers and consumers, but of increasing the power and maintaining the security of the state. From the standpoint of national political economy, free trade is a tactical policy that may at certain times be in the interests of a state to adopt. List admitted that if he were an Englishman he would be a free trader.[4]

In the nineteenth century liberal political economy and national political economy came to offer alternative conceptions of national interest, and become associated with different social bases and political forces. National political economy became the perspective of all those groups entrenched in the apparatuses of the state and practised in defining and formulating the national interest. It supplied the economic principles for nationalist and right-wing political forces, but because its bias was collectivist rather than individualist it also proved increasingly attractive to those liberals and social democrats who wished to use public agencies to reform and restructure social institutions.

What marks national political economy so clearly is its tendency to treat the nation as a single strategic commercial and industrial enterprise, competing with other similar enterprises in the world economy. Liberal political economy treats the nation as an association of individuals pursuing their own separate purposes within a framework of law. The nation has no purpose other than the purposes of the individuals who compose it. If these purposes demand exchanges with foreigners, the government must not obstruct but facilitate them. For national political economy there is a national interest beyond the purposes of individuals, which it is the task of the permanent agencies of the state to identify, formulate and secure.

Once British industry began to lose ground in world markets, because of the very high tariffs erected against British goods, and subsequently because of direct competition from the industries that developed behind them, the free trade policy began to be re-examined. New forces on the Right in Britain began to clamour for a policy of imperial protection and national efficiency to meet the growing challenge from foreign rivals, and safeguard Britain's future prosperity. A struggle erupted between the

adherents of a policy of free trade and the adherents of tariff
reform. A national policy was inescapable. The dispute was
over whether it should aim to maximise the opportunities
and the returns for British companies, banks, and workers
by maintaining the greatest possible degree of openness to
the world economy, or whether it should be subordinated by
public agencies to a national assessment of British interest,
British welfare and British security.

This battle was on a much grander scale than the battle
over the Corn Laws, where the pleas for protection were so
much more clearly the pleas of a sectional interest. What
was new about the tariff reform debate sixty years later was
that in the meantime industrial capitalism had completed
the transformation of British society and the organisation of
a world economy, and the urgent questions of policy
concerned not whether industrial advance should be reined
back, but how it was to be sustained and the gains from the
past consolidated and extended.[5]

The Social Imperialist movement at the turn of the
century was the first major political response to the problem
of British decline, the first major attempt to change the
course of British policy. The Social Imperialists proposed to
meet the threats to Britain's strategic position and commercial superiority by consolidating a political empire within
the world economy, which could make Britain self-
sufficient. For the Social Imperialists the tariff reform
programme was not merely a means of maintaining and
extending British prosperity, but also of meeting the
military and strategic challenge of other states. The dream
of Greater Britain, of a federation of Anglo-Saxon settler
states, organised as a bloc within the world economy and
strong enough to maintain its independence and prosperity,
is a dream that has faded. It was a major alternative
geopolitical strategy, but it was not pursued, and the
opportunity for it disappeared. Its rationale was to preserve
Britain's great power status, and to secure permanent world
markets for British industry, but once that status was no
more, protectionism rapidly lost its practicality and its
appeal for most of the Right. The American alliance, and a
junior role in helping to maintain the open trading and

financial system of the world economy, became the new framework for Conservative thinking after 1945.[6]

National political economy was regarded as inescapable for states that desired independence to pursue ambitions and to order their own internal affairs as they saw fit. Milner declared, 'This country must remain a Great Power or she will become a poor country' and all the Social Imperialists constantly stessed the links between military strategy and commercial strategy. The Boer War (1899–1902) was regarded as one of the greatest successes of the new Social Imperialism. Julian Amery has described it as:

> a masterstroke of policy. Few victories in British history have done more to increase Britain's economic or military power. After the peace of Vereeniging British settlers and British capital poured into the country. Today it has become Britain's second most important market in the world and the ground where well over £1000 million of British capital are profitably invested.[7]

The Social Imperialists were successful in getting Britain to adopt a more aggressive and conscious policy of imperialist expansion. Liberal as well as Conservative governments were equally committed to the principle of a strong navy and the maintenance of the colonial possessions, even though there was disagreement between the parties over specific acts of imperial policy. But the real conflict came over whether Britain should seek to make its dominant position permanent by an economic and political policy aimed at converting the Empire into a single world state. The rationale was always that Britain could only hope to solve the problems of her economy within a much wider framework of trade and payments than the British national economy permitted, and only a Greater British state could guarantee that Britain remained dominant within such a framework.

The Social Imperialists believed that Britain could only preserve its power and its wealth if its leaders realised the dangers into which the policy of expansion had led the nation. Chamberlain emphasised this point again and again in his speeches:

> Why do the people not realise that Germany is making
> war upon us, that her economic attack is just as surely an
> act of aggression as if she had declared hostilities? She
> will never rest until she dominates the world . . . Tariff
> Reform is our defence. It is just as vital as the navy. We
> must arm if we are not to be beaten without striking a
> blow.

> Workers cannot live off investments in a foreign country.
> If that labour is taken from you, you have no recourse
> except perhaps to learn French or German . . . you cannot
> go on forever watching with indifference the disappear-
> ance of your principal industries.[8]

But the Social Imperialists never did succeed in wresting
Britain from its traditional liberal policy. Protection was
always resisted and only triumphed briefly, during the First
World War after 1916, and again after 1932. In both cases
the liberal order in the world economy had first to be
destroyed.

Social Imperialism also involved an internal strategy for
winning the support of the working class and increasing
industrial efficiency. The reason for Britain's decline was
ascribed directly to the long period of *laissez-faire* policies,
the pursuit of short-term commercial gains leading to the
neglect of military preparedness, and the shameful
exploitation of the working class. Social Imperialism set out
to win the mass support for imperialist policy of the kind
which Chamberlain had long enjoyed in Birmingham. It
sought mobilisation of the population behind collective
national goals and recognised as a result that concessions
were necessary to secure loyalty. The leading Social
Imperialists despised the ineffectiveness of national policy
and the lack of strong leadership which parliamentary
politics produced. Germany was feared but also much
admired by them. It had abandoned a liberal economic
policy and it had never had to endure liberal political
institutions.

The result was a concerted attempt to put forward a programme and build a movement that could overcome the grievances of the working class and dramatically increase national power. The Social Imperialists regarded class conflict as one of the most serious elements weakening the nation in its competition with other nations. Free trade policy might provide cheap food but it also provided slums, low wages, unemployment, illiteracy, and malnutrition. The physical condition of the English workers was regarded as so poor by many Social Imperialists that they doubted whether an efficient army could be formed.[9] The Social Imperialists proposed social reforms that would be paid for out of the revenue from tariffs and could heal the rift between capital and labour, and establish a new spirit of class harmony and class collaboration.

The failure of the external programme of the Social Imperialists did not prevent the steady realisation of the internal programme, as pressure from the working class was increasingly exerted and as the scale of the needs that were not being met through markets became more appreciated. This part of Social Imperialism, increasing public expenditure to bear the costs of free market competition in the interests of social stability and greater economic efficiency, became part of the general political consensus and was appropriated by other political forces fully committed to maintaining free trade, especially the 'New Liberals' and social democrats who came increasingly to dominate the policy discussions of the Labour movement.[10]

6.2 Fascism and the slump

Under Chamberlain, Social Imperialism had captured the Unionist party, but the Unionist party failed to oust the Liberals from office. In the aftermath of war, revolution abroad and the rise of Labour at home, the new dominant Conservative party in the 1920s remained trapped within liberal orthodoxy and failed to implement the programme of Social Imperialism. The rejection of tariffs, the return to gold, and the General Strike, were all viewed by many Social

Imperialists as a fatal policy of negative anti-Socialisr holding the line for property and defending Britain traditional world interests. They saw it as a policy doom to eventual defeat, since it could delay but not avert tl steady decline of British world power and the advance Labour.[11]

It was under these circumstances that Oswald Mosl launched his New Party in 1931 to overthrow the 'old gang of politics and forge an entirely new course. The links wi the strategy of Social Imperialism are obvious, althoug Mosley went further than Chamberlain in several respect He attempted to create a mass movement outside tl existing party system, he advocated much greater sta direction of the economy, and he was much more explicit identifying the City of London as one of the chief obstacl to implementing an economic policy that preserved tl interests and future of the national economy.

Mosley was strongly influenced by Keynes in his econ mic thinking, particularly in his approach to the problem unemployment, but he also shared the strategic ar geopolitical perspectives of the Social Imperialists.[12] F argued that the breakdown of the liberal world econom and the sharp reduction of Britain's major export marke as a result of the war, made a change in Britain's extern policy still more urgent. The orthodox liberal policy patiently rebuilding the international monetary systen restoring the liberal trading network, encouraging rationa isation of domestic industry, and waiting for a revival of tl four leading industrial sectors – textiles; iron, steel ar engineering; coal; and shipbuilding – had to be rejected. condemned the British economy to perpetual stagnatio and high unemployment. It would benefit finance because would maintain the unlimited mobility of capital but would seriously weaken domestic industry. Mosley argue that experience of the 1920s and the world slump prove that Britain's position of dominance in the world econom had been irretrievably lost. Other countries had develope their own local manufactures, new powerful industri. competitors had arisen to challenge Britain's hold on mar markets, and British industry could not match the low cos of some foreign producers and had to face the dumping of their surplus production on the British market. At the same time, the progress of technology and mass production meant that modern industries throughout the world had a far greater capacity than ever before. The world economy was gripped by a general crisis of overproduction and Britain no longer had either the industrial or the military power to regain its control over world markets.[13]

Mosley's solutions were set out in the Memorandum on unemployment he submitted to the Prime Minister in 1930 when he was a junior minister, and in *The Greater Britain*, a founding document of the British Union of Fascists in 1932. He came to advocate a policy of economic self-sufficiency. Britain should tackle its unemployment problem by ruthlessly protecting its home market (using quotas rather than tariffs), developing trade links with the self-governing Dominions and controlling all colonial markets. He advocated, for example, the closing of the Indian market to Japanese competition and a new suppression of the local Indian textile industry, to maximise the demand for British products. In this way Britain could guarantee sufficient markets for its own industries. The chimera of a new world ascendancy for British capital would give place to the more attainable objective of a strong world empire, able to rival all other states.[14]

Such a policy meant confronting the City of London and subordinating finance to the objectives of national policy. The currency would be managed, and internal money supply and credit creation would be determined, by the need to secure full employment of resources and the development of productive capacity, rather than by the need to achieve an external trade balance and to maintain confidence in sterling. Mosley wanted to sweep away the minimal state and to concentrate the whole energies of government on finding a solution to the unemployment problem. He proposed establishing a small War Cabinet with its own civil service by passing the Treasury and the Board of Trade. This powerful executive would carry through measures to alleviate unemployment by whatever programme of public works proved necessary. It would seek

controls over credit and investment, establishing ne
public agencies to achieve this, and would carry throug
major rationalisations of industry and agriculture. Su
rationalisations would succeed, Mosley thought, becau
the government would ensure that markets were availab
and would not rely on market forces to carry them throug
The greatly increased capacity of modern industry, whi
was causing the great shortfall in markets, could be handl
if the state undertook to maintain effective demand at
high enough level through its spending and credit polici
Full employment of manpower and productive capacit
rather than stable money, was to be the priority of sta
policy.

Some of Mosley's ideas were acted on in the 1930s on
the gold standard had finally collapsed. Protected home ar
imperial markets did bring a substantial recovery of Briti
industry and the advance of many of the science-based ma
production industries. But the drastic overhaul of the sta
machine which Mosley wanted, and the ambitious pro
ramme of state intervention which he proposed, we
resisted. Mosley's Fascist movement failed to break throug
and the bases of liberal orthodoxy were not touched.[15]

6.3 Labour and the national economy

The failure of first Social Imperialism and then Fascism
Britain to change the liberal world orientation of the Briti
state made the subordination of Britain to the United Stat
inevitable after 1945. Since that time support for protectic
on the Right has noticeably dwindled, and within tl
Conservative party the tradition founded by Chamberla
has few heirs. Only the National Front on the Right ha
openly advocated protection.[16] Although some Conserva
tives were opposed to entry into the EC, they rarely did
as advocates of protection. The new nationalism of Enoc
Powell, while rejecting the Common Market, was joined
the most uncompromising statement of the principles
liberal political economy.[17]

The weakness of national political economy in Britai

reflects the loss of military power and the new stage of the world economy. The fusion that took place after 1945 between industrial and banking capital, the spread of production overseas by companies based in Britain, the revival of world trade and the growing interpenetration of the markets of the developed world, all weakened the attractiveness and the practicality of a protectionist strategy.

The cause of protection and the national economy migrated to the Left. This was a fairly new development, since formerly the Labour movement had never wholeheartedly embraced national political economy. Social Imperialism had generally been resisted and the early Labour leaders – Philip Snowden in particular, who was Chancellor of the Exchequer in 1924 and 1929 – were often strict adherents of liberal political economy. Churchill, himself a free trader, wrote of Snowden that 'the Snowden mind and the Treasury mind embraced one another with the enthusiasm of two long-separated kindred lizards'. Snowden pursued orthodox financial policies, eventually resigning from the National government in 1932 when it introduced protection.[18] Mosley failed to carry any significant part of the Labour leadership with him in his plans to fight unemployment.[19] Labour leaders continued to hold liberal conceptions of Britain's external policy and world role, and shared the belief in free trade and cosmopolitanism which it proclaimed. At the time when an autarkic policy was most practicable Labour's leaders refused to contemplate it. They sought to defend the interests and rights of the working class but they had no conception of using the state power even to achieve modest shifts in the priorities of state policy, still less to attempt to influence the general balance of class forces in civil society.

There did exist perspectives in the Labour movement other than accommodation to the prevailing orthodoxy. Most important were the various socialist critiques of political economy, including Marxism, whose standpoint was the interest of the working class.[20] These critiques furnished arguments against the continued rule of capital, and generally emphasised either the inequitable distribution of the social product and the harshness and waste of market forces, or the exploitation and subordination of the worker in the production process. Ideals of greater equality of distribution and co-operative ownership were central to the idea of a socialist commonwealth as an alternative to capitalism as a way of organising industrial society. The critiques of political economy were divided in their attitude towards the state, and how capitalism might best be replaced. Many socialists believed that the existing state had to be destroyed because it was necessarily subordinate to the market order and therefore to the needs of capital. A new democratic state subordinate to the working class had to be established. But other socialists argued that the nature of the state as a public realm gave it an independence which a socialist movement could use to push through reforms that would permit gradual movement towards the building of socialism.[21]

This latter perspective was to become increasingly dominant in the party, and allowed the spread of the perspective of national political economy in the Labour movement with its emphasis upon the national economy and productive capacity. National political economy has always been relatively weak in Britain – there has never, for example, been a permanent government department to speak for and represent the interests of the national economy and national industry. Mosley's remodelled executive was rejected, Labour's Ministry of Economic Affairs (1947) and Department of Economic Affairs (1964) did not survive.[22] Nevertheless, the national economy could not be ignored, and a perspective based upon it continually reappeared because of the size of the state sector and the organised influence of the working class and national capital, as well as the pressures of the national electorate.

In the 1930s after the meagre achievements of its first two administrations, the Labour party began to develop a serious programme of policies for reforming the worst abuses of capitalism and creating high employment and prosperity. Public ownership, higher public spending, and planned trade were all among them.[23] Several of the party's new leaders became strongly influenced by Keynes and the idea that the chronic unemployment and stagnation which had been experienced in the 1920s and 1930s could be overcome by a rational state policy to control the level of demand.[24] The view that capitalist crises were essentially crises of insufficient demand suggested that if the political weight of social democracy were strong enough, the political barriers in the path of higher government spending could be removed, and an expanding economy created in which resources could be redistributed and new forms of public enterprise and welfare provision established.

Keynesianism was of enormous assistance after 1945 in legitimating the expanded role of the state over which Conservative and Labour governments presided. But the external policy remained unchanged and the internal policy of demand management permitted redistribution without reorganisation. The idea of an enterprise state remained anathema. Nevertheless, the deteriorating economic position of the British economy began to revive interest in strategies that could arrest the decline and safeguard those achievements of social democracy already secured.[25] In the process both national political economy and the socialist critiques of political economy began a major resurgence within the Labour movement.

6.4 The Left challenge

The revival of interest in strategies for socialism in the Labour movement dates from the failure of the modernisation strategy in the 1960s. After the prolonged battles within the party over unilateral nuclear disarmament and the proposals to end the party's commitment to public ownership, Harold Wilson skilfully united the party behind the programme for a 'New Britain'.[26] This envisaged a far-reaching modernisation of industry and the successful pursuit of economic expansion, accompanied by and financing major social reforms and large increases in public expenditure. For this new national economic policy Labour built wide national support. But by 1968 the whole strategy was in ruins and the extent of disenchantment and disillusion throughout the Labour movement was intense.[27] Not only had the government sacrificed all its plans for expansion to the need to maintain the confidence of the financial markets and bring the balance of payments back into surplus, but it had diluted all the measures that had some socialist content and was pursuing policies that held down wages and raised taxes on the working class, culminating in an attempt to impose legal curbs on union power.[28]

The late 1960s saw the development of many new radical movements and increasingly these developed outside the Labour party.[29] There was also a considerable growth in a socialist political culture, the revival of the Marxist critique of political economy being particularly pronounced.[30] When the Labour party lost office in 1970 a major review and discussion of its record took place. It was only the second period of majority Labour government Britain had ever experienced and it was inevitably compared unfavourably with 1945. Very little in the way of positive socialist achievement could be pointed to in the record of the Wilson government.

The evident failure of the attempt to modernise the British economy and to alter patterns of distribution revived interest in socialism and gave new impetus to the Left. One result was the drawing up of *Labour's Programme 1973*, the most left-wing statement the party had adopted since 1945.[31] The reason why the Left was once again making itself heard in the party was partly due to the leftward shift of several of the large unions in response to the increasing attacks by governments on union power.[32] But it also reflected increasing political tensions. The new programme emerged against a background of the industrial and political crises of the Heath government[33] and growing signs of weakness in the world economy.

The intellectual emphasis behind the new strategic thinking was provided by Labour party intellectuals like Michael Barratt Brown, John Hughes, Ken Coates, and Stuart Holland,[34] while political leadership was provided by Tony Benn who emerged as a leading advocate of a socialist strategy.[35] The increasingly severe plight of the national economy acted as a spur. The key to the new thinking was the idea that the way to a further socialist advance in Britain was by adopting a programme to restore health to the national economy through measures that increased state control and the power of the organised Labour movement, and would extend social rights and increase democratic participation, so breaking the stalemate between capital and labour that had lasted since the war. If Britain remained tied to the world economy, no such advance was possible, so dependent on world trade, so penetrated by international capital, so vulnerable to international financial pressures had Britain become. Another starting point was opposition to Britain's membership of the EC. The EC was increasingly opposed by the bulk of the Labour party, partly because it threatened to link the British economy still more firmly with the economies of the developed capitalist world, and partly because it was feared that British governments would progressively lose the power to introduce socialist policies, and plan the national economy as they wanted. To the extent that the EC was able to extend its co-operation from agricultural policy to monetary policy and industrial policy, the British national economy would become part of a much wider European national economy and the British state merely a regional arm of a European state.

Withdrawing from the EC was a major part of Labour's new programme from the outset. When Labour returned to office in 1974 the leadership compromised by attempting to 'renegotiate' the terms of entry. This elaborate exercise ended in a national referendum on the new terms, which were backed by a majority of the Labour Cabinet, but opposed by the Labour party.[36] The winning of the referendum was the signal for the removal of Tony Benn from the Department of Industry, where he had begun to implement the party's new industrial policies. These were abruptly curtailed, and the government drifted steadily towards orthodox policies to cope with the world recession. It introduced the first package of monetarist measures, including cash limits, monetary targets and round after round of spending cuts. It also organised, with the help of the trade unions, a new incomes policy. The slide into defensive orthodoxy intensified when the pound collapsed in 1976, and the government negotiated a loan from the IMF. Moderation was further consolidated after the government lost its small majority in the House of Commons in 1977 and was forced to conclude a pact with the Liberals.[37]

Amidst this familiar record of the Labour party in government, one thing was different. The Left in the party and in the Cabinet possessed in the 1973 *Programme* an 'alternative economic strategy', which was employed to criticise the direction of government policy. Just as a free economy strategy arose on the right so an alternative economic strategy arose on the left. Both were more than just technical economic policies; both represented major attempts to map our new political courses to overcome Britain's decline and transform British institutions and British society.

6.5   Regaining national economic sovereignty

The main condition for the implementation of the alternative economic strategy was the substantial severing of the ties that bound the British economy to the world economy. Only then could full economic sovereignty be regained, only then could the British state plan the national economy, only then would the measures not be undermined by foreign pressures. From the Labour Left's standpoint a social democracy could only be created if the British state regained control over the national economy.

The social democracy which the Labour Left aimed at was not the same as the social democracy advocated by Crosland and others in the 1950s. Crosland's ideal of social democracy was a dynamic and rapidly expanding private sector, which would provide the basis for high taxation and high government spending aimed at redistributing income and resources between classes and between generations, so as to ensure equality of opportunity and a high level of effective demand.[38] Such a goal, however, was not seen as conflicting with the integration of the British economy in the world capitalist economy.

The record of the Labour government after 1964, and again after 1974, as well as the experience of membership of the EC, persuaded a wide band of Labour opinion that the social democracy sought by Crosland was unobtainable, so long as the links which Britain maintained with the world economy remained unchanged. If those links were challenged, then the scope for internal reorganisation of the economy became much greater also. Integration in the world economy was seen to impose a market order and a liberal orientation on British policy whatever democratically elected governments in Westminster decided. There was always a potential clash between the national democratic state and the international market order.[39] The alternative economic strategy sought to abolish the tension by transforming Britain's links with the world economy.

The alternative economic strategy aimed to use political power to rebuild economic strength and extend civil, political and social rights to the fullest possible extent. The strategy was often caricatured as seeking the extension of bureaucracy and the centralised power of the state. But what all the theorists of the alternative economic strategy emphasised was the need to combine measures that socialised and collectivised the economy, with measures that gave greater civil, political, and social rights, and which encouraged democratic participation, not just in government but in all social institutions, including schools, factories, hospitals, and housing estates. The underlying idea was that full participation as a citizen in all social decisions was more fulfilling and satisfying for the individual than the pursuit of private interests within a market order. For full participation to be possible every individual had to enjoy equal rights, not just the equal rights they needed to be property owners and commodity producers, but the political and social rights they needed to be citizens – freedom of speech and publication, free elections, freedom of association and freedom of information, equal opportunities in education and health care, and social security against sickness, injury, handicap, and old age.[40]

Movement towards the granting of such rights has meant some movement beyond the provision of legal rights, in an attempt to reduce some of the social and economic inequalities that legal rights do not touch. Social democracy is an egalitarian ideal, whilst in a market order much greater emphasis is laid upon *individual* liberty. Freedom in a social democracy is enjoyed and experienced as a collective possession that belongs to the whole community and is consciously created by it. To the extent that social democracy is realised the state acquires a democratic and egalitarian basis. The guaranteeing of these rights becomes the foundation of its legitimacy.

Most capitalist states have become social democracies by creating universal suffrage and greatly expanding public spending. But while the deep and enduring problem of the legitimacy of the distribution of power and property in capitalist society has been eased by extending the public realm and accommodating new interests, neither the sphere of market exchange, nor the organisation of the production process, have altered fundamentally, and the degree of social and political inequality has only been marginally reduced.[41] Democracy and capitalism coexist at times uneasily, and social democratic policies must not encroach too far if the tension between them is to remain manageable. In Britain the welfare policies, the tax structure and the bargaining position, legal privileges and political influence of the trade unions, were widely regarded on both Left and Right as being policies which even if they had not changed the pattern of distribution very much, still laid burdens on British capital that other national capitals did not suffer, and contributed to slow growth during the boom. When the economy could no longer sustain them, repeated attacks began to be made on public expenditure and on trade-union rights.[42] An era of greater political turbulence and more open class confrontation began.

The Labour Left argued that since British capitalism could no longer tolerate either high public spending or strong trade unions, and was even becoming unenthusiastic about democratic government, the basis for the social democracy of Crosland and others had disappeared. The effective choice was between a thoroughgoing capitalist rationalisation, in which many of the gains and conquests of the Labour movement since 1940 were reversed, or a strategy to transform capitalism in a socialist direction. Only by tackling the inequalities that continually arose from the private ownership and private direction of the economic process could a basis be created for further advance towards social democracy.

The centrepiece of the alternative economic strategy was therefore seen to be 'breaking the chains of the world economy'. Because of its unique history of expansion and decline, the sovereignty of the British state was more penetrated and compromised than any other capitalist state outside the Third World. A socialist government would plan to introduce most stringent controls on foreign trade and on the export of capital. Trade would be planned through the imposition not of tariffs but of quotas, which might not reduce the existing volume of imports, and could even allow for the growth of some imports. Capital control would be imposed to end the vulnerability of sterling to sudden outflows of capital. Sterling would cease to be an international currency and would no longer be freely convertible; foreign holdings in sterling would be frozen. The exchange rate would then be controlled in line with British trade and industrial policy rather than determined through the foreign exchange markets.

These measures would be undertaken to safeguard the national economy. Import controls would be intended to halt 'de-industrialisation' – the remorseless rise in import penetration achieved by foreign manufacturers especially since the 1974–5 recession, which had threatened the survival of large parts of British industry and had contributed to steadily mounting unemployment.[43] Foreign exchange controls would be intended to halt not only runs on the pound and the panic deflations they so often produced in the past, but also to prevent so many British firms expanding abroad rather than in the domestic economy.

Both policies could only be accomplished if Britain had already left the EC or was prepared to leave it. Any import quotas or foreign exchange controls which could be negotiated with the rest of the EC would be unlikely to be effective enough to achieve their purpose. Such controls would also cause major problems with transnationals. Advocates of the alternative economic strategy regarded the advent of the transnational corporations, and the new world division they had organised, as not only one of the crucial contemporary features of the world economy, but one of the main causes of Britain's specific problems. The number of British firms that had become transnational, and the number of foreign transnationals operating in Britain, meant that any British government determined to take control of the British economy would have to confront the power of transnational companies. Foreign exchange controls and import controls would only go so far. Multinationals, it was argued, would find ways of evading the controls and would use their power to undermine government policies. One suggestion was that all the assets belonging to foreign transnational companies should be nationalised as well as the assets of most of the leading British transnational companies. To minimise retaliation from foreign governments, the assets of foreign transnationals would be paid for at full market value, by first requisitioning and then selling British overseas portfolio investments (as was done during both wars).[44]

In these ways a transformation would be wrought in Britain's external relations with the world economy. The international role of sterling would finally disappear, many of the activities of the City would be ended or drastically curtailed, and though foreign trade would not cease (no government could achieve that), it would become strictly monitored and regulated in line with the needs of the domestic economy as the government defined them. There would be many more bilateral trade agreements, particularly with Third World countries. The international orientation of the leading sector of British business would be ended and the penetration of the British economy by foreign transnationals would be reversed. The British economy would remain a major trading economy still dependent for supplies of food and raw materials, but no longer burdened by an international currency, a deteriorating balance of payments on visible trade, and an internationally oriented financial and business sector. If carried through this would indeed make possible a major change of direction in external policy. It was more radical than anything envisaged by Joseph Chamberlain or Oswald Mosley.

6.6 The regeneration of British industry

The loosening of Britain's ties with the market order of world capitalism would permit the pursuit of different internal policies. Safeguarded by import quotas from balance of payment problems the government would make the creation of full employment and economic growth its top priorities. It would try to do this by expanding demand, until all unused resources in the economy had been brought into play. This would be an orthodox Keynesian policy and would restore the priority given after the war to full employment and growth. Once full employment had been achieved by stimulating demand, the problem of inflation, whether caused by excess demand or the bargaining power of different groups in the economy, would be met by wide-ranging price and wages controls. A permanent prices and incomes policy that succeeded in at least suppressing inflation would be an essential part of the alternative economic strategy.

Demand-management policies, however, would be supplemented by measures aimed at improving British industrial performance, and which would involve a major expansion of state intervention. A national enterprise board, similar to the ill-fated IRC of the late 1960s and the NEB established after 1974,[45] though with greater powers and greater funds, would become the chief public instrument for directly raising the rate of investment in British manufacturing industry, establishing new companies alongside existing private firms or venturing into entirely new fields. To give the state overall control of productive investment, twenty-five of the largest manufacturing companies together with the banking system would be nationalised. Those large companies that remained privately owned would be expected to sign planning agreements, detailing their objectives on investment, output, and employment.

The aim of all these measures would be to remedy the comparatively low rates of investment in the British economy achieved since the war, so rebuilding British industrial capacity and raising productivity in British industry to world levels. Interest rates would be held at very low levels (as they were in the 1940s),[46] while demand would be maintained at high levels. Increasing public spending on investment and welfare would be the chief instruments used for raising demand. Although defence spending would be greatly reduced there would be little scope for any reductions in taxes. Control of the banking system and low interest rates would permit an expansive credit policy, although the areas of the economy where credit went would remain strictly controlled.

In all these ways a greater degree of central planning and central co-ordination would replace the more haphazard planning and co-ordination emerging through the interaction of the state and the private companies which dominate the economy. Government responsibilities would be greatly enlarged, beyond simply guaranteeing the conditions of the market order, or attempting to manipulate the economy indirectly from the centre to attain specified national objectives. The bulk of the economy would still be in private hands, but the state would be the dominant agent and no longer subordinate to the market order.

The role of the trade unions in this new regime was a major question. As organisations they grew up within market orders, but also challenged the attempt to enforce a separation between the political realm and the economic realm. A permanent incomes policy would remove many of their functions, while state direction of investment would establish a public and a national interest overriding all local and sectional demands. Trade unions would have to be fully incorporated into the national planning system, surrendering their privileges and powers as independent organisations in return for participation in the making and implementation of economic policy. Whether such a transition would be an easy one was another matter.

Accompanying the new policies on internal economic management and the new expanded role for the state would be a wide range of measures to extend and consolidate democracy. Many of the social privileges and antiquated institutions of Britain would disappear. The House of Lords would be abolished, the civil service remodelled to fit it for its new tasks in administering a much larger public sector, private schools and private health care would disappear, more open government as well as more open media would be introduced. They would be accompanied by egalitarian welfare measures that would extend the welfare state and force through a much greater redistribution of wealth than any so far achieved in Britain. At the same time ideas for workers' control in factories, subordinating management to new forms of industrial democracy, and popular administration of services like education, health and housing would be implemented.

6.7 The political problem

These were the policies which would be relied upon to win popular support while the economy was being reorganised and the foundations laid for a prosperous and expanding economy. The strategy was a response to the problem of British decline and the failings of its industry and the growing unemployment and social distress which were occurring. It was a strategy which had deep roots in Labour movement tradition and was seen as the best means both for securing the gains that the movement had won in the past and preparing the way for a transition to socialism.[47]

It inevitably attracted wide criticism. Opponents on the right saw it as a recipe for a siege economy, and a totalitarian state with a standard of living sinking to that of Eastern Europe. On the left criticisms came from two sides. There were those who thought it too bold, and those who thought it not nearly bold enough.[48] It was accepted that many of the proposed measures might prove indispensable for remedying the backwardness and inefficiencies of British capitalism. What was questioned was whether such

measures, even if they could be introduced, would streng-
then the position of the Left, or assist in the construction of
socialism. The belief that they would rested on the
assumption that the new social democratic consensus of the
1940s was achieved by a decisive change in the balance of
class forces, through the organisation of a broad popular
democratic alliance, which overcame resistance to the
imposition of new policies and new priorities. With this
consensus under attack and weakening, the time was
considered right for the construction of a new popular
democratic alliance, which could win national support by
demonstrating that the most pressing national problem,
economic decline, could only be overcome by adopting
policies that extended the role of the state, redistributed
wealth, made state and society more democratic, and broke
the dominant pattern of relationships with the world
economy that had evolved over 300 years.

Those who argued the strategy was too bold pointed to
the enormous dislocations its implementation would bring.
Import quotas would not only restrict choice but raise
prices; if they were effective, retaliation by other countries
could not be avoided. While trade was being reorganised
shortages of many commodities would be inevitable. The
external policies alone would therefore imperil popular
support for the government. Extrication from so complex a
trading network would necessarily be slow and painful. If
Britain could easily revert to self-sufficiency it might be
different, but as it could not, these critics doubted whether
the foundation of the alternative economic strategy was
sound: could Britain stand alone? Was Britain any longer
powerful enough to sustain an independent economic
policy against the political opposition of the leading
capitalist states? Some suggested that a surer strategy for
socialist advance was for Britain to remain within the EC,
combining with other socialist movements on an international basis, and accepting and endorsing the moves to greater
integration in the belief that this could create a new terrain
on which an international socialist movement could be built.

For such critics the alternative economic strategy was
flawed, chiefly because it treated the United Kingdom as

though it were an underdeveloped economy seeking a path of industrialisation. Once its role as one of the leading metropolitan centres of world capitalism was recognised, then it was difficult to avoid the conclusion that its links with the world economy could not be broken to create the basis for a policy of re-industrialisation without causing quite major short-term dislocations in trade, employment and living standards which would require the government to enjoy very broad-based popular support as well as considerable support from business if it were to cope with them successfully, for external disruption would be accompanied by internal disruption. The government would face herculean political tasks: securing the co-operation of the existing civil service to implement a programme that ended Britain's traditional external policy; securing the co-operation or acquiescence of the military establishment in policies that took Britain out of NATO and drastically cut defence spending; securing the quiescence of the judiciary in the face of new legislation that overrode provisions of the Common Law in many new areas; securing the co-operation of business in a programme which nationalised a large section of its assets and gave the state major new powers; securing the neutrality of the media.

To overcome the combined opposition of the bulk of the British ruling class to the implementation of the alternative economic strategy would require far more than an electoral victory under the unrepresentative and antiquated electoral rules of the British Parliament. It would need more than the abolition of the House of Lords and the passing of a Freedom of Information Act. It would require a crisis of far greater magnitude than any so far experienced in Britain, which would divide the ruling class on the measures that should be taken; and it would also require united trade-union and broad popular support.

Critics of the alternative economic strategy doubted whether the Labour movement was in any position to implement its programme as a solution to such a crisis. Bringing back prosperity, full employment and economic growth were all popular aims. What was in doubt was not the goals but the sacrifices and hardships that might well be needed in the attempt to realise them. Could such a government find sufficient support not just for the ends of its policies but for the means as well? The free economy strategy faced the same problem but in a less acute form. If the alternative economic strategy were attempted against united ruling-class opposition and with only slender support for socialist change, internal conflict and dislocation could become enormous. The hopes for increased investment and productivity would prove illusory and the government could be faced by investment strikes and tax strikes, which if not quickly averted would plunge it into a major fiscal crisis.

Many advocates of the alternative economic strategy were fully aware of all this. They never proposed it just as a technical policy ·for overcoming decline.[49] What they argued was that an attempt to implement such a strategy inevitably polarises class forces and itself creates the new bases of working-class and popular support that can carry the government through. The argument therefore turns on the class capacity and class consciousness of the British working class, and whether despite all its ideological and organisation rifts, despite its continuing high vote for the Conservative party, despite the ideological perspectives of so many of its leaders, it would nevertheless burst into new life and rally effectively to support a socialist government that was implementing the alternative economic strategy.

Critics of the strategy who thought it not bold enough did not disagree that the obstacles to the successful implementation of the strategy were formidable. But they argued that this pointed to the essential weakness of the strategy. It was a strategy for socialism that was to be implemented by the existing state. Instead of organising to overthrow this state and constructing a new state to oversee the construction of socialism, the alternative economic strategy would depend upon securing the goodwill or neutrality of the existing civil service, the existing military, the existing judiciary, the media and large sections of the capitalist class, as well as the neutrality of the major external capitalist powers.

These critics from the left argued that any attempt to implement socialist policies had to involve an immediate and direct challenge to the sources of class power in society and, in particular, the class character of the existing state.[50] A government attempting to implement the alternative economic strategy, which was not prepared to organise and base itself on a mass movement outside Parliament to mount such a challenge, would go one of two ways. Either it would follow the road of previous Labour governments with its leaders forced to submit to the prevailing realities of power, and therefore to policy orthodoxies not of their own choosing, or it would collapse or be toppled by the weight of resistance and sabotage from the capitalist class and the state machine, like Allende's Popular Unity government in Chile.[51]

The disagreements over the alternative economic strategy reflected differences about the nature of the crisis that faced world capitalism in the 1970s, and the significance of the changes which increasing state regulation and the advances made by labour movements had brought. There was no agreement on the Left about whether the recession and the slowdown in the rate of capital accumulation was a sign of a deep-seated crisis of profitability, or a less intractable deficiency of demand which had arisen from a number of contingent causes. Had the achievements of social democracy so altered the state as to permit a strategy of intervention that used the agencies of state power to create openings to the Left? Could a broad national coalition be assembled within the mass democracy that could sustain a government which implemented policies aimed at transforming the basic network of capitalist power and shifting the political balance in favour of the working class and towards socialism? Similarly, there was no agreement on the nature of the modern state. The alternative economic strategy was enmeshed in these debates. It was the first clear sign for a generation that serious strategic thinking about socialism had re-emerged on the British Left.

7

The end of decline?

Remember the conventional wisdom of the day. The British people were 'ungovernable'. We were in the grip of an incurable 'British disease'. Britain was heading for 'irreversible decline'.

Well, the people were *not* ungovernable, the disease was *not* incurable, the decline *has* been reversed.

Conservative Election Manifesto 1987

7.1 The Thatcherite project

The free economy strategy and the alternative economic strategy were responses to the deep political and economic crisis which gripped Britain in the 1970s. Their success in influencing policy was very different. The alternative economic strategy won much support in the Labour movement, but only a mild version of it was ever adopted as party policy. That was in 1983 when the party suffered its heaviest post-war electoral defeat.

The free economy strategy captured large sections of Conservative opinion after Margaret Thatcher became Leader in 1975. The Conservatives won the general elections in 1979, 1983, 1987 and 1992. Their success permitted an extended trial of their ideas for creating a free economy and breaking free of the chains of corporatism and social democracy. At the 1979 general election the Conservatives made decline one of their central themes. They refused to accept that decline was inevitable, and they pledged themselves to reverse it.

In 1980 and 1981 the economy plunged into a severe recession. Output and investment slumped and unemployment soared. Sterling moved up sharply as did interest rates, and inflation accelerated. When riots erupted in several cities during 1981 some feared that Britain was locked into a spiral of decline which was leading to a breakdown of public order. The slump threatened not just the future of the Conservative party but the stability of the state.

During 1981, however, the bottom of the recession was reached and also the nadir of the government's political fortunes. In 1982, even before the Falklands War, both the economy and the government's popularity began to improve. After receiving such a battering in the previous two years government ministers were quick to seize on every sign of recovery. The Prime Minister began claiming that there had been a dramatic improvement in productivity and that the economy had turned the corner.

In the 1981 budget the government had chosen to increase taxation and risk further deflation of demand although unemployment had reached three million and was still rising. Several cabinet ministers had come close to resigning over it. This budget quickly became an important landmark for the Thatcherite project. Supporters of the Treasury declared that this was the budget that had turned the tide, because it had convinced the financial markets that the government was serious about financial discipline, and had sent a signal to trade unions, employers and bankers that sound money was the government's top priority.[1]

As the economy continued to improve during 1983 the tone of government proclamations became steadily more triumphant. The theme of the Conservative manifesto at the 1983 general election was that national recovery had begun:

When we came to office in May 1979, our country was suffering both from an economic crisis and a crisis of morale. British industry was uncompetitive, over-taxed, over-regulated, and over-manned ... This country was drifting further behind its neighbours. Defeatism was in the air.[2]

But the manifesto remained cautious. There were still many obstacles that remained to be overcome:

> In the last four years, many British firms have made splendid progress in improving their competitiveness and profitability. But there is some way to go yet before this country has regained that self-renewing capacity for growth which once made her a great economic power, and will make her great again.[3]

The recovery at this stage was fairly modest. The main achievement was the substantial fall in the rate of inflation from over 20 per cent at its peak to single figures. Unemployment stopped climbing but it did not fall. Output had begun rising again but was far below its 1979 level, and although productivity had sharply increased, many observers attributed it to a once-for-all increase reflecting the huge shedding of labour in 1979–81.

By 1987, however, and its third election triumph the government could claim that the economic recovery had lasted six years and appeared to be gathering pace. Inflation had not been eliminated but it had been kept generally below 5 per cent. Unemployment had at last begun to fall, and manufacturing output was almost back to its 1979 level. Profits had risen sharply and productivity was increasing steadily. Falling interest rates and two tax-cutting budgets in 1986 and 1987 were used to promote a vigorous consumer boom and a rise in living standards just before the election. Rarely had a government managed to align the economic cycle with the election cycle to such good effect.

The Conservative manifesto at the 1987 general election was euphoric about the state of the economy. It boasted that 'the British economy has never been stronger or more productive.' A vast change it suggested separated the Britain of 1987 from the Britain of the late 1970s:

> Is it really only such a short time ago that inflation rose to an annual rate of 27 per cent? That the leader of the Transport and General Workers Union was widely seen as the most powerful man in the land? That a minority

Labour government, staggering from crisis to crisis on borrowed money, was nonetheless maintained in power by the Liberal party . . . ? And that Labour's much-vaunted pay pact with the unions collapsed in the industrial anarchy of the 'winter of discontent', in which the dead went unburied, rubbish piled up in the streets, and the country was gripped by a creeping paralysis which Labour was powerless to cure?

It seems in retrospect to be the history of another country.[4]

The manifesto went on to make specific claims about the British revival:

1. Britain was in the seventh successive year of economic growth and had moved from the bottom to the top of the league for output growth among major European economies, and from the bottom to the top of the productivity league among major world economies.
2. Inflation had reached its lowest level for twenty years, and unemployment had fallen in every month since July 1986.
3. The number of strikes had dropped to their lowest levels for fifty years.
4. Overseas assets had been built up to their highest level since the Second World War, worth over £100 billion, second only to those of Japan.
5. Living standards were higher than ever before in British history, a 21 per cent increase in real terms for the takehome pay of the average family with two children.
6. Profitability of industrial companies had risen to the highest level for over twenty years.

In addition the manifesto spoke of a new climate of enterprise in the country, born of the confidence that Britain was internationally competitive again.

Many of these claims were contested, but in 1987 many observers acknowledged that the weight of evidence was impressive. Something significant had happened to the British economy, and the Conservative claims could not be dismissed simply as political hype. British decline might just be a thing of the past. *Fortune* and *Newsweek* in the United States ran cover stories on the theme 'Britain is Back', reflecting the substantial confidence which the overseas business and financial communities now had in the British economy, and specifically in the policies and leaders of the Conservative government.

The bubble burst almost as quickly as it had formed. The rapid expansion of demand in 1987–8 fuelled by tax cuts, credit, and public spending reintroduced rising inflation in 1989–90. Thatcher entered office and left office with inflation rising. Thatcher's long rearguard action against membership of the Exchange Rate Mechanism (ERM) was partly to blame. Those states which were members of the ERM experienced no upsurge in inflation in 1989–90. Britain's inflation was entirely due to monetary mismanagement at home.

It precipitated a recession which lasted until 1993. Unemployment and bankruptcies began to climb sharply again which put pressure on public spending. By 1990 public spending as a proportion of gross domestic product had returned to the levels the Government had inherited. But the reduction of the fiscal base during the years of growth had left the Government with less flexibility, and led to a very rapid rise in public borrowing as the only means of bridging the gap between expenditure and revenue and preserving the image of the Conservative party as a low tax party. The Government was forced to raise taxes sharply after the 1992 election in order to reduce the borrowing which had risen to £50 billion.

Another aspect of the recession was the widening trade gap. With the declining value of North Sea Oil and the continuing appetite for the British economy for imported manufactures the balance of payments surplus was transformed into a large deficit. It represented a serious obstacle to any early reflation of the British economy, and indicated that Britain would suffer a long period of slow growth until the financial imbalances created by the Lawson boom had been corrected.

The recession at the end of the 1980s punctured the extravagant hopes of some monetarists that Britan's new financial framework would ensure economic growth that was proof against inflation and recession. The 1980s boom ended in a crisis of an all too familiar kind, and raised questions as to how much had really changed.

In a longer perspective how will the Thatcher decade of the 1980s come to be judged? Will it be seen as the moment, notwithstanding the recession, when a lasting recovery began and decline ceased to be a problem in British politics? Will it be recorded as another failed attempt to break out of the cycle of decline? Or will it perhaps be looked on as a period of transition in which the nature of the problem which decline represents was redefined? In the new period in the development of the world economy which has been inaugurated by the collapse of communism, the trends towards globalisation of production and finance, and regionalisation of economic regulation may make the debates of the rise and fall of nations that flourished during the national-protectionist era obsolete.

The Thatcher project for reversing British decline was a product of the national-protectionist era and drew significantly upon a rhetoric of national revival and national effort. The claims and counter-claims about Britain's economic performance during the Thatcher decade raise important issues for all theories of decline. If a trend apparently so well established as Britain's relative economic decline can be reversed by a combination of political determination and the adoption of a particular set of policies, then either the obstacles to modernisation were less substantial than previously supposed, or the general context had changed in such a way as to make the earlier obstacles less important. This second possibility will be discussed in the final section of this chapter. But first it is necessary to look more closely at Conservative policies and at what they did and did not achieve.

7.2 The market cure

After its two general election defeats in 1974 and a change of leadership the Conservative party became firmly identified with a version of the free economy strategy for reversing British decline. It was unclear however how far the Conservative government elected in 1979 would go in implementing it, particularly since the party leadership and the new Cabinet were deeply divided over aspects of the strategy.[5] Some party opponents of the strategy predicted that the monetarist experiment would last no more than six months.

The role of the Prime Minister in ensuring that market principles influenced the framework for policy formulation was crucial. Her personal commitment to the market approach was strong. Only supporters of the strategy were appointed to the key economic ministries, in particular the Treasury. Those who were opposed to the strategy or who grew sceptical were isolated and many of them were eventually dismissed. Those that survived learnt to become supporters of the new policies. Three consecutive general election victories gave the party leadership unchallenged legitimacy, and seemed to justify its claim that there was no alternative to its policies.

It would be very misleading to suppose, however, that the Thatcher government had an economic strategy which it proceeded to implement in detail as soon as it entered office. What actually occurred was very much more complex than this. Events and circumstances were often more important determinants of policies and decisions than the ideas and principles of the market strategy. Although the 1987 manifesto presented the evolution of policy as a smooth and coherent progression, the reality was very different. Like all governments there was considerable improvisation and opportunism.

Policy under the Thatcher government during the 1980s passed through three distinct phases: 1979–82, 1982–7, and 1987–90. The first was dominated by the second oil price rise and the world recession; the second by the sustained recovery in the world economy led by the United States; and the third by the stock market crash of October 1987 which was triggered by fears over the enormous trade and financial imbalances which were emerging in the world economy and signalled a new recession.

The British economy fared differently in each phase. In the first phase the British recession was earlier and deeper than in most other countries. By contrast the British recovery in the second phase was longer and more rapid (see Table 7.1). In the third phase the British economy at first continued to accelerate but the boom was unsustainable and once again

Table 7.1 Comparative economic performance of major OECD countries 1979–92

	USA	Japan	Germany	France	UK	OECD
Growth of real GDP (percentage changes)						
1979	2.5	5.5	4.1	3.2	2.8	3.6
1980	−0.5	3.6	1.1	1.6	−1.9	1.2
1981	1.8	3.6	0.2	1.2	−1.0	1.6
1982	−2.2	3.2	−0.9	2.5	1.5	0.0
1983	3.9	2.7	1.6	0.7	3.5	2.7
1984	6.2	4.3	2.8	1.3	2.3	4.4
1985	3.2	5.0	1.9	1.9	3.8	3.3
1986	2.9	2.6	2.2	2.5	4.1	2.8
1987	3.1	4.1	1.4	2.3	4.8	3.2
1988	3.9	6.2	3.7	4.5	4.4	4.4
1989	2.5	4.7	3.4	4.3	2.1	3.3
1990	0.8	4.8	5.1	2.5	0.5	2.4
1991	−1.2	4.0	3.7	0.7	−2.2	0.7
1992	2.1	1.3	2.0	1.3	−0.6	1.5
Standardised unemployment rates (percentage of total labour force)						
1979	5.8	2.1	3.2	5.9	5.0	5.1
1980	7.0	2.0	2.9	6.3	6.4	5.8
1981	7.5	2.2	4.2	7.4	9.8	6.6
1982	9.5	2.4	5.9	8.1	11.3	8.1
1983	9.5	2.6	7.7	8.3	12.4	8.5
1984	7.4	2.7	7.1	9.7	11.7	8.0
1985	7.1	2.6	7.1	10.2	11.2	7.8
1986	6.9	2.8	6.4	10.4	11.2	7.7
1987	6.1	2.8	6.2	10.5	10.3	7.3
1988	5.4	2.5	6.2	10.0	8.6	6.7
1989	5.2	2.3	5.6	9.4	7.2	6.2
1990	5.4	2.1	4.9	8.9	6.8	6.1
1991	6.6	2.1	4.4	9.4	8.7	6.8
1992	7.3	2.2	4.8	10.2	9.9	7.5
Current balances (percentage of GDP)						
1979	0.0	−0.9	−0.7	0.9	−0.2	−0.4
1980	0.1	−1.0	−1.7	−0.6	1.2	−0.9
1981	0.2	0.4	−0.5	−0.8	2.6	−0.3
1982	−0.4	0.6	0.8	−2.2	1.7	−0.4
1983	−1.3	1.8	0.8	−0.9	1.2	−0.3
1984	−2.6	2.8	1.6	−0.2	0.6	−0.7
1985	−3.0	3.7	2.7	−0.1	0.8	−0.7
1986	−3.5	4.3	4.5	0.3	0.0	−0.3
1987	−3.6	3.6	4.1	−0.6	−1.1	−0.5
1988	−2.6	2.7	4.2	−0.5	−3.4	−0.4
1989	−1.9	2.0	4.9	−0.6	−4.1	−0.5
1990	−1.6	1.2	3.2	−1.3	−3.1	−0.7
1991	−0.1	2.2	−1.2	−0.5	−1.1	−0.2
1992	−1.0	3.2	−1.3	0.2	−2.0	−0.2

Source: OECD, *Economic Outlook*, 53, June 1993.

Britain was the first major OECD economy to move into recession.

The government's claim to have produced if not an economic miracle at least a significant reversal in the trend of decline rested on its monetary cure for inflation and its supply-side policies for making the British economy more competitive and enterprising.

The monetary cure had a high profile during the first phase of policy. But it was less of a break in policy than supporters and critics have sometimes claimed. One of the great advantages enjoyed by the new government was that it could pursue its monetarist experiment in a political climate in which opinion had already shifted decisively towards monetarism as the necessary framework for controlling the impact of the recession.[6]

The Thatcher government did not need to abandon Keynesian demand management policies. That had already been done by Labour. It was the Labour government that had presided over a doubling of unemployment between 1975 and 1977 without resorting to prescribed Keynesian remedies. It was the Labour government that had introduced cash limits in 1975 to exert stricter control over public expenditure. It was the Labour government during the sterling crisis of 1976 that had accepted a formal commitment to observe monetary targets and pledged itself to contain and reduce the burden of public expenditure in order to reassure the international financial markets about the direction of government policy and ministers' intentions.

The main contribution made by the Thatcher government was to consolidate the new policy regime by the fierceness of its ideological commitment to it. Monetarism was justified not on pragmatic but on doctrinal grounds. Not even token endorsements of previous social democratic objectives such as full employment were given. The control of inflation was proclaimed from the outset as the central objective of the government's economic policy.

The one major innovation introduced by the government was the Medium Term Financial Strategy, announced in the 1980 budget, which set targets for the growth of money supply over a period of four years ahead, as well as indicating desired levels for public borrowing.[7] The government seems to have expected that a strict financial policy would gradually restore sound money and squeeze inflationary expectations out of the economy. The cost would be a small rise in unemployment, but this would only be transitional, and the economy would quickly bounce back, helped by major cuts in public spending and taxes to stimulate private initiative and investment. Falling inflation and slightly higher unemployment would promote faster growth, and growth prospects would be further enhanced by measures to remove obstacles to free markets. Public spending would be reduced and trade-union power curbed.

The actual course of events was spectacularly different. The government found itself presiding over the worst economic collapse since the Great Depression. The high interest rates which the monetarist strategy prescribed to reduce inflation assisted the rapid appreciation of sterling following the oil price rise. British companies suffered a sudden loss in competitiveness of 20 per cent.

The consequence was a major contraction of manufacturing industry. Company liquidations soared, reaching 12 000 in 1982, the highest ever. Unemployment doubled, rising to over three million. It did not begin to fall until 1986. The output of manufacturing industry fell by 14.5 per cent and investment in manufacturing by 36 per cent.

One of the most telling statistics, however, was the further rise in import penetration which the recession brought. In 1983 more manufactured goods were imported than were exported—the first time ever. A surplus on trade in manufactures of £5 billion in 1980 had become a deficit of £4 billion by 1985. In some major sectors like electrical engineering, textiles, and clothing there was a jump in import penetration of 25 per cent. By 1988 the deficit on manufactures was £14.4 billion.

Many service industries continued to expand and there was a sharp increase in the flow of capital abroad, assisted by the removal of all exchange controls in 1979. Between 1979 and 1983 £35.4 billion was exported, a net outflow of £18.8 billion. By the time of the stock market crash in 1987 Britain's overseas assets were worth more than £100 billion.

The scale of the recession meant that public spending on social security and industrial subsidies increased while revenues were reduced. The government managed selective cuts in taxes and in public spending programmes, but these were outweighed by the increases it was forced to make. By the end of the first phase the burden of both direct and indirect taxation was higher than under the previous Labour government, and public expenditure as a proportion of GDP had increased (see Table 7.2). Inflation having accelerated to over 20 per cent in 1980 fell back very quickly under the impact of the recession to less than 5 per cent in 1983. It was the government's one clear success, achieved at a very high cost.

Such a record would have sunk most governments and it almost wrecked that of Margaret Thatcher. But ideological convictions helped keep it afloat. Having broken from the spell of the post-war consensus the Thatcher government was able to turn even mass unemployment to its advantage. The slump was blamed partly on the world recession, for which the government disclaimed any responsibility, but also on the weaknesses, mistakes, and extravagances which had accumulated during thirty-five years of social democracy. The recession became proof of what the new Conservative leadership had been saying all along. The nation had been living on borrowed time and it needed a sharp shock to bring it to its senses.

The government made relatively little progress in this first phase towards some of its key objectives. It suffered many reverses and encountered major obstacles. But the ideological thrust of its programme and its strategic understanding of what needed to be done remained firm. During the second phase of the government, 1982–7, the nature of the strategy became much clearer.

At its centre was Britain's relationship to the world economy. The government insisted that there could be no salvation outside the world market; only those goods and services which were internationally competitive should be produced. Although for short-term tactical reasons the government continued to subsidise many sectors of British manufacturing industry in addition to traditionally protected

Table 7.2 Changes in government spending and taxation in major OECD countries 1979–92

	USA	Japan	Germany	France	UK	OECD
Government receipts (percentage of nominal GDP)						
1979	30.3	26.3	44.6	44.1	37.7	33.7
1980	30.5	27.6	45.0	46.1	39.5	34.6
1981	31.1	29.0	45.0	46.7	41.5	35.5
1982	30.5	29.4	45.7	47.6	42.1	35.7
1983	29.9	29.6	45.3	48.2	41.4	35.7
1984	29.7	30.2	45.5	49.2	41.2	35.8
1985	30.1	30.8	45.8	49.3	41.2	36.3
1986	30.2	31.0	45.0	48.6	40.1	36.3
1987	31.0	32.6	44.8	49.0	39.4	36.9
1988	30.5	33.1	44.1	48.3	39.0	36.7
1989	30.9	33.4	44.9	47.8	38.5	37.0
1990	30.9	34.6	43.2	48.3	38.6	37.3
1991	30.8	34.4	45.6	48.5	37.9	37.5
1992	30.7	34.0	46.6	48.1	37.4	37.5
Government outlays (percentage of nominal GDP)						
1979	29.9	31.1	47.2	45.0	40.9	36.0
1980	31.8	32.0	47.9	46.1	42.9	37.3
1981	32.1	32.8	48.7	48.6	44.2	38.5
1982	33.9	33.0	49.0	50.3	44.5	39.8
1983	33.9	33.3	47.8	51.4	44.7	40.0
1984	32.6	32.3	47.4	51.9	45.2	39.3
1985	33.2	31.6	47.0	52.1	44.0	39.5
1986	33.7	32.0	46.4	51.3	42.5	39.5
1987	33.4	32.2	46.7	50.9	40.7	39.2
1988	32.5	31.6	46.3	50.0	38.0	38.4
1989	32.4	30.9	44.8	49.1	37.6	38.0
1990	33.3	31.7	45.2	49.8	39.9	39.0
1991	34.2	31.4	48.7	50.6	40.8	40.0
1992	35.4	32.2	49.4	52.0	44.1	41.2
Government financial balances (percentage of nominal GDP)						
1979	+0.4	−4.7	−2.6	−0.8	−3.2	−2.3
1980	−1.3	−4.4	−2.9	0.0	−3.4	−2.7
1981	−1.0	−3.8	−3.7	−1.9	−2.6	−3.0
1982	−3.4	−3.6	−3.3	−2.8	−2.5	−4.1
1983	−4.1	−3.6	−2.6	−3.2	−3.3	−4.4
1984	−2.9	−2.1	−1.9	−2.8	−3.9	−3.5
1985	−3.1	−0.8	−1.2	−2.9	−2.9	−3.3
1986	−3.4	−0.9	−1.3	−2.7	−2.4	−3.2
1987	−2.5	+0.5	−1.9	−1.9	−1.3	−2.3
1988	−2.0	+1.5	−2.2	−1.7	+1.0	−1.7
1989	−1.5	−2.5	+0.1	−1.3	+0.9	−1.0
1990	−2.5	+2.9	−2.0	−1.5	−1.3	−1.8
1991	−3.4	+3.0	−3.2	−2.1	−2.9	−2.6
1992	−4.7	+1.8	−2.8	−3.9	−6.7	−3.7

Source: OECD, *Economic Outlook*, 53, June 1993.

areas such as agriculture and defence, it went further than any previous post-war government in accepting the logic of Britain's position in the international division of labour, even when this involved a substantial contraction of the manufacturing base of the economy.

The government disclaimed responsibility for preserving prosperity and employment throughout the national economy. It pinned its hopes for future prosperity on the continuing success of those sectors of the British economy already internationally competitive, on the development of new small businesses, and on the growth of internationally traded services.

The role of the financial policy within this wider economic strategy was crucial. It was seen as the best help that could be given by government to reconstruct the economy and assist recovery. High levels of unemployment and bankruptcies were justified as necessary to purge economy of wrong attitudes and misallocated resources, and to lay the foundations for profitable investment and production. Unemployment was desirable also for shifting the balance between labour and capital, and introducing a new realism to industrial relations. Managements would have the opportunity and the need to reduce their workforce and to increase efficiency.

Financial discipline was only the first stage, however, in the market strategy for national recovery. It had to be reinforced by a major cut in public spending and taxation, made possible by a significant contraction in public activities. The aim was not just to facilitate tax cuts but to remove as much economic decision-making as possible from the political process.

The severity of the slump meant, however, that the government was obliged to increase both spending and taxes. Financial stabilisation required social stabilisation. Spending on the police and armed forces increased, the employment programmes of the Manpower Services Commission were greatly enlarged, and the budgets for social security, unemployment pay, and industry were allowed to expand.

Some of the government's strongest supporters were dismayed at the slow pace of change, particularly in the field of welfare expenditure. Many of the government's measures, such as council house sales, higher prescription charges, and higher fees for overseas students, while welcome to the market lobby, were marginal to the main spending programmes. Hopes during the first two phases of the Thatcher government that ministers might introduce private health insurance or educational vouchers were dashed.

Many market lobbyists advised much more drastic action to cope with unprofitable nationalised industries and the trade unions. Propping up loss-makers in steel, coal, cars and shipbuilding only converted their managements into civil servants administering subsidies, increased public spending, and hindered reconstruction through market forces.

There was some disappointment too about changes in trade-union law. In June 1980 Hayek warned that the unions should be quickly confronted and stripped of their power, if the market strategy was to have any prospect of success.[8] If the confrontation was prolonged the ability of the unions to resist market forces might entail a level of unemployment and a degree of stagnation in the economy that could make the government so unpopular as to endanger the changes of a Conservative victory at the next election. To break the union veto he proposed the holding of a national referendum to seek approval for the immediate abolition of all legal privileges granted to the trade unions since 1906. Trade unions could once again become liable for damages suffered by an employer from strike action.

The government had wider political objectives in view, however, and preferred to move cautiously, taking on opponents one at a time, seizing opportunities as they presented themselves.[9] Trade-union law was reformed in stages in three bills, in 1980, 1982 and 1984, and major confrontation with the whole trade-union movement was avoided. The government gave full support to employers in a succession of major disputes, in steel, printing, and mining. The defeats suffered by unions that fought against the restructuring being imposed on their industries, coupled with the effects of the new legislation and high unemployment, helped transform the climate of industrial relations and the perception of union power.

The other key aspects of the supply-side policies as they

unfolded during the second and third phases were privatisation, cuts in direct taxation, and training policy. Having discovered that privatisation was feasible, and contributed useful sums to the Exchequer, privatisation became the flagship of the Thatcher government's supply-side revolution.[10] Privatisation, however, was more successful in the denationalisation of state-owned industries than it was in moving many public services into the private sector. Nevertheless by the end of the decade the 'new public management' had become firmly established, and was reshaping the character of all public sector institution, with the introduction of devices such as internal markets, tendering, and contracting out. The Next Steps Report proposed splitting the civil service into policy-making agencies at the centre and delivery agencies which would be responsible for implementing the policies, and which could in principle be privatised.[11]

Another revolution which gathered pace during the 1980s were the new training programmes, associated with the Manpower Service Commission, which survived the massacre of the quangos at the beginning of the decade, mainly because of the pressing practical need to respond to rapidly rising unemployment. Training provision was gradually shifted from a tripartite regime which involved unions, government, and employers to a new neo-liberal regime from which trade unions were virtually excluded. The Manpower Services Commission had been abolished by the end of the decade and the supervision of training programmes transferred to the new Training and Enterprise Councils (TECs) which were dominated by local employers, and aimed primarily at rectifying short-term skills shortages.[12]

Many of the supply-side changes did not change the size of the state, but they did restructure it in important ways. The symbolism of the shift in the boundaries of the public and private sectors was important politically. This was true also of the assault on the principle of progressive taxation. Overall the tax burden had not been significantly altered after ten years of Conservative government. But for those on high incomes the changes had been substantial, and were justified as part of the process of creating an enterprise and incentive economy.

The scope for tax cuts came partly from the proceeds of privatisation sales and oil revenues, but mainly from the sustained growth during the second policy phase (1982–7) and the government's ability if not to reduce public spending, at least to contain its growth. The determination to resist pressure from special interest lobbies for sharply increased spending strengthened rather than weakened during the government's term of office.

The strategists of the government believed that if the recovery could be sustained and the public sector contained, there would be a relatively painless expansion of private sector activity and provision financed through tax cuts and rising incomes. The political problem was how to win the political argument for keeping public expenditure constrained in key areas such as health and education and pensions, and how to regain control over those areas of public expenditure in the hands of autonomous public bodies or locally elected councils outside direct central control. The realisation that more needed to be done here if the momentum of the move away from the state was to be maintained prompted the announcement of the new radical programme on which the Conservatives fought and won the election in 1987.

The government calculated that keeping inflation low, containing public spending and funding direct tax cuts would help it retain the electoral support that was necessary for the longer-term supply-side changes to be implemented and to take effect. Institutional reforms designed to remove as many obstacles to free markets as possible and to weaken political opposition to Conservatism still depended on the growth of the second phase being sustained.

7.3 The debate on recovery

The success or failure of the Thatcher economic experiment has been fiercely debated. Like many of the debates on British decline the conclusions that are reached often depend on the starting point. Decline has always been a contested concept, and recovery is equally so.

The government's case that the economic recovery is real

and lasting has received considerable support from economists. The tone of the OECD reports on the British economy became steadily more favourable through the 1980s. Until 1989 the British government was perceived by the international community as having pursued a consistent and increasingly successful set of policies which were permitting the British economy to make up lost ground.

In its 1987 report the OECD declared that recent developments compared favourably with the long-term performance of the UK. The performance was less impressive when economic performance was measured from the previous cyclical peak in 1979 (see Table 7.3). But even when account was taken of the slump between 1979 and 1981 GDP growth now appeared in line with the average of the European Community countries rather than lagging behind it. The output losses in the initial years of the medium-term financial strategy were subsequently made up. Following that period, the OECD concluded, the strategy was implemented more flexibly, but the basic framework remained intact.

The 1988 report was even more positive, despite the stock market crash and gathering economic problems. The UK performance was still judged to compare favourably with other OECD states, especially the growth of output. The report concluded:

> Notwithstanding the risks attached to the short-term outlook it is already now clear that the 1980s will stand out as a decade of impressive improvement in economic performance, reversing a long-term trend of decline relative to other countries.[13]

It singled out what it called a new flexibility in the labour market and the new trends in productivity. It argued that the evidence that was now accumulating suggested that there was a change in trend rather than simply a transitory cyclical development as many observers had initially suggested. Productivity was rising because of changes in work organisation rather than because of capital investment. The scope for further increases was present as British companies caught up with the performance of their international rivals. Only

Japan, the OECD noted, had recorded higher productivity growth rates than the UK in the 1980s.

The OECD report then asked whether the improved performance meant that the British disease had been overcome, as the government had claimed. On the positive side it noted that the old stop–go cycle which had plagued British post-war economic management appeared to have been overcome; productivity growth had accelerated markedly; there had been a substantial reduction in government intervention in the economy, with markets being given much greater freedom to determine resource allocation; Britain had enjoyed the benefits of North Sea oil, and the British economy had become further integrated into the world economy.

But the OECD also cautioned that too much should not be read into the recovery since 1981: 'as the improved performance has coincided with a cyclical recovery there is uncertainty as to the extent to which these changes are permanent'.[14]

The improvement in productivity performance was the key, although the OECD estimated that in 1986 output per employed person in the UK still fell short of productivity levels in the USA by one-third and in the European Community by one-quarter. But the OECD believed that the government's supply-side policies were gradually transforming Britain's economic performance.

These supply-side policies included the abolition of exchange controls; the reorientation of the objectives of the nationalised industries; legislation on trade unions; reduction in personal tax rates; deregulation; privatisation; and reforms in education, housing, and regional and urban policies. The effect of this supply-side strategy, the OECD report argued, had forced the private sector to take more responsibility for adjusting to the changing economic environment. Both management and unions had had to reassess their attitudes.

This positive judgement of the achievements of the Conservative government in the 1980s has been echoed and amplified by others. Supporters of the market cure argue that in order to assess properly the record of the Thatcher government it should be compared with that of the 1974–9 Labour government. One common view is that the policies pursued after 1979 represented a return to economic reality.[15]

The era of corporatism and government intervention had steadily moved large sectors of the economy away from profitability and responsibility towards subsidy and dependence. Britain was becoming ungovernable because of a weak state and an assertive trade-union movement.

The economic recovery of the 1980s therefore is a recovery of the basic rules and attitudes necessary for success and efficiency in a market order. It is a political triumph before anything else. As Nigel Lawson put it:

> the British experiment . . . consists of seeking, within an explicit medium-term context, to provide increasing freedom for markets to work within a framework of firm monetary and fiscal discipline . . . the true British experiment is a political experiment. It is the demonstration that trade union power *can* be curbed within a free society, and that inflation *can* be eradicated within a democracy.[16]

There remains a difficulty, however, as to how this political triumph, if such it is, is to be explained. The New Right analysis of the political process is noted for its pessimism. Democracy encourages the political parties to outbid one another in their campaign promises, which encourages the electorate to have excessive expectations about the capacity of governments to deliver the costless benefits. Democratic institutions also encourage the proliferation of organised interests, all pressing their own special interest on government in the guise of the public interest. All groups seek to gain the maximum benefits from the political process by loading the costs onto other less well organised and protected groups. In Mancur Olson's account the longer established a democratic political system the more tenacious and wide-ranging will be its special interests, and the greater the political interference in the workings of free markets.[17]

If the causes of decline are structural in the way Olson suggests they cannot be overcome by changes in the culture of a country or in the political will of its leaders. The logic of collective action will always reassert itself. Organised distributional coalitions will always be more effective in the political process than the unorganised majority. The political process will always lack the kind of constraints which in economic markets are provided by prices and competition. Some market enthusiasts therefore dream of abolishing politics altogether. But only through a political process can a market order be established and maintained.

If the iron laws of political economy do not bend before the good intentions of politicians and the soundness of their ideological credentials, it follows that the Conservative government's claims to have launched a genuine recovery depend on its having discovered some way of breaking the grip of the special interests which paralysed government before.

One solution is to argue that the institutional sclerosis created by a long-established democracy can be broken by an external shock, typically war or invasion. Such a shock allows a political system to be reorganised, and its distributional coalitions dispersed. Geoffrey Maynard, among others, claims that the Thatcher government benefited from just such an external shock – the shock created by the slump of 1979–81, which temporarily destroyed the power of the special interests, and allowed the Thatcher government to reassert the rules and institutions of the free, competitive market economy as the overriding public interest.[18]

On this view the economic recovery of the 1980s was a real recovery and made possible by the sharp break with the previous social democratic era which the 1979–81 slump permitted. The most obvious casualty among the special interests was the trade-union movement. It was systematically excluded from national policy-making, it suffered a considerable drop in membership and a decline in its bargaining position as a result of the slump, and a general deterioration in its political influence due to the decline of the Labour party and the contraction of the public sector.

The main grounds therefore for believing that the improved economic performance of the 1980s signals a lasting economic recovery are firstly the improvement in productivity, and secondly the decline in the bargaining strength and political influence of the Labour movement.

Those who question the extent of the recovery argue that the improvement between 1981 and 1987 must be placed in the context of Britain's past economic performance and of its continuing structural problems. As the OECD pointed out, the UK economic performance is only markedly better than other economies when the period 1979–81 is excluded from the figures. When entire economic cycles are compared, the figures show that in the 1979–87 cycle Britain performed as well as the average. This was an improvement on previous cycles when it had performed less well than the average. It is also true however that UK performance, although better relatively, fell short of its performance in the 1950s and 1960s (see Table 7.3).

The least that can be said of Britain's economic performance in the 1980s is that the decline was halted. But only the next cycle will show whether this better performance has become permanent. As reflected in the OECD statistics Britain would need to maintain the above-average growth rates it achieved in 1986–8 for a considerable period to make further inroads into unemployment and to catch up the performance of its main rivals.

Critics of the government's policies argued that the structural foundations of the recovery remained very weak. Particular concern was expressed about the position of manufacturing industry which suffered such severe contraction in 1979–81 and did not regain its 1973 level until 1989.

This concern was forcibly expressed in the report from the House of Lords Select Committee on Overseas Trade, published in 1985. The Select Committee was set up to

Table 7.3 Productivity in major OECD countries

	Total factor productivity			Labour productivity		
	1960–73	1973–79	1979–91	1960–73	1973–79	1979–91
USA	1.6	−0.4	0.2	2.2	0.0	0.7
Japan	5.8	1.3	1.9	8.6	2.9	3.0
Germany	2.7	1.8	0.8	4.5	3.0	1.4
France	4.0	1.7	1.4	5.4	3.0	2.3
UK	2.3	0.6	1.3	3.6	1.6	1.9
OECD	3.1	0.6	0.9	4.5	1.6	1.6

Source: OECD, *Economic Outlook*, 53, June 1993.

consider the causes and implications of the deficit in the United Kingdom's balance of trade in manufactures.

The Committee noted that between 1963 and 1983 the UK had run a surplus of between £1.5 billion and £6 billion every year on manufactures. In 1984 the surplus had become a deficit of £4 billion. They attributed this change to the fall in manufacturing output of 14.5 per cent in 1980 and 1981. As a percentage of GDP manufacturing output decline in the UK fell from 28 per cent in 1972 to 21 per cent in 1983. Among similar economies only the UK suffered a sustained absolute fall in manufacturing in this period. Yet manufacturing remained very important to the UK economy because although it represented only one-fifth of all activity in the UK it provided 40 per cent of overseas earnings.

Britain had only been able to survive the contraction of manufacturing because of the contribution made by North Sea oil. Some economists argued that the contraction in manufacturing was made necessary by the existence of oil.[19] But no one disputed that in the long term Britain needed to retain and extend its manufacturing base. What concerned the House of Lords was that the contraction of manufacturing might make this much more difficult in future. Britain's share of exports of world manufactures which had stopped falling in the 1970s resumed its downward drift in the 1980s. In most major sectors import penetration was becoming more marked, and in some sectors previous trade surpluses were being turned into deficits.

The arguments presented by the Treasury to the Committee were summarised in its report. The Treasury took view that Britain was suffering a long-term decline in manufacturing both as a share of GDP and in the balance of trade in manufactures. In addition the impact of North Sea oil on the balance of payments made a further deterioration in the balance of trade in manufactured goods necessary. Otherwise Britain would have run very large current account surpluses. It was right that manufacturing rather than any other sector should contract to make way for oil because the comparative advantage of the UK in most sectors of manufacturing was weak.

The Treasury agreed that the recovery since 1981 had

produced an upturn in imports and a further deterioriation in the trade balance, but argued that the trade deficit in manufactures was not as important a measure of economic performance as output. Moreover, once the contribution of oil to the balance of payments began to decline there would be 'compensating adjustments'. Income from overseas assets built up during the oil years would increase and manufacturing would recover. New industries and new businesses would emerge. The task for government was not to plan in detail the future shape of the British economy, but to pursue macro-economic policies which favoured competitiveness and growth in all sectors, and did not attempt to give priority to any one.

The evenhandedness of the Treasury was entirely rejected by the House of Lords Select Committee. They argued that a sustainable growth in GDP was not possible without a favourable trade balance in manufactures. Many services were not tradable and could not fill the gap left by manufacturing. Many service industries were also highly dependent on manufacturing. Twenty per cent of all service industry output had manufacturing industry as its main customer.

The Committee rejected the idea that there was anything inevitable or automatic about the decline of manufacturing as a result of the windfall of North Sea oil. It was a deliberate policy choice to use the oil wealth to increase overseas investments, maintain a high pound, and run down manufacturing. The Committee believed this policy to be a mistake. There was no guarantee that there could be a spontaneous rebirth of manufacturing at some point in the future. The costs of re-entry might be prohibitive once overseas markets were lost and an integrated manufacturing base was destroyed. There was no guarantee either that Britain could suddenly become competitive in new industries. The Committee pointed to the example of the information technology sector which was expected to be in substantial deficit by 1990.

The Committee's conclusion was stark and pessimistic about the future:

> The Committee's view is that the continuing deficit in the balance of trade in manufactures is a symptom of the

decline in Britain's manufacturing capacity on the one hand and of the poor competitiveness of important areas of manufacturing on the other. Unless the climate is changed so that the manufacturing base is enlarged and steps are taken to ensure that import penetration is combatted and that manufactured exports are stimulated, as the oil revenues diminish the country will experience adverse effects which will worsen with time. These will include

i.   a contraction of manufacturing to the point where the successful continuation of much of manufacturing activity is put at risk

ii. an irreplaceable loss of GDP

iii. an adverse balance of payments of such proportions that severely deflationary measures will be needed

iv. lower tax revenue for public spending on welfare, defence and other areas

v.   higher unemployment with little prospect of reducing it

vi. the economy stagnating and inflation rising driven up by a falling exchange rate.[20]

Given this grim litany it hardly came as a surprise that the Committee should warn that if these dangers were not recognised and tackled there could be 'a devastating effect on the future economic and political stability of the nation'.

The government refused to recognise that there were such dangers. The fears of the Committee it thought were entirely illusory.

Many economists, however, broadly shared the Committee's view. Most Keynesians had believed the British economy would not recover spontaneously from the slump of 1979–81. The sustained economic recovery after 1982 caught many by surprise and appeared to vindicate the monetarist claim that sustainable non-inflationary growth was possible if monetarist prescriptions were followed. With the difficulties which the boom ran into after 1987, however, the Keynesian critics came back into their own.

In the 1970s Wynne Godley and the Cambridge Economic Policy Group had argued that Britain's economic problem was a structural one and could only be cured by structural means.[21] The heart of the problem was an economy whose industrial base was so weak that whenever demand expanded beyond a certain point it could not be satisfied by domestic production and led to a sharply increased deficit. Governments had repeatedly dealt with this problem by financial means, deflating the economy to reduce demand, which also had the effect of weakening business confidence and reducing investment.

From this perspective the recovery of the 1980s appears a re-run on a larger scale of the policy cycle and mistakes of the 1960s. An expansion driven by consumer demand and fuelled by a massive credit expansion and substantial tax cuts produced faster rates of growth than were achieved even during the Barber boom of 1972–3, but resulted in a record balance of payments deficit of £15 billion in 1988, coupled with the re-emergence of inflationary pressures and a resurgence of labour unrest. The basic cause of the problem according to the Cambridge analysis was that the British economy was simply not productive enough. It could not generate sufficient exports to ensure continuous economic growth, full employment of resources, and a broad balance in its trade. Every economic expansion was brought to a halt by a deterioration in the trade balance.

The supply-side policies of the Conservatives did little to remedy this problem. By encouraging indifference to the fate of manufacturing they helped to make the problem more acute. The level of investment in manufacturing in the 1980s was below even the level achieved in the 1970s. The problem was hidden for a while when the economy was growing smoothly, but it reappeared larger than even at the end of the 1980s.[22] The Thatcher government had presided over a doubling of imports while exports had risen by only 50 per cent.

This analysis has been given its most precise formulation by two other Cambridge economists, Bob Rowthorn and John Wells.[23] They analyse three scenarios for a return to full employment by the year 2025; a green scenario, and a supergrowth scenario.

In the green scenario, GDP is only 26 per cent higher in 2025 than in 1985. Productivity growth of 1.4. per cent per annum has been used almost entirely to reduce hours worked rather than to boost output and consumption.

In the growth scenario, the economy expands at the rate achieved by the UK economy between 1950 and 1973. With productivity increasing at 2 per cent per annum, GDP would be 178 per cent above the 1985 level.

In the supergrowth scenario, the economy grows at 4 per cent a year. By 2025 GDP is 450 per cent above its 1985 level and productivity is 350 per cent higher.

Each of these scenarios has different consequences for the balance of payments. The green scenario has only modest consequences for the balance of payments, but is the least likely to be realised because of its radical implications for the way the economy is organised. In the growth and supergrowth scenarios imports would increase rapidly and could only be financed if there were a large increase in exports of manufactures. For the growth scenario the UK would need a surplus in its trade on manufactures of £3 billion per annum by 2005 and £8 billion per annum by 2025. For the supergrowth scenario the surplus required would be £6 billion and £13 billion per annum.

The inescapable conclusion which Rowthorn and Wells draw from their analysis is that Britain needs a large and growing surplus in its trade on manufactures if it is to sustain an expanding economy at full employment. They note that the most likely scenario, the growth scenario, is not predicting an economic miracle; it merely reproduces the UK performance of the 1960s. But even this fairly modest ambition is seen to require a very large improvement in the present ability of the manufacturing sector to earn a surplus on its trade.

From this perspective the 1980s recovery appears to have very shallow roots, because it is unsustainable. It has been associated with a sharp deterioration in the manufacturing trade balance, not an improvement. The scrapping of so much manufacturing capacity during the 1980s may have created a more efficient manufacturing sector, but one that is perilously small for the role it needs to perform for the UK economy.

To remedy this situation would require a major programme of investment to increase industrial capacity, diverting scarce resources from other potential uses, notably consumption and social investment. Such austerity policies would be politically unpalatable, since they would involve not just a short sharp shock but a prolonged period of reconstruction. The Thatcher government may have weakened the trade unions and other producer interests for a time. But it did little to challenge the tax privileges and consumption expections of major consumer interests. It protected their privileges and fuelled their expectations, and was richly rewarded electorally. Despite its rhetoric it did not face the majority of the population with hard choices, still less with hard times. Those who bore the brunt of the policies and suffered poverty and unemployment were a minority, and could safely be ignored.

Scepticism about the claims made for the economic recovery is often rooted in a view of how the economy works which places much less faith in the spontaneous powers of the market to regenerate the British economy. The poor performance of the British economy is seen as an institutional failure, the failure to develop the kind of 'regulative intelligence' for the economy which other countries have achieved through the forging of close relationships between the state, finance, industry and labour.[24] The nature of those relationships in Britain have prevented the emergence of a viable corporatism and have led consistently to the subordination of an independent manufacturing interest to the dominant financial interest of the City and British transnational companies.

From this standpoint the Thatcher decade of the 1980s represented no revolution, and only a partial break with what went before. It was, rather, one further triumph for the financial and commercial strategy to which the British state has always been wedded. What the Thatcher years achieved was the dismantling of many of the collectivist institutions of the Fordist era in Britain. But nothing was put in their place.

The economic recovery in the 1980s did very little to remedy the deficiencies in investment, in training, and in research that had long hindered the performance of the manufacturing sector in Britain. As a result many economists concluded that there was only likely to be a marginal improvement in Britain's relative economic performance as a result of the supply-side reforms of the 1980s. This judgement was confirmed by the sudden deterioration of the trade

Table 7.4 Inflation: consumer prices percentage changes at average annual rate

| | Average | | 1990 | 1991 | 1992 |
	1971–80	1980–9			
United States	8.2	4.6	5.4	4.2	3.0
Japan	9.3	1.9	3.1	3.3	1.7
Germany	5.1	2.6	2.7	3.5	4.0
France	10.1	6.6	3.4	3.2	2.4
UK	14.2	6.2	9.5	5.9	3.7
OECD	9.8	5.7	5.8	5.2	4.0

Source: OECD, *Economic Outlook*, 53, June 1993.

balance in 1988 and 1989, the rise of inflation (see Table 7.4) and the renewed plunge into recession in 1990. The oil wealth had been spent, but there were few signs of a lasting improvement in the competitiveness of Britain's leading economic sectors.[25]

7.4 The criteria for success

The record of the Thatcher government in the 1980s can also be analysed in terms of the three strategic political economy perspectives on decline outlined in Chapter 1. How far have the policies of the Thatcher government succeeded in tackling the problems identified in the four theses of decline?

As might be expected the Conservative record appears best when evaluated in the light of the market perspective. The government moved some way to increasing the openness of the British economy through its abolition of exchange controls, its hostility to many forms of industrial protectionism and subsidy, and the encouragement it gave to inward investment by transnational companies. Its economic strategy was directed to providing the most favourable environment possible in terms of labour costs, local taxes, and state aid in order to make Britain a more attractive site for transnational investment than comparable economies in the European Community.

The exposure of the British economy to greater international competition was one of the most important successes of government policy in the 1980s. Substantial protection continued initially for sectors such as defence, agriculture and even coal. But by the end of the decade even these sectors were being market tested. The doubts some ministers retained about the wisdom of allowing all production decisions to be decided by comparative advantage had largely disappeared. The Major Government continued and extended the principle, most notably in the rapid rundown of the coal industry announced in 1992, the defence cuts, and the government's support for the reduction of agricultural subsidies in the 1993 GATT agreement.

Internally the supply-side policies made market disciplines more important throughout the economy by dismantling corporatist structures, weakening trade unions, and containing public spending. Industrial conflict declined and the quality of management improved. The government made efforts to promote an enterprise culture through a mixture of exhortation, tax cuts and institutional reform.

From the market standpoint many of the changes were limited and tentative. They did not launch any great cultural revolution. The gains were piecemeal and cumulative. Some saw this as a virtue and as part of the process whereby the whole framework within which people made choices and formed attitudes would be transformed. Others worried that too little would be achieved before a swing of the political pendulum brought a return to collectivist policies.

Least change of all was registered in the organisation of the political system itself. The government displaced some distributional coalitions but it reinforced others. It showed no interest in constitutional reform to impose permanent limits on government. It made full use of the powers of the British state to push through many measures which lacked popular support. It turned out to be a government which rolled the state back in some areas and rolled it forward in others. It deomonstrated how few obstacles the old constitutional state in Britain placed in the way of a government determined to exercise its powers to the full and push through controversial legislation.

So long as these powers were in the hands of those who

sought to extend the role of markets they might seem tolerable, but there was no guarantee either that the Conservatives could continue to win elections indefinitely, or that the free market wing would continue to dominate the party as it had done under Margaret Thatcher's leadership.

From the state and class perspectives on British decline the assessment of the Thatcher record is much less favourable. It appears far more as continuity with the past than a radical break with it, liquidating some of the manifestations of Britain's backwardness but either failing to tackle many of the structural reasons for Britain's decline, or in some cases reinforcing them.

On each of the four theses on decline the Thatcher record is found to have major deficiencies as a strategy for modernisation. Far from using the opportunity of the 1980s and the opportunities for European co-operation as a means for finally ridding Britain of the imperial legacy of its world role, the Thatcher government chose to reaffirm that the Atlantic relationship with the United States remained the lynchpin of Britain's foreign policy. By the end of the 1980s there were still many areas where Britain appeared to be clinging to aspects of its former world role and was reluctant to accept the reality of its position in the post-imperial world order. The troubled relationship with the European Community was the clearest example, but so too was the continuing level of British defence spending, and the resulting bias of spending on research and development towards military projects.

In a powerful polemic against what he calls the 'declinist' literature[26] David Edgerton has argued that Britain always was a developmental state, and always did attach a high importance to technological and industrial development, only that its energies and priorities were aimed primarily at building a strong military-industrial complex to service the needs of Britain's imperial state and its world role. His view is an important corrective to that of Corelli Barnett, whose gloom about Britain's industrial performance is so unrelieved that it is sometimes difficult to understand how Britain managed to fight two world wars at all, still less to emerge on the winning side. But Edgerton exaggerates his own case. The key point in understanding British decline as a historical process is that the decline in competitiveness and the decline in world power were interlinked. It was precisely because the British state spent so much of its energies on defence industries like military aircraft that the needs of domestic industrial reconstruction were given a lower priority. It never was the case that all British industry was equally backward. Some sectors including the defence industries have always been world leaders. The argument about decline from the developmental state perspective was about the balance of the economy. The Thatcher Government did little to change that balance, and in important respects because of its renewed commitment to what remained of the world role of the imperial state it reinforced it.

No less serious from a state perspective was the failure of the Conservative government to tackle the supply-side problems that had prevented effective modernisation of the economy in the past.[27] The liberal ethos of British institutions which had so hindered the emergence of a developmental state was not shattered but further strengthened. The government turned away from the experiments with greater co-operation between the key institutional sectors of the economy. It gave no attention to forging new links between the financial sector and manufacturing. It abandoned attempts to build consensus around an industrial strategy and its industrial relations reforms were confined to a one-sided attempt to weaken the trade unions through new union laws. It did little to tackle the long-term structural problem of industrial relations in Britain – the low level of co-operation between management and shopfloor.

The cultural revolution which the government promoted was also limited. It proved more hostile to established British institutions than previous Conservative governments, but from a state perspective on Britain's decline what was require above all was a determined assault to raise the importance of manufacturing the production relative to finance and consumption.

In political matters the government was at its most conservative. It centralised power still further, withdrawing powers and legitimacy from local government and other public agencies to which power had been devolved. It resisted calls for constitutional reform except for a limited increase in the powers of parliamentary Select Committees. Political modernisation was thwarted.

From the class perspective also the apparent radicalism and the novelty of the Thatcher government's policies masked deeper continuities. The government remained tied to the logic of Britain's traditional foreign economic policy. The City's role was unquestioned; manufacturing again was sacrificed without scruple. The reconstruction of the British economy was guided by the priorities of the bloc of class interests that had for so long dominated Britain's metropolitan heartland and the policy of the British state. The accommodation with organised labour and all the institutions and policies which that had spawned over eighty years were stripped away to reveal once again the old constitutional state and the old commercial policy.[28]

Seen in this way, the Thatcherite project proposed only a limited modernisation. Some of the gains of the labour movement were rolled back, but the kind of class confrontation which a decisive restructuring of British capitalism would have required was avoided. Instead manufacturing industry was downgraded still further. It was found that profitability could be restored by opening the British economy and taking full advantage of the rentier and financial opportunities which the world market afforded. The special nature of British capitalism's relationship to the world economy was reinforced. The industrial power of the British working class was contained and its political influence marginalised, but little was done to remedy the cycle of low pay, low skill, low investment and low productivity in which many sectors had become caught.[29]

What the Thatcher government assailed most vigorously were the institutions and traditions of Labourism – which for long had been British Conservatism's ritual foe but at the same time one of its most dependable supports. The curtailment of the powers and responsibilities of local councils, the abolition of the metropolitan councils, the legislation to weaken unions, the (unsuccessful) attempt to stop the unions making financial contributions to the Labour party, the privatisation of public companies and services, and the denigration of public sector workers, all fit into this pattern.

Many Conservatives came to believe during the 1980s that socialism and the Labour movement could be permanently marginalised in British politics, particularly following the split in Labour's ranks in 1981 and the formation of the SDP. The fear that had mesmerised Conservatives since the 1920s that the next general election might produce a Labour government was lifted. The need to accommodate Labour and the interest of the Labour movement was openly repudiated. For many Conservatives the secret of Britain's recovery was simply this – the removal of Labour's veto.

7.5 The future of decline

The euphoria over Britain's economic recovery and Labour's continuing political eclipse at the time of the 1987 election soon faded. Familiar problems returned to trouble policy-makers: balance of payments deficits, inflation, industrial militancy, and pressure on sterling. As many government critics pointed out, an economy which so rapidly overheated, running up a record balance of payments deficit and generating inflation considerably above the OECD average when unemployment was still close to two million, could hardly be described as fundamentally sound. The ensuing recession confirmed that view.

The 1980s increasingly appears the end of an era rather than the beginning of a new one. Margaret Thatcher's resignation as Prime Minister in 1990 marked the end of the heroic period of Thatcherism and the end of perhaps the last political attempt to solve the problem of British 'decline'. At the same time the disintegration of the Soviet Union and the collapse of communism signalled the beginning of a new era for the world economy.

Yet some things did change irreversibly during the 1980s. During the decade a watershed was crossed and some important political questions resolved. The national protec-tionist option was pushed once more to the margins of British politics, perhaps permanently. Three general election victories for the Conservatives over a divided and increasingly demoralised Labour party ensured that it was the free market strategy which determined the agenda. By the time support for the Labour party began to revive in 1988–9 the party had abandoned all versions of the alternative economic strategy.[30] In its 1989 policy review it returned to its social democratic tradition and embraced economic policies which accepted capitalism, the profit motive, the role of markets, and the importance of competition and the consumer.

The key departure, however, was that the Labour leadership now accepted that the internationalisation of the British economy was irreversible. Labour conceded that economic management would have to proceed within the constraints imposed by Britain's membership of a regional grouping, the European Union, and by its wider involvement in the free movement of capital and goods in the world economy. If Britain was to prosper it would be as an integrated part of the world capitalist economy.

The plans devised at different times by both left and right for Britain to regain economic sovereignty within the world economy had depended on particular political structures – the British Empire and the British Labour movement. By the end of the 1980s the empire had disappeared and the Labour movement was a declining force. The basis for an independent and self-sufficient national economy within a capitalist world order had collapsed. By the end of the 1980s no substantial section of right or left opinion any longer supported generalised protection for the British economy.

The Thatcherite project was one particular strategy, whose origins lay in the 1970s, but which was powerfully re-shaped by the events and experiences of the 1980s. The objective of restoring the Conservatives' political hegemony was achieved, and so complete was Conservative dominance of British politics for a time that discussion of alternatives seemed unnecessary. But the Thatcherite project did not exhaust the options for modernising the British economy and making it competitive within the constraints of the world economy. It appeared more dominant than it really was because the main party of opposition remained divided over the merits of the alternative economic strategy and withdrawal from the European Community. But it was very important as a catalyst

for change, not least for the change in the Labour party itself.
It helped clear the ground by dismantling many established
institutions and practices and by challenging entrenched
attitudes.

Keith Middlemas has argued that one of the most
important changes of the Thatcher years was that it moved
decisively away from the tradition of the previous seventy-five
years during which the state had acted as a broker between
the three great economic submarkets – labour, industry and
finance. The state was reorganised to achieve a smaller
number of essential tasks, at less cost, with less conflict or
disruption, and more under the control of party politicians.[31]
The rules of the political game were rewritten, as the balance
shifted to marginalise labour, and to prioritise the interest of
finance and some sectors of industry. Middlemas' judgement
is that after the Thatcher decade the state is closer to being
effective as well as efficient although in relation to a narrower
range of objectives.

The 1990s had a different agenda from the 1980s. It was
centred around the shape of the new world economy, and the
balance between regionalisation and globalisation, evident in
the arguments over the future of the European Union and the
North American Free Trade Association (NAFTA), over
migration, over sovereignty and national identity, over new
forms of democracy, and over the protection of the environment.

Within such a context the debate on decline became a
debate about how a post-imperial and post-Labourist Britain
can best survive within the capitalist world economy. By the
end of the 1980s the two leading parties of the state offered
alternative capitalist futures, less qualified than either had
offered before. They differed on the degree of state involvement
that was necessary to ensure the smoothest adaptation of the
economy to international competition, to regulate markets,
and to provide for the disadvantaged.

Among political parties with any prospects of commanding
substantial electoral support only the Scottish Nationalists
and the Green party articulated an alternative. The Greens
offered a new version of the ideal of a socialist commonwealth,
a transformed industrial society, a politics of moral absolutes

and ultimate ends, which brought together elements of the peace movement, community activists, environmental groups, the anti-nuclear lobby, as well as many libertarian socialists.

By the end of the 1980s the crisis of the 1970s had been resolved through the imposition of the solutions favoured by the Thatcher government. Its success suggested that the long-term effects of the decline would continue to be manageable. The kingdom would not break up. The country would not become ungovernable. The reasons for its success also suggested, however, that the time was past when Britain might plausibly emerge once more as one of the leading capitalist industrial powers. The defeat of the national protectionist option in the 1980s implied that Britain was now relegated permanently to a secondary status within the hierarchy of capitalist states.

The national protectionist option might not have succeeded. There are many reasons for thinking that it would not. But it was perhaps the last attempt to forge a political will in Britain to overturn the political and ideological dominance of the financial/commercial interest, for so long the dominant bloc of capitalist interests in the British state. With the failure of the challenge certain consequences followed. Both parties sought to ensure that Britain would retain a continuing important role as a leading financial and trading centre. As an industrial centre activity would depend increasingly on Britain's ability to attract inward investment and production facilites from transnational companies. Neither party had a strategy for using state power to restore an integrated manufacturing sector in the United Kingdom.

Since the end of the 1940s the scope for national economic management has become more restricted, although it has certainly not vanished entirely.[32] But the acceleration of the pace of internationalisation in the 1970s and 1980s has a further implication. As economies became more inter-dependent so the measurement of the performance of national economies becomes less meaningful and the concept of a national decline more elusive.[33] As Britain becomes more integrated into the European Union the final end of Britain's long post-imperial era will approach, and with it the end of the era of decline.

In any scenarios of Britain's future the way in which the European Union develops is crucial. Two main possibilities are envisaged. In the first scenario the momentum towards greater European political and economic integration is maintained through the 1990s. The completion of the single market in 1992 is only the start of more far-reaching changes – economic and monetary union, the implementation of the social charter, and the emergence of more accountable and more powerful European state agencies.

The second scenario envisages little further economic integration beyond the completion of the internal market as the limit in the extent of European integration. Nation-states and national economies remain, and national governments still have substantial economic sovereignty to pursue whatever policies they deem appropriate. No new federal structures or executive state agencies are established. Europe remains decentralised. There is a set of unified markets but fragmented state authority.

Which of these two scenarios is more likely to be realised and which is the more desirable had already become fiercely contested within British politics by the time of the 1989 European elections and fuelled and debates on the Maastricht Treaty in 1993.[34] The veteran anti-Europeans of Left and Right are greatly diminished in number, but during the 1980s they received some new recruits, particularly from the New Right. Many market liberals had come to fear that economic and monetary union and the European social charter would introduce regulation and corporatist institutions across Europe. The result would be a much more tightly regulated and inflexible economy than was desirable. The survival of Britain's market experiment would be at risk.

What is at stake is the institutional character of European capitalism in the 1980s: whether it should be a free trade area with substantial economic sovereignty remaining with the national governments, or whether it should acquire the character of a developmental state, able to protect Europe's economic independence. British capital appears ambivalent. The leading transnationals and the leading financial houses want to reap the advantages of the single market. The City wants to be the major financial centre for the European Union

after 1992. At the same time they do not want to be confined
to operating within the EU. They want to retain their global
reach. The City wants to be within Europe and outside it at
the same time, just as it has for so long been inside yet outside
the British economy. It does not want to be subservient to the
needs of European industry. In this way many of the
arguments that were once deployed at the national level look
set to re-emerge at the European level.

In this contest the market solutions of the free economy
strategy look more likely to dominate because of the
rudimentary character of European state institutions and
organisation. Unless this is remedied the European Union will
be predominantly a large single market, a battleground for the
world economy's leading transnational companies. Europe
may enter the same path of development as Britain, ceding its
economic independence and its ability to retain leading
sectors in world economic development.

The Thatcher and Major governments vigorously urged
their European partners to copy their policies of deregulation,
privatisation, and free trade. Only the Thatcherite model,
because it would open the European Union to full international
competition, could assure Europe's prosperity. Such a policy
if pursued would guarantee that Europe while remaining rich
would evolve into a subordinate part of the world economy
dominated by Japanese and American transnational
companies. Only the German model with its emphasis on
long-term investment, a highly skilled work-force and high
social spending offers an alternative route. It has its
supporters in Britain, in all parties.[35] But it faces formidable
obstacles, in particular the absence of a European state.

Whichever model is realised it may become increasingly
difficult to distinguish the economic performance of the
British economy as a separate unit within the European
Union. More and more of the parameters and the policies
which determine economic performance will be decided at a
European level. There will be substantial regional disparities
and comparisons but these are unlikely to correspond to the
boundaries of nation-states.

Many areas of Britain remain poorly equipped to compete
within this new European economic space, but assistance is

more likely to come in the future from action by European agencies or from other regional agencies than directly from national governments. A prospect is emerging in which the national level of policy-making may become less important, while the European level and the local level become more important. The Thatcher government tried to weaken the local level and block moves towards a stronger European level. But it is only likely to have delayed the process.

The possible emergence of new state structures at both regional and European level offer opportunities to Britain and the British left. The history of the decline and the shake-out imposed on manufacturing industry in the last two decades leaves Britain with more declining industrial regions than most other member states. Considerable scope exists for local economic strategies and partnerships between the public and private sectors to assist these regions.

Britain will also have some very rich regions and prosperous sectors. While the Westminster Parliament remains the central focus of British politics, the imbalance in Britain's territorial politics will be a source of instability. The Thatcher government handled the growing divisions between regions in the country by directing its appeal to groups which were employed and regions which were prosperous. It became increasingly remote from those areas of the country which had to endure the painful process of adjusting to the loss of major industries. The gulf between rich and poor widened under the Thatcher government, so did the gulf between regions. Electorally, however, the government was able to win sufficient seats in its electoral heartland in the South East to be able to ignore the loss of support in areas like Scotland and the declining industrial areas of the North.[36]

This kind of political management, rewarding the two-thirds of the electorate in secure jobs, at the expense of the one-third of unemployed and casual workers, was not unique to Britain's Conservative government. Governments of Right and Left throughout Europe practised it in the 1980s. Constructing an alternative electoral coalition that would bring forward a different set of economic and social priorities is no easy task.

The basis for a new radical politics exists in the new groups, identities and life-styles that have emerged in the last twenty years. The green movement is one sign of it. It has already had some success in shifting the policy argument about the relative merits of market and interventionist solutions in favour of more intervention and regulation in the environmental field. But it will be difficult for greens and socialists outside Labour's coalition to build an electoral coalition strong enough to interrupt the narrowly focused debate on policy between the two major parties.

The scope for radical politics of both left and right derives from the opportunities in Britain for political and cultural as well as economic modernisation. There has been growing awareness that Britain is viewed by many in Europe not just as economically backward, but politically and culturally backward also. The assumptions of superiority bred in the imperial era have been slow to weaken. But European integration is hastening the process.

If Britain's integration into Europe does progress, the pressure for institutional reform will intensify. Britain may emerge as a more typical European state, shedding in the process some of the burdens that have delayed its adaption in the past. Membership of the European Union might finally enable Britain to modernise successfully and lose the stigma of decline. If this happened it would be because Britain had successfully integrated itself within a regional economy whose main centre of gravity is elsewhere, not because Britain had once again re-emerged as a major economic and political power.[37]

Whatever its remaining problems Britain will still be part of one of the richest regional economies in the world. The imbalances within the European Union are negligible compared with the imbalances between the rich and poor regions of the world economy. The task of finding solutions to these imbalances and to the ecological problems associated with the present organisation of industrial activities will dominate politics in the 1990s and into the next century.

Notes and references

The purpose of these notes is partly to indicate the main sources used in writing this book, and partly to give a guide to further reading on its major themes.

Introduction

1. Carlo Cipolla (ed.), *The Economic Decline of Empires* (London: Methuen, 1971) p. 14.
2. Spoken by Ray Gunter, Minister of Labour, 1964–8.
3. W. A. P. Manser gives a scathing account of the obsession with the balance of payments in *Britain in Balance* (Harmondsworth: Penguin, 1973).
4. A phrase used by Roy Jenkins in 1975. The plural society he claimed was endangered because public spending had reached 60 per cent of GNP. Joel Barnett who was Chief Secretary to the Treasury at the time commented: 'It was a typically elegant phrase, if rendered more meaningless than might normally have been the case when in the following year we changed the definition of public expenditure, so as to reduce the percentage substantially.' Joel Barnett, *Inside the Treasury* (London: Deutsch, 1982) p. 80.
5. Striking examples of it may be found in Paul Einzig's book, *Decline and Fall* (London: Macmillan, 1967), and Robert Moss, *The Death of Democracy* (London: Abacus, 1975).
6. In a speech in 1979 subsequently published as a Centre for Policy Studies pamphlet.
7. See, for example, C. Barnett, *The Collapse of British Power* (London: Methuen, 1972); G. C. Allen, *The British Disease* (London: IEA, 1976); M. Wiener, *English Culture and the Decline of the Industrial Spirit, 1850–1980* (Cambridge University Press, 1981); C. Barnett, *The Audit of War* (London: Macmillan, 1986).

226

8. David Edgerton, *England and the Aeroplane* (London: Macmillan 1991); David Edgerton, 'Liberal Militarism and the British State', *New Left Review 185* January/February 1991, 138–69. Corelli Barnett's reply is contained in *New Left Review 187* May/June 1991, 143–4.
9. Between 1800 and 1970 world population tripled, and the quantity of manufacturing production rose 1730 times. See W. W. Rostow, *The World Economy* (London: Macmillan 1978).
10. Charles Feinstein, 'The Benefits of Backwardness and the Costs of Continuity' in A. Graham (ed.), *Government and Economies in the Post-War World* (London: Routledge 1990) p. 291. When Britain actually began to fall behind continues to be disputed by historians. See Sidney Pollard, *Britain's Prime and Britain's Decline: the British Economy 1870–1914* (London: Arnold, 1989).
11. Joseph Chamberlain, *Imperial Union and Tariff Reform* (London: Grant Richards, 1903) p. 59.
12. For world system approaches see I. Wallerstein, *The Modern World System* (New York: Academic Press, 1974); S. Gill & D. Law, *The Global Political Economy* (Brighton: Harvester Wheatsheaf, 1988); Robert Cox, *Production, Power, and World Order* (New York: Columbia University Press, 1987). The approach taken in this book is discussed further in 'The Decline of Britain', *Contemporary Record*, 2:5 (Spring 1989) 18–23; 'From Empire to De-industrialisation: the problem of British development' in U. Ostergard (ed.), *Culture & History* 9/10 (Copenhagen: Academic Press 1991) 85–104; 'Britain's Decline: Some Theoretical Issues', in M. Mann (ed.), *The Rise and Decline of the Nation-State* (Oxford: Blackwell 1990) 71–90.

Chapter 1: The hundred years' decline

1. Resignation speech in the House of Commons, 28 May 1930.
2. By 1960; two-thirds of the import trade of the industrialised countries were goods exchanged amongst themselves. By 1971 these were three-quarters. See A. Shonfield *et al.*, *Politics and Trade* (Oxford University Press, 1976) p. 103.
3. See S. Hymer, *The Multinational Corporation* (Cambridge University Press, 1979), and C. Tugendhat, *The Multinationals* (London: Eyre & Spottiswoode, 1971).
4. See P. Deane and W. A. Cole, *British Economic Growth* (Cambridge University Press, 1967), and W. W. Rostow, *The World Economy* (London: Macmillan, 1978) ch. 28.

5. The main issues between those emphasising temporary deficiencies in supply or demand and those emphasising more fundamental social and political obstacles to accumulation are well brought out in a debate between Bill Warren and Ernest Mandel, 'Recession and its Consequences', *New Left Review*, 87–88, September–December 1974, pp. 114–24. Most of Mandel's expectations were borne out by subsequent events.

6. E. Mandel, *The Second Slump* (London: New Left Books, 1978).

7. In the nineteenth century every boom terminated in a slump which enforced a restructuring of capital through bankruptcies and unemployment (often as much as 25 per cent of the labour force), and by a general fall in prices (sometimes as much as one-third), which in time made investment and expansion profitable once more. As the scale and complexity of capitalist production grew, so markets proved too unstable and too inflexible to create all the conditions necessary for profitable accumulation, and increasing reliance was placed on the state to provide them.

8. The nature of the long boom and the forces which undermined it are explored from different standpoints in E. Mandel, *Late Capitalism* (London: New Left Books, 1975), P. Sweezy and H. Magdoff, *The Dynamics of the Capitalist Economy* (New York: MR Press, 1972), and Rostow, *The World Economy*.

9. See Paul Mattick, *Marx and Keynes* (London: Merlin, 1969).

10. See M. Barratt-Brown, *The Economies of Imperialism* (Harmondsworth: Penguin, 1972).

11. United States policy after 1945 can be studied in D. Horowitz, *From Yalta to Vietnam* (Harmondsworth: Penguin, 1967), and R. Gardner, *Sterling Dollar Diplomacy* (Oxford University Press, 1956). See also B. Johnson, *The Politics of Money* (London: Murray, 1970).

12. The downfall of the dollar is analysed by R. Segal, *The Decline and Fall of the American Dollar* (New York: Bantam, 1974).

13. See the discussion in Paul Bullock and David Yaffe, 'Inflation, the Crisis and the Post-war Boom', *Revolutionary Communist*, nos 3–4, November 1975, pp. 1–45; and in Andrew Gamble and Paul Walton, *Capitalism in Crisis* (London: Macmillan, 1976).

14. This is discussed by Tom Nairn in 'Marxism and the Modern Janus', in *The Breakup of Britain* (London: New Left Books, 1977). See also A. Gerschenkron, *Economic Backwardness in Historical Perspective* (Harvard University Press, 1966).

15. There are two detailed studies of the reaction to the challenge: R. Heindel, *The American Impact on Great Britain, 1898–1914* (New York: Octagon, 1968), and R. J. S. Hoffmann, *Great Britain and*

    the German Trade Rivalry, 1875–1914 (New York: Russell, 1964).

16. *Daily Mail*, 5 May 1901.

17. M. Wiener, *English Culture and the Decline of the Industrial Spirit, 1850–1980* (Cambridge University Press, 1981).

18. Sidney Pollard, *The Wasting of the British Economy* (London: Croom Helm, 1982).

19. Another symbolic expression of the declining importance of Britain in the world economy was the demotion of Britain from second to fifth in the order in which member countries are listed and surveyed in OECD statistics and reports.

20. For the calculations see *Labour Research*, January 1983, vol. 72, no. 1.

21. Prest and Coppock, *The UK Economy*, table 1.14, p. 50.

22. In *Saint Joan*.

23. A considerable anti-growth literature emerged in the 1970s. See, for example, Bernard Nossiter, *The Future that Works* (London: Deutsch, 1978), and E. Mishan, *The Costs of Economic Growth* (Harmondsworth: Penguin, 1969). The methodological problems of comparing the growth paths of different countries are examined in P. O'Brien and C. Keyder, *Economic Growth in Britain and France, 1780–1914* (London: Allen & Unwin, 1978).

24. See S. Gomulka, 'Britain's Slow Industrial Growth', in W. Beckerman (ed.), *Slow Growth in Britain* (Oxford University Press, 1979) pp. 166–93.

25. See D. McKie and C. Cook, *Election Guide* (London: Quartet, 1978) pp. 57–8.

26. F. Blackaby, *De-Industrialisation* (London: Heinemann, 1978) p. 243.

27. See R. Caves and L. B. Krause (eds), *Britain's Economic Performance* (Washington, DC: Brookings Institution) p. 136.

28. Central Policy Review Staff, *The Future of the British Car Industry* (London: CPRS, 1975).

29. C. F. Pratten, *Labour Productivity Differentials Within International Companies* (Department of Applied Economics, Cambridge University, 1976) pp. 5, 6.

30. F. E. Jones, 'Our Manufacturing Industry: The Missing £100 000 Million', *National Westminster Bank Review*, May 1978, pp. 8–17.

31. Second to the United States, which overtook Britain after 1945. See Rostow, *The World Economy*, ch. 7.

32. See index compiled by *Labour Research*, and published monthly in that journal. In June 1980 the index had only risen to 107 (1974 = 100).

33. The discrepancy between élite and popular perceptions of

decline has become a standard theme in the literature. See James Alt, *The Politics of Economic Decline* (Cambridge University Press, 1979).

34. Particularly important have been Andrew Shonfield, *British Economic Policy Since the War* (Harmondsworth: Penguin, 1958); W. A. P. Manser, *Britain in Balance* (Harmondsworth: Penguin 1971); and Stephen Blank, 'The Politics of Foreign Economic Policy', *International Organization*, vol. 31, no. 4, 1977, pp. 673–722.

35. R. C. O. Matthews, 'Why has Britain had Full Employment Since the War?' *Economic Journal*, vol. 78, Sept. 1968.

36. Manser, *Britain in Balance*.

37. W. Beckerman, *The Labour Government's Economic Record* (London: Duckworth, 1972). R. Caves *et al.*, *Britain's Economic Prospects* (London: Allen & Unwin, 1968).

38. M. Holmes, *Political Pressure and Economic Policy* (London: Butterworth, 1982).

39. This is most associated with the Cambridge Economic Policy Group. See also B. Gould *et al.*, *Monetarism or Prosperity* (London: Macmillan, 1981).

40. Jones, 'Our Manufacturing Industry – The Missing £100 000 Million', pp. 8–17.

41. An excellent survey of monetarism is provided by N. Bosanquet, *After the New Right* (London: Heinemann, 1983).

42. One variant of the unproductive public expenditure thesis is R. Bacon and W. Eltis, *Britain's Economic Problem: Too Few Producers* (London: Macmillan, 1978).

43. See, for example, F. Blackaby (ed.), *Demand Management* (Cambridge University Press, 1978) ch. 9.

44. S. Brittan and P. Lilley, *The Delusion of Incomes Policy* (London: Temple Smith, 1977).

45. S. Holland, *The Socialist Challenge* (London: Quartet, 1975).

46. B. Semmel, *Imperialism and Social Reform* (London: Allen & Unwin, 1960); G. R. Searle, *The Quest for National Efficiency* (Oxford University Press, 1971).

47. See the further discussion in Chapters 2 and 6. The way in which decline was perceived by the political élite before 1914 is the subject of an important study by Aaron Friedberg, *The Weary Titan* (Princeton University Press, 1988).

48. D. Cameron Watt, *Succeeding John Bull* (Cambridge University Press, 1984).

49. Stuart Hall and Bill Schwarz, 'State and Society, 1880–1930', in M. Langan and Bill Schwarz (eds), *Crises in the British State* (London: Hutchinson, 1985).

50. For an excellent analysis of the concept of Fordism, see Henk Overbeek, *Global Capitalism and Britain's Decline* (London: Unwin Hyman, 1989).

51. One of the influential accounts of the development of policy is Keith Middlemass, *Politics in Industrial Society* (London: Deutsch, 1979). The best short survey of the literature on decline is Alan Sked, *Britain's Decline* (Oxford: Blackwell, 1987).

52. For the crisis of the 1970s see especially Colin Leys, *Politics in Britain* (London: Verso, 1989); and David Coates and John Hillard (eds), *The Economic Decline of Modern Britain* (Brighton: Harvester, 1986).

53. W. A. P. Manser, *Britain in Balance* (Harmondsworth: Penguin, 1981).

54. R. Bacon and W. Eltis, *Britain's Economic Problem: Too few Producers* (London: Macmillan, 1978); IEA, *The Dilemmas of Government Expenditure* (London, IEA, 1976).

55. F. A. Hayek, *A Tiger by the Tail* (London: IEA, 1972).

56. Keith Joseph, *Stranded on the Middle Ground* (London: CPS, 1976).

57. M. Olson, *The Rise and Decline of Nations* (Yale University Press, 1982).

58. S. Brittan, *The Economic Consequences of Democracy* (London: Temple Smith, 1977).

59. See Joseph, *Stranded on the Middle Ground*; and Corelli Barnett, *The Audit of War* (London: Macmillan, 1986).

60. Paul Kennedy, *The Rise and Fall of the Great Powers* (London: Unwin Hyman, 1988); Joel Krieger, *Reagan, Thatcher, and the Politics of Decline* (Cambridge: Polity, 1986).

61. Stephen Blank, 'The Politics of Foreign Economic Policy', *International Organisation*, vol. 31, no. 4, 1977, pp. 673–722; Andrew Shonfield, *British Economic Policy Since the War* (Harmondsworth: Penguin, 1958).

62. David Marquand, *The Unprincipled Society* (London: Cape, 1987); Andrew Schonfield, *Modern Capitalism* (Oxford University Press, 1964); Peter Hall, *Governing the Economy* (Cambridge: Polity, 1986); S. Pollard, *The Wasting of the British Economy* (London: Croom Helm, 1982).

63. D. Ashford, *Policy and Politics in Britain* (Oxford: Blackwell, 1981); S. E. Finer, *Adversary Politics and Electoral Reform* (London: Wigram, 1979); S. Beer, *Britain Against Itself* (New York: Norton, 1982).

64. D. Marquand, *The Unprincipled Society*.

65. M. Wiener, *English Culture and the Decline of the Industrial Spirit* (Cambridge University Press, 1981).

66. G. K. Ingham, *Capitalism Divided* (London: Macmillan, 1984); Colin Leys, 'Thatcherism and British Manufacturing: A Question of Hegemony', *New Left Review*, 151, 1985, pp. 5–25; Perry Anderson, 'The Figures of Descent', *New Left Review*, 161, 1987, pp. 20–77; Michael Barratt Brown, 'Away With All the Great Arches', *New Left Review*, 167, 1988, pp. 22–52; G. K. Ingham, 'Commercial Capital and British Development', *New Left Review*, 172, 1988, pp. 45–66.

67. Henk Overbeek, *Global Capitalism and Britain's Decline*; Ben Fine and Laurence Harris, *The Peculiarities of the British Economy* (London: Lawrence & Wishart, 1985).

68. Andrew Glyn and Bob Sutcliffe, *Workers, British Capitalism, and the Profits Squeeze* (Harmondsworth: Penguin, 1972); Andrew Glyn and John Harrison, *The British Economic Disaster* (London: Pluto, 1980); Coates and Hillard (eds), *The Economic Decline of Modern Britain*; T. Nichols, *The British Worker Question* (London: Routledge, 1986).

69. Tom Nairn, *The Breakup of Britain* (London: NLB, 1977).

70. Hall and Schwarz, 'State and Society, 1880–1930'.

71. Bob Jessop, 'The Dual Crisis of the State', in *Essays in the Theory of the State* (Cambridge: Polity, 1989).

72. Nairn, *The Breakup of Britain*.

73. Caves and Krause (eds), *Britain's Economic Performance*.

Chapter 2: The world island

1. *The Testament of Adolf Hitler* (London: Cassell, 1961) p. 34.

2. Wales was incorporated in England in 1536. Scotland and England were united by the Act of Union in 1701, so forming Great Britain. The United Kingdom was created in 1801 when the formal independence of the Irish Parliament was abolished, although Ireland had long been an English dependency.

3. This was certainly true for Scotland and England, though less true for Wales. Wales did have heavy industry, but has been described (by Eric Hobsbawm) as a 'mining annexe' of the British economy with its own distinctive class structure. Nevertheless it was still very different again from Ireland.

4. A very good and concise survey of Irish history is given by Liam de Paor, *Divided Ulster* (Harmondsworth: Penguin, 1971).

5. Four million emigrated from Ireland during the nineteenth century. Irish labour was employed in England particularly in building and railway construction.

6. The most important was the split in the Liberal party in 1886 over Gladstone's Home Rule Bill. Joseph Chamberlain led the breakaway Liberal Unionists into alliance with the Conservatives. The Union was to be a central political issue for the next twenty years, the Conservatives even adopting a new name, the Unionists, to emphasise its overriding importance. For Chamberlain's career see D. Judd, *Radical Joe* (London: Hamish Hamilton, 1977).

7. See A. T. Q. Stewart, *Ulster Crisis* (London: Faber, 1967).

8. The history and dynamics of this world economy have been explored in the major study by Immanuel Wallerstein, *The Modern World System* (New York: Academic Press, 1974).

9. This strategy is set out by Halford Mackinder (Geographer, Imperialist, Director of LSE, Unionist MP, Commissioner to the White forces during the Russian Civil War) in *Democratic Ideals and Reality* (London: Constable, 1919).

10. A judgement made by the Cambridge historian J. R. Seeley in his highly influential work *The Expansion of England* (London: Macmillan, 1909). The growth of this trade was not uniform and its expansion was generally interrupted by wars. There was a peace party in England which disliked the expense of the commercial policy because of the wars it involved. Nevertheless, it was the successful prosecution of the wars that laid the foundation for the periods of greatest expansion of trade. Some historians seem curiously blind to this. W. E. Minchinton in his Introduction to *The Growth of English Overseas Trade in the Seventeenth and Eighteenth Centuries* (London: Methuen, 1969) notes how trade always expanded fastest in times of peace and concludes that the idea that the commercial expansion began with Cromwell is mistaken. At the same time he notes the crucial steps that were taken under Cromwell which made the great expansion from 1660 to 1685 possible – the Navigation Acts, the war with Holland, and the seizure of Jamaica from Spain.

11. See B. Semmel, *The Rise of Free Trade Imperialism* (Cambridge University Press, 1970), the outstanding study of the subject. In 1815 the Empire covered some two million square miles with a population of approximately 100 million.

12. The Anti-Corn Law League, in which Cobden and Bright were leading members, never became strong enough to force through repeal against the united resistance of the landed class. Repeal came because of a split within this class. See N. McCord, *The Anti-Corn Law League, 1838–1846* (London: Allen & Unwin, 1968).

13. By the 1840s 3.4 million Britons were fed on foreign wheat.

14. See E. Hobsbawm, *Industry and Empire* (Harmondsworth: Penguin, 1969) ch. 7.

15. The most notorious use of British naval power to open markets was the Opium war of 1839–41. The Chinese Emperor had attempted to halt all trade, especially the trade in opium. At the conclusion of the war Hong Kong was handed over to Britain and China opened to trade and western penetration.

16. Tariffs rose very steeply after 1870. The general American tariff was 57 per cent by 1897. Russia imposed protective tariffs in 1877. France in 1878, Germany in 1879.

17. There were many different protectionist programmes. Some wanted a uniform tariff imposed on all imports, others wanted it imposed only against those countries that discriminated against British goods. The latter principle was often acceptable to pragmatic free traders, but it was the former that marked out the true tariff reformers, since the object was not primarily retaliation against those states that had themselves imposed tariffs, but a permanent protection of trade. Ideally they wanted the Empire to be a single free trade economic bloc protected by an external tariff barrier. Imperial preference was a second-best solution whereby every self-governing state of the Empire would impose its own external tariff but admit goods from other imperial countries at preferential rates. Protectionist sentiment began to stir in the 1880s, and the Tariff Reform League, established in 1903, was preceded by the Campaign for Fair Trade in the 1880s and such organisations as the United Empire Trade League.

18. The Free Trade doctrine is set out with great clarity in Richard Cobden's *Political Writings*, 2 vols (London: Ridgeway, 1867), and also in the *Sophismes Economiques* of Frederic Bastiat, which the Cobden Club (motto: Free Trade, Peace, Goodwill among Nations) reprinted at the height of the controversy on tariff reform under the title *Fallacies of Protection* (London: Cassell, 1909).

19. Jingoism was so named after the popular music hall song.
    We don't want to fight but by Jingo if we do,
    We've got the ships, we've got the men, we've got the money too.

20. A point emphasised by D. K. Fieldhouse, *Economics and Empire* (London: Weidenfeld & Nicolson, 1973).

21. Charles Dilke, the radical liberal politician, wrote a very influential book, *Greater Britain* (London: Macmillan, 1868), which set out these ideas. See also the earlier theories and

practical enterprises of Edward Gibbon Wakefield for middle-class settlement of the Empire, described in Semmel, *The Rise of Free Trade Imperialism*.

22. For the very varied ideology of imperialism see A. P. Thornton, *The Imperial Idea and its enemies* (London: Macmillan, 1957).

23. Before the Tariff Reform League was established this was already made embarrassingly clear at the Congress of the Chambers of Commerce of the Empire in 1896. The Dominions feared that any scheme of imperial free trade would be mainly to the advantage of British manufacturers. They wanted protection against British competition so as to establish their own industries. The Social Imperialists were forced to recognise this reluctance, but believed that if a strong enough political initiative were taken by Britain, all parts of the Empire would be prepared to make sacrifices for the sake of greater unity.

24. Although free trade triumphed over protection, the Liberals remained committed to the Empire and to a policy of free trade imperialism safeguarding Britain's colonial possessions while maintaining the openness of the world economy to British goods.

25. The Empire, though vast, was extremely undeveloped. Only Malaya was a significant source of supply of raw materials for the British economy, and even by 1914 the bulk of British investment still continued to flow to the more developed parts of the world economy. See S. Pollard, *The Development of the British Economy* (London: Arnold, 1969) pp. 19–23. The British empire was always very unlike the continental empires which America and Russia already had, and to which Germany aspired.

26. See A. Imlah, *Economic Elements in the Pax Britannica* (New York: Russell, 1958). The total foreign investments of Germany, France and Italy combined were £5500 million in 1914.

27. H. Mackinder, *Britain and the British Seas* (London: Heinemann, 1902) p. 343.

28. The British battle fleet had to be superior to the two next largest navies in the world combined. The arms race before 1914 was begun by the German decision to build a fleet. The German bourgeoisie, not the German aristocracy, was the class that pressed for this, with the explicit aim of challenging England. See David Calleo, *The German Problem Re-Considered* (Cambridge University Press, 1978) chs 3, 4.

29. Mackinder's strategic ideas had most influence not in Britain, but in Germany, on Haushofer. One of Haushofer's research assistants in the early 1920s was Rudolf Hess, shortly to spend some time in a prison cell with Adolph Hitler. In this way

Mackinder's ideas helped to shape the geopolitical thinking of Hitler.
30. This is most strongly argued by Corelli Barnett in his book, *The Collapse of British Power* (London: Methuen, 1972). He goes so far as to state: 'The British and imperial armies which marched and conquered in the latter half of the war . . . were not manifestations of British imperial power at a new zenith, as the British believed at the time and long afterwards, but only the illusion of it. They were instead manifestations of *American* power – and of the decline of England into a warrior satellite of the United States' (p. 592). This is an exaggeration, but it is a correction to the view of Britain as an equal ally and equal power in the war.
31. See D. Watt, *Personalities and Policies* (London: Longman, 1965), especially 'America and the Elite, 1895–1956'.
32. Joseph Chamberlain, when Colonial Secretary in the 1890s, briefly favoured a German alliance. British ties with Germany were close, particularly through the royal family. When the Great War broke out the British royal family changed their surname from Saxe-Coburg to Windsor (in 1917).
33. German war aims are discussed by Fritz Fischer, *Germany's Aims in the First World War* (London: Chatto & Windus, 1967), and by David Calleo, *The German Problem Re-Considered*.
34. Alexis de Tocqueville, *Journeys to England and Ireland* (1835).

Chapter 3: The unfinished revolution

1. Gaetano Mosca, *The Ruling Class* (New York: McGraw-Hill, 1939), p. 119.
2. Christopher Hill's many books on the civil war are outstanding. See particularly his book on Cromwell, *God's Englishman* (Harmondsworth: Penguin, 1972). See also Barrington Moore Jr, *Social Origins of Dictatorship and Democracy* (Harmondsworth: Penguin, 1969) ch. 1.
3. See the discussion in R. R. Palmer, *The Age of the Democratic Revolution* (Princeton University Press, 1959).
4. Adam Smith, *The Wealth of Nations* (London: Methuen, 1961) p. 26.
5. Two of its most noted practitioners were Lord Macaulay and Lord Acton. One of its most stringent critics was Herbert

Butterfield, *The Whig Interpretation of History* (London: Bell, 1931).

6. See the discussion by E. P. Thompson in *The Making of the English Working Class* (Harmondsworth: Penguin, 1969) part I, especially chs 4, 5.

7. The two key changes were the widening of the franchise and the move to free trade, which were accompanied by major administrative and financial reforms, particularly the re-introduction of income tax in the 1840s, and the Bank Act of 1844.

8. Joseph Schumpeter, *Capitalism, Socialism and Democracy* (London: Allen & Unwin, 1949) p. 229.

9. This theme has been most thoroughly explored by Tom Nairn in 'The Twilight of the British State', *New Left Review*, 101–2, February–April 1977.

10. The struggle over the Corn Laws was bitter and intense but it did not lead to any armed conflict. The landed interest accepted its defeat. An important reason for this undoubtedly lay in the high rentier incomes which monetary stability provided for all owners of property. See B. Johnson, *The Politics of Money* (London: Murray, 1970) p. 40.

11. Quoted in B. Semmel, *The Rise of Free Trade Imperialism* (Cambridge University Press, 1970) p. 8.

12. See the analysis of the public schools in Corelli Barnett, *The Collapse of British Power* (London: Methuen, 1971) ch. 2. He writes, for instance; 'The qualities imparted to this future ruling class by their education – probity, orthodoxy, romantic idealism, a strong sense of public responsibility – admirably fitted them for running the British Empire as they saw it; an unchanging institution of charitable purpose and assured income. Such qualities were however ill-suited to leading the Empire, a great business and strategic enterprise, through drastic internal reorganisations and against ferocious and unscrupulous competition' (p. 43). The shortcomings and social divisiveness of the public school system have long been major themes in the writing on British decline. A recent example is G. C. Allen, *The British Disease* (London: IEA, 1979).

13. The classic analysis was provided by Perry Anderson and Tom Nairn in their essays in *New Left Review* in the 1960s. See especially, Perry Anderson, 'Origins of the Present Crisis', *New Left Review*, 23, January–February 1964, and Tom Nairn, *The Breakup of Britain* (London: New Left Books, 1977).

14. Whether they found their way directly into industrial investment is uncertain. Historians tend to regard accumulated savings of

the new industrialists themselves as more important. But there is little doubt about the later utilisation of these accumulated hoards once industry had become securely established.

15. This history is vividly described by Thompson, *The Making of the English Working Class*, and by Karl Marx, *Capital*, vol. 1 (Harmondsworth: Penguin, 1976), particularly his chapters on the working day (ch. 10), and on machinery (ch. 15).

16. See, for example, the account in Eric Hobsbawm and G. Rude, *Captain Swing* (London: Lawrence & Wishart, 1969), and Eric Hobsbawm, *Labouring Men* (London: Weidenfeld & Nicholson, 1964).

17. For a review of the growth and the extent of state involvement in the nineteenth century see J. Brebner, '*Laissez-faire* and State Intervention in Nineteenth Century Britain', in E. Carus-Wilson (ed.), *Essays in Economic History* (London: Arnold, 1962) pp. 252–62.

18. For Chartism see G. D. H. Cole and R. W. Postgate, *The Common People* (London: Methuen, 1961) section V.

19. Karl Marx, 'The Chartists', *New York Daily Tribune*, 25 August 1852, reprinted in *Surveys from Exile* (Harmondsworth: Penguin, 1973) p. 264.

20. The increase in the total electorate was tiny; it rose from 510 000 to 720 000, 2.1 per cent to 3.3 per cent of the population.

21. Over three-quarters were estimated to belong to the manual working class. See Eric Hobsbawm, *Industry and Empire* (Harmondsworth: Penguin, 1969) pp. 154, 157–8. By 1850 more lived in cities than in the country and by 1881 2 out of 5 lived in the six giant conurbations.

22. Universal suffrage was slow in coming. The electorate was doubled in 1867 and again in 1885, when it stood at five million, still only 16 per cent of the population. In 1918 full manhood suffrage was conceded and votes for women over thirty. Votes for all women came in 1928.

23. See J. H. Goldthorpe, 'The Current Inflation: Towards a Sociological Account', in F. Hirsch and J. H. Goldthorpe (eds), *The Political Economy of Inflation* (London: Martin Robertson, 1978) pp. 186–213.

24. See Cole and Postgate, *The Common People*.

25. Richard Cobden, *Political Writings*, 2 vols (London: Ridgeway, 1867).

26. The rise in real wages after 1850 was significant. Trade-union rights were gradually extended. The 1871 Criminal Law Amendment Act and the 1875 Conspiracy and Protection of Property Act legalised trade unions.

27. See Raphael Samuel, 'The Workshop of the World', *History Workshop*, no. 3, Spring 1977, pp. 6–72.

28. See Hobsbawm, *Industry and Empire*, ch. 9, and P. Mathias, *The First Industrial Nation* (London: Methuen, 1969) ch. 15. Recent research has challenged this interpretation.

29. Custom and excise were indirect taxes levied on consumption, but with the move to free trade went the reintroduction of an income tax to make good the shortfall in revenue. This was to grow into the Treasury's most dependable source of revenue.

30. There were attempts to reform all these in the early decades of this century but no radical changes emerged.

31. The Liberals established their caucus, the National Liberal Federation, in 1877. The Birmingham Liberal Association, which became Chamberlain's power base, was founded in 1865.

32. See Ross McKibbin, *The Evolution of the Labour Party 1910–1924* (Oxford University Press, 1974).

33. In 1918 the Labour party still had only sixty-three seats compared with forty-two in 1910, but, mainly as a result of contesting many more constituencies, its share of the vote rose from 7.1 per cent of 22.2 per cent, and it received over two million votes.

34. The most important socialist element of the new programme was contained in Clause IV of the new constitution. See R. Miliband, *Parliamentary Socialism* (London: Merlin, 1961) for a discussion of its significance.

35. The only concession of its protectionist views was the policy of Safeguarding. See note 9 to Chapter 5.

36. See Maurice Cowling, *The Impact of Labour* (Cambridge University Press, 1970) for a painstaking analysis.

37. See Chapter 6 (pp. 162–5).

38. The three positions were represented in the Conservative party by, for example, Lord Birkenhead, Leo Amery, and Stanley Baldwin. See Amery's own account in *My Political Life* (London: Hutchinson, 1953).

39. All recent histories of the strike agree on this. See Patrick Renshaw, *The General Strike* (London: Eyre Methuen, 1975), and Margaret Morris, *The General Strike* (Harmondsworth: Penguin, 1976).

40. The *British Gazette*, for instance, declared: 'There can be no compromise of any kind. Either the country will break the General Strike or the General Strike will break the country.' When the strike was over Churchill urged conciliation.

41. See R. P. Arnot, *The General Strike* (London: Labour Research Department, 1926), and E. Burns, *Trade Councils in Action*

(London: Labour Research Department, 1926). There is little doubt that the solidarity of the strikers was growing; more workers were in fact out on strike the day after it was called off than during the strike itself.

42. This paradox has given rise to an enormous literature. See especially R. T. McKenzie and A. Silver, *Angels in Marble* (London: Heinemann, 1968), and F. Parkin, 'Working Class Conservatives: a Theory of Political Deviance', *British Journal of Sociology*, vol. 18, no. 3, 1967, pp. 278–90.

43. The *Financial Times*, 6 May 1926.

44. The Trade Disputes Act (1927) outlawed sympathy and political strikes, it restricted picketing, and it forced trade unionists wishing to pay the political levy to the Labour party to contract in. Formerly those wishing to avoid paying the levy had had to contract out.

45. See D. Coates, *The Labour Party and the Struggle for Socialism* (Cambridge University Press, 1975); Miliband, *Parliamentary Socialism*; and T. Nairn, 'Anatomy of the Labour Party', reprinted in R. Blackburn (ed.), *Revolution and Class Struggle* (London: Fontana, 1977) pp. 314–73.

Chapter 4: Managing social democracy

1. J. M. Keynes, quoted by Robert Skidelsky, in C. Crouch (ed.), *State and Economy in Contemporary Capitalism* (London: Croom Helm, 1979) p. 58.

2. Many of these assets were acquired cheaply by American companies. By 1945 one-quarter of British overseas assets worth £1118 million had been sold. Sterling liabilities had increased from £476 million to £3355 million, and British exports needed to be raised by 75 per cent over pre-war levels to pay for imports.

3. I have explored this transformation of the Conservative party in *The Conservative Nation* (London: Routledge & Kegan Paul, 1974).

4. Labour's vote in 1945 was 47.8 per cent of the poll.

5. Labour's constitutional reforms were marginal – the business and university votes were abolished, and the power of the House of Lords to delay legislation was reduced from two years to one year. The paucity of Labour's constitutional reforms showed the extent to which the Labour leadership had become reconciled to the existing state.

6. One of the fullest studies of the emergence of the consensus is Paul Addison's *The Road to 1945* (London: Cape, 1975).

7. Public spending stabilised at 45 per cent of GNP after 1945 compared with a level of around 25 per cent in the inter-war years. See A. Peacock and D. Wiseman, *The Growth of Public Expenditure in the UK* (London: Allen & Unwin, 1966).

8. After 1945 the bulk of public revenue was derived from direct taxes levied on the whole population. Before 1913 direct taxes accounted for only one-third of public revenue; by 1975 they accounted for three-fifths. For further discussion see Ian Gough, *The Political Economy of Welfare State* (London: Macmillan, 1979).

9. The main industries nationalised were the Bank of England (1946); the coal mines (1946); electricity (1947); gas (1948); railways (1948). They joined the Post Office, the airlines and the BBC. Iron and Steel was nationalised in 1949 but was denationalised in 1953, then renationalised in 1966.

10. The commitment to full employment made in the 1944 White Paper on Employment Policy. See Addison, *The Road to 1945*, pp. 243–6.

11. See the influential analysis by Samuel Beer, *Modern British Politics* (London: Faber, 1965), especially ch. 12; and the new study by Keith Middlemas, *Politics in Industrial Society* (London: Deutsch, 1979).

12. Commodity exports had fallen by one-third, and invisible exports and rentier incomes had greatly diminished.

13. Exports increased 77 per cent between 1946 and 1950. See S. Pollard, *The Development of the British Economy* (London: Arnold, 1969) p. 362.

14. Ibid, p. 376ff. Real output per head between 1937 and 1950 rose 25 per cent.

15. The period of pay restraint between 1948 and 1950 was the most successful incomes policy ever operated in Britain. Links between the unions and the Labour party were still close and the memories of wartime collaboration still strong.

16. The decision to rearm was announced in January 1951. The Labour government committed Britain to a £4700 million rearmament programme. This necessitated immediate increases in taxes, including health service charges, in the 1951 budget. The programme was scaled down by the Conservatives when they came into office.

17. Despite the damage to the market order the 1930s did see a considerable economic expansion. The part played in this by the protectionist policies is disputed. The high unemployment was concentrated in the older industries and older industrial areas.

The extent of the recovery should not, however, be overstated. For contrasting views see B. W. E. Alford, *Depression and Recovery: British Economic Growth 1918–1939* (London: Macmillan, 1972), and D. H. Aldcroft, 'Economic Growth in the InterWar Years: A Reassessment', *Economic History Review*, vol. XX, 1967.

18. See T. H. Marshall, *Citizenship and Social Class* (Cambridge University Press, 1950).

19. The literature on these themes has been unending since the end of the 1950s. Among the more significant are Anthony Sampson, *The Anatomy of Britain* (London: Hodder, 1961); M. Shanks, *The Stagnant Society* (Harmondsworth: Penguin, 1961); and more recently, G. C. Allen, *The British Disease* (London: IEA, 1976).

20. See Susan Strange, *Sterling and British Policy* (Oxford University Press, 1971).

21. Cordell Hull described the Ottawa agreements of 1932 as 'the greatest injury in a commercial way that has been inflicted on this country since I have been in public life'. Quoted by Julian Amery, *Joseph Chamberlain and the Tariff Reform Campaign* (London: Macmillan, 1969) p. 1034.

22. Quoted by D. Watt, *Personalities and Policies* (London: Longman, 1965) p. 61.

23. Convertibility meant that the pound should be convertible into other currencies, i.e., freely traded on the foreign exchange markets so giving maximum opportunity to American companies to sell their goods in England.

24. See R. N. Gardner, *Sterling-Dollar Diplomacy* (Oxford University Press, 1956) for a very full account of the negotiations. For an account which challenges conventional interpretations see Peter Burnham, *The Political Economy of Post-War Reconstruction* (London: Macmillan 1990).

25. The Marshall Aid programme scheduled $17 thousand million to finance European recovery.

26. See David Horowitz, *From Yalta to Vietnam* (Harmondsworth: Penguin, 1967).

27. Susan Strange, *Sterling and British Policy*; and Andrew Shonfield, *British Economic Policy Since the War* (Harmondsworth: Penguin, 1958).

28. In the 1960s British defence spending averaged 6 per cent of GNP, compared with 4.4 per cent in France, 3.6 per cent in Germany, 3.3 per cent in Italy, and 1.1 per cent in Japan. See Strange, *Strange and British Policy*, ch. 6.

29. Overseas military spending rose from £12 million in 1952 to £313 million in 1966.

30. Net overseas investment averaged £120 million in 1952–5, and £305 million in 1972–3.

31. W. B. Reddaway *et al.*, *Effects of UK Direct Investment Overseas* (Cambridge University Press, 1967).

32. W. A. P. Manser, *Britain in Balance* (Harmondsworth: Penguin, 1973).

33. See the discussion in Pollard, *The Development of the British Economy*, pp. 468ff.

34. Susan Strange's analysis is the most detailed. See Strange, *Sterling and British Policy*. She distinguishes between top currency, master currency, and negotiated currency status for international currencies. Sterling had been a top currency before 1914; after 1945 it was still a master currency for the sterling area, but outside that, and even within part of the sterling area, it was becoming increasingly a negotiated currency, which meant that the terms of its use had to be negotiated between the holders and the British government.

35. See Pollard, *The Development of the British Economy*.

36. See, for example, R. Caves (ed.), *Britain's Economic Prospects* (London: Allen & Unwin, 1968) part I; and R. C. O. Matthews, 'Post-War Business Cycles in the UK', in M. Bronfenbrenner, *Is the Business Cycle Obsolete?* (New York: Wiley, 1969).

37. Cf. G. Turner, *Business in Britain* (London: Eyre & Spottiswoode, 1969) ch. 2.

38. Quoted by R. Heindel, *The American Impact on Great Britain, 1898–1914* (New York: Octagon, 1968) p. 215.

39. Only 20 per cent of assets were nationalised. See A. Rogow and P. Shore, *The Labour Government and British Industry* (Oxford: Blackwell, 1955).

40. A detailed review of this period is given by J. C. R. Dow, *The Management of the British Economy, 1945–60* (Cambridge University Press, 1964). See also, S. Brittan, *Steering the Economy* (Harmondsworth: Penguin, 1971); Alan Budd, *The Politics of Economic Planning* (London: Fontana, 1978); and J. Leruez, *Economic Planning and Policy in Britain* (London: Martin Robertson, 1975).

41. The scale of the immigration was smaller than the immigration into many other European economies. By 1961 there were 600 000 Commonwealth immigrants in the United Kingdom. By 1971 this had risen to 1.2 million. In 1962 the Commonwealth Immigration Act imposed the first set of restrictions on entry. These were tightened by further legislation in 1968, 1971 and 1979.

42. Governments were forced to attempt trade-offs between unemployment and inflation, and between growth and the balance

of payments, but the underlying trends were very favourable
Unemployment in particular was very low until after 1966.

43. The most obvious aspect was the satirical boom represented by
television programmes like *That Was The Week That Was* and
magazines like *Private Eye*. Of the great tide of ephemera
writing, the collection of essays edited by Arthur Koestler
Suicide of a Nation (London: Hutchinson, 1963), is representative
The economic problem over which some of its contributor
agonised looks rather puny today.

44. The new enthusiasm for growth and supply-side management of
the economy is traced by Samuel Brittan in *Steering the Economy*

45. For the origins and fate of Labour's policies see W. Beckerman
The Labour Government's Economic Record 1964–70 (London: Duck
worth, 1972), and David Coates, *Labour in Power* (London
Longman, 1980) chs 4, 5.

46. F. Cripps, in F. Blackaby (ed.), *De-Industrialisation* (London
Heinemann, 1978) p. 170.

47. It is quite salutary now to read Harold Wilson's collection of
speeches, *The New Britain* (Harmondsworth: Penguin, 1964)
which was published as a Penguin Special in the run-up to the
1964 General Election, and to compare the plans with what
actually transpired.

48. It began in 1969 and subsequently gave rise to the notion that
pay rises were the chief factor driving inflation forward. But
grave doubt was thrown on this by subsequent research. See D
Jackson *et al.*, *Do Trade Unions Cause Inflation?* (Cambridge
University Press, 1971).

49. See Robin Blackburn, 'The Heath Government', *New Left
Review*, vol. 70, 1971, pp. 3–26.

50. See David Calleo, *Britain's Future* (London: Hodder, 1968), for a
survey of the arguments being used in the 1960s.

51. The main provisions of the act were specified legal rights for
individuals; a concept of unfair industrial practices; a National
Industrial Relations Court; registration of trade unions; and the
granting of special powers to the Secretary of State for
Employment to declare states of emergency and order ballots of
the work-force in certain strikes.

52. The current account surplus was £437 million in 1969 and £631
million in 1970.

53. See B. Tew, *The Evolution of the International Monetary System 1945–
77* (London: Hutchinson, 1977).

54. Between 1958 and 1967 the average annual loss of working days
in the United Kingdom was 3 274 000. This rose to 10 136 000
between 1968 and 1977.

55. The level of unemployment that had been reached is generally regarded as the most important factor. See B. Sewill and R. Harris, *British Economic Policy 1970–74* (London: IEA, 1975).

56. The Industry Act (1972) increased the incentives for investment in all regions of the United Kingdom by offering free depreciation and an initial 50 per cent tax cut. It also made provision for grants to industry in exchange for state shareholdings.

57. See Samuel Brittan, *The Economic Consequences of Democracy* (London: Temple Smith, 1968). There was an orgy of speculation particularly amongst the fringe banks, but very little productive investment.

58. Heath's counter-inflation policy was extremely successful. Six million workers settled under Phase 3. Only the failure to accommodate the miners wrecked it.

Chapter 5: The sovereign market

1. Sir Keith Joseph, *Solving the Union Problem is the Key to Britain's Recovery* (London: Centre for Policy Studies, 1979), p. 5.

2. Grahame Thompson, 'The Relationship between the Financial and Industrial Sectors in the British Economy', *Economy and Society*, vol. 6, no 3, August 1977. It is emphasised by writers from many different schools, especially Andrew Shonfield, Susan Strange, Brian Johnson, Sidney Pollard and Tom Nairn.

3. It performed this role most notably when Montagu Norman was Governor, 1920–43. But the City has never needed a direct representative of its interests within Whitehall, in the manner of the CBI or TUC, partly because of the loose nature of the 'City', partly because the City outlook is so embedded in the Treasury and the Board of Trade, but mainly because the pressures brought to bear on governments by the decentralised workings of the financial markets have generally been quite sufficient to keep government policy within certain paths.

4. Repeal of the Corn Laws in 1846 did not spell immediate ruin for British agriculture. The 1850s and 1860s were a period of prosperity. The real decline came in the 1870s and 1880s when other sources of food made possible by the new railways and steamships began to be developed, particularly in North America. This coincided with the raising of protectionist barriers by many other states, leaving Britain by far the largest open market for surplus world food production. Acreage in

Britain under cultivation fell from 17.1 million in 1872 to 13.4 million in 1913. See A. Imlah, *Economic Elements in the Pax Britannica* (New York: Russell, 1958) p. 184.

5. Although the majority of MPs and still more of Cabinet Ministers continued to come from the landed aristocracy. See W. L. Guttsman, *The British Political Elite* (London: MacGibbon & Kee, 1963).

6. Support for free trade was strongest in the great export industries. The textile industry employed 1.5 million, coal 1 million, shipbuilding 1 million. There were 200 000 seamen. Only 100 000 by contrast were employed in the industry that was foremost in demanding protection, iron and steel. See B. Semmel, *Imperialism and Social Reform* (London: Allen & Unwin, 1960) ch. 7.

7. The most important measure was the Trade Disputes Act of 1906, which reversed several adverse legal judgements against trade unions, most notably the decision in the Taff Vale case of 1901. Henceforward unions were given crucial legal immunities which meant that they could not be held liable to employers or to third parties for damages which strikes necessarily caused.

8. Measured by the fairly crude yardstick of government expenditure as a proportion of GNP, state expenditure which had averaged approximately 12 per cent before 1914 and 25 per cent in the inter-war years rose during the Second World War to 60 per cent, falling back after 1945 to 45 per cent. It continued to fall during the 1950s until it reached 36 per cent in 1958, but then began rising again until it stabilised at around 50 per cent in the late 1960s and early 1970s. In 1975 with the impact of the recession it reached 57.9 per cent. For the overall growth of public expenditure see A. Peacock and J. Wiseman, *The Growth of Public Expenditure in the UK* (London: Allen & Unwin, 1966), and Ian Gough, *The Political Economy of the Welfare State* (London: Macmillan, 1979) ch. 5.

9. The government did retain a weakened form of protection known as Safeguarding, designed to protect British industries in their home markets from competition from protected industries abroad. But no duties were placed on food imports and the more ambitious schemes of imperial preference were not implemented, especially after Stanley Baldwin lost an election on the issue in 1923. In 1930 only 17 per cent of imports by value were dutiable, mostly by revenue duties. Protective duties only covered 2–3 per cent of imports. See S. Pollard, *The Development of the British Economy* (London: Arnold, 1969) p. 194.

10. What was most remarkable about the decision to return to the

gold standard in 1925 was the lack of coherent opposition to it, either from industrialists, the Labour movement, the civil service, politicians, or intellectuals. See S. Pollard, *The Gold Standard and Employment Policies between the Wars* (London: Methuen, 1970).

11. The May Committee was established in 1931 to advise the government on what economies it could find to balance the budget. Large increases in taxes were ruled out; so was an increase in government borrowing; so was a raid on the Sinking Fund; so the burden had to fall on spending. Because unemployment was rising so steeply the most obvious area for savings was the dole. The Committee proposed to cover the deficit of £120 million by increasing taxes by £24 million, and by making economies of £96 million, which included a cut in the dole of 20 per cent.

12. It split 9–11 and the nine opposed to the cuts made clear their intention to resign. The new National government implemented the May Report (although it only managed economies of £70 million), but it also cut the pay of all public employees including the armed forces. The resulting mutiny in the fleet at Invergordon caused the final avalanche of funds that pulled down sterling and the gold standard.

13. See, for instance Don Patinkin, *Money, Interest, and Prices* (New York: Harper & Row, 1965).

14. Social Democrats like Evan Durbin and Hugh Dalton were particularly attracted by Keynesian ideas, and it was the means by which many former Marxists, such as John Strachey, renewed their connection with the Labour party and adopted a perspective of a constitutional and peaceful transformation of capitalism into socialism. See especially John Strachey, *Contemporary Capitalism* (London: Gollancz, 1956).

15. Adherents of demand-pull blamed excess demand in product and labour markets for inflation. Adherents of cost-push pointed to the degree of monopoly exercised by companies and unions in determining prices and wage rates. For a general review see R. J. Ball (ed.), *Inflation* (Harmondsworth: Penguin, 1969).

16. For a general survey see Stuart Hall, 'The Great Moving Right Show', *Marxism Today*, January 1979.

17. Most recently the case against economic liberalism has been argued by Ian Gilmour, *Inside Right* (London: Hutchinson, 1977). But see also earlier arguments by Aubrey Jones, *The Pendulum of Politics* (London: Faber, 1946); and Quintin Hogg, *The Case for Conservatism* (Harmondsworth: Penguin, 1947).

18. See the detailed examination of Conservative policies by Nigel

Harris, *Competition and the Corporate Society* (London: Methuen, 1972).

19. For early history and a discussion of the role of the Bow Group in the Conservative party see Andrew Gamble, *The Conservative Nation* (London: Routledge & Kegan Paul, 1974) ch. 4.

20. The IEA was founded in 1957, since when it has published well over 250 papers, analysing questions of economic policy from a free market perspective. Its key figures are Ralph Harris and Arthur Seldon. I have briefly discussed its role and its main ideas in 'The Free Economy and the Strong State', *Socialist Register*, 1979.

21. See the analysis by Patrick Seyd, 'Factionalism in the 1970s', in Z. Layton Henry (ed.), *Conservative Party Politics* (London: Macmillan, 1980) pp. 231–43.

22. A detailed examination of the support he acquired is given by Douglas Schoen, *Enoch Powell and the Powellites* (London: Macmillan, 1977).

23. In the 1970–74 parliament he voted against the government on no fewer than 113 separate occasions. See Philip Norton, *Dissension in the House of Commons* (London: Macmillan, 1975).

24. For the circumstances of Thatcher's election see R. Behrens, *The Conservative Party From Heath to Thatcher* (Farnborough: Saxon House, 1980). Only two members of the Shadow Cabinet, apart from herself, are thought to have voted for her.

25. The division in the leadership which led to the issue of such vague and inconclusive policy documents was satirised by Peter Jay in 'All Things to All Tories', *The Times*, 7 October 1976.

26. Norman's career and attitudes are surveyed by Andrew Boyle, *Montagu Norman* (London: Cassell, 1967).

27. The intention of Operation Robot was to make sterling convertible to non-sterling holders at a floating exchange rate, while freezing certain sterling balances. See S. Brittan, *Steering the Economy* (Harmondsworth: Penguin, 1971) pp. 195–200.

28. I have discussed this at greater length in 'The Free Economy and the Strong State', *Socialist Register*, 1979. The most important statement of this position is to be found in F. A. Hayek, *The Constitution of Liberty* (London: Routledge & Kegan Paul, 1961).

29. The growth of public regulation in housing and the level of welfare benefits are particularly cited in addition to nationalisation. But the spread of trade unionist is blamed most of all.

30. Powell's views on the Common Market have been collected in *The Common Market: the Case Against* (Kingswood: Elliott Rightway Books, 1971).

31. For a clear exposition of the principles of monetarism see T. Congdon, *Monetarism* (London: Centre for Policy Studies, 1978), and Milton Friedman, *Inflation and Unemployment* (London: IEA, 1977).

32. Whether any such control of money supply is possible, and whether money supply can be exactly defined, has long been a matter of controversy. Grave doubts were expressed by the Radcliffe Committee in 1956. See R. S. Sayers, 'Monetary Thought and Monetary Policy in England', in H. G. Johnson (ed.), *Readings in British Monetary Economics* (Oxford University Press, 1972). The more coherent position in liberal political economy is to argue not for control of monetary aggregates, which have proved extremely hard to pin down and still involve a degree of macro-management of the economy, but to embrace the cause of sound money, as Enoch Powell does. Here the government does not need to worry about the wider money supply but merely has to concentrate upon balancing its own budget. But the commitment of modern monetarists to the principle of balanced budgets has always been rather less than wholehearted.

33. Hayek has suggested that even this power could be limited by making all national currencies legal tender, with the intention that good money would drive out bad and provide yet another means of subordinating government policy to the market order. See F. von Hayek, *The De-Nationalisation of Money* (London: IEA, 1976).

34. This is best expressed by F. A. Hayek, *A Tiger by the Tail* (London: IEA, 1972).

35. See R. Bacon and W. Eltis, *Britain's Economic Problem: Too Few Producers* (London: Macmillan, 1978) for this argument. But see also Gough, *The Political Economy of The Welfare State*, for an analysis of its limitations.

36. Crowding out became a fashionable doctrine in the late 1970s. See G. Pepper, *Too Much Money*, Hobart Paper no. 68 (London: IEA, 1976).

37. A 'public good' is a good whose consumption by one person does not diminish the amount available to others. Whether any 'public good' can be defined unambiguously and independently of individual preferences and perceptions without destroying the whole edifice of liberal economic theory is another question.

38. Enoch Powell, *Freedom and Reality* (Kingswood: Elliott Rightway Books, 1969) ch. 10.

39. This emerges in the doctrine of the national rate of unemployment which states that in any economy there is a level of unemployment

that cannot be reduced by expanding demand without at the same time increasing inflation. This natural rate exists partly because of the numbers of handicapped and 'unemployables', partly because of inefficiencies in the labour market which are caused by housing policies, trade union rules, government regulations on employment of women and children, minimum wage and maximum hour legislation. If pushed to its extreme the theory states that if workers were prepared to work for negative wages there would be no unemployment. For further clarification see J. Wood, *How Little Unemployment?*, Hobart Paper no. 65 (London: IEA, 1975).

40. This means that a market order cannot be sustained on the basis of the market itself. This leads to a double prescription – every state should be *laissez-faire* in relation to the exchanges and contracts between individuals, but interventionist when dealing with the conditions for making markets function.

41. Montagu Norman's hopes for the gold standard were one example. Recent speculation about a Currency Commission is another. This preference for fixed, eternal criteria to govern economic policy and reduce discretionary action has always been powerful. The monetary targets of the monetarists are only the latest example.

42. See Lord Hailsham, *The Dilemma of Democracy* (London: Collins, 1978), and Nevil Johnson, *In Search of the Constitution* (Oxford: Pergamon, 1977).

43. This conflict between the rationality of bureaucracy and the rationality of the market has been analysed by many as one of the chief strains in Western capitalist societies. See in particular Jürgen Habermas, *Legitimation Crisis* (London: Heinemann, 1977).

44. See the discussion of possible constitutional reforms in Samuel Brittan, *The Economic Consequences of Democracy* (London: Temple Smith, 1977).

Chapter 6: The enterprise state

1. Tony Benn, Interview with Eric Hobsbawm, *Marxism Today*, October 1980, p. 6.

2. Prominent among them was the economist, and intellectual opponent of Ricardo, Thomas Malthus. See B. Semmel, *The Rise of Free Trade Imperialism* (Cambridge University Press, 1970).

3. Friedrich List was born in Germany but spent many years in the

United States, and was also strongly influenced by the doctrines of the Saint-Simonians in France. His principal book was *The National System* (1856).

4. See M. E. Hirst, *Life of Friedrich List* (London: Smith, Elder, 1909).
5. The major study in B. Semmel, *Imperialism and Social Reform* (London: Allen & Unwin, 1960).
6. The last stand of the Social Imperialists, led by Leo Amery, was made at the Conservative Conference in the early 1950s. They were brushed aside. See Andrew Gamble, *The Conservative Nation* (London: Routledge & Kegan Paul, 1974) ch. 7.
7. Julian Amery, *Joseph Chamberlain and the Tariff Reform Campaign* (London: Macmillan, 1969) p. 998.
8. Joseph Chamberlain, quoted by Henry Page-Croft, *My Life of Strife* (London: Hutchinson 1948) p. 47. See also Chamberlain's series of speeches delivered in 1903, collected in *Imperial Union and Tariff Reform* (London: Grant Richards, 1903).
9. Their fears proved justified. When conscription was introduced in 1917, 10 per cent of young men were fouud to be totally unfit for service, 41.5 per cent had marked disabilities, 22 per cent had partial disabilities, and only one-third were completely fit. See E. Hobsbawm, *Industry and Empire* (Harmondsworth: Penguin, 1969) pp. 164–5.
10. What divided them from the Social Imperialists was not the need for greater state spending and collective provision, but how it was to be financed – out of progressive taxes on income or through regressive customs duties. There was a tension between the two principal parts of the Social Imperialist programme. They wanted tariffs to shut out foreign goods so that British industries could dominate both home and Empire markets; at the same time they were relying on revenue from the tariff to fund the measures that would promote collaboration between classes. This inevitably meant taxes on food. Even at the height of the free trade the imposition of tariffs for revenue purposes was accepted as quite legitimate by all parties, but with the increasing yield from income tax, and its obvious scope for extension, the importance of tariff revenues for funding the state had begun to diminish.
11. Leo Amery was particularly prominent in this group. See his account in *My Political Life, vol. I, England Before the Storm* (London: Hutchinson, 1953).
12. See Robert Skidelsky, *Oswald Mosley* (London: Macmillan, 1975) ch. 11.
13. The evidence of such overcapacity was striking. In the United

States in 1932 one-half of the total productive capacity of the economy was unused. See M. Flamant and J. Singer-Kerel, *Modern Economic Crises* (London: Barrie & Jenkins, 1968).

14. See *The Greater Britain* (London: British Union of Fascists, 1932) especially book 2.

15. The BUF failed to create a mass movement or to make any significant breakthrough, although Skidelsky has argued that it was the war not the British political culture that finally defeated it. 'Would British Fascism have done so disastrously at a general election in 1940 fought in the trough of a new depression?' Skidelsky, *Oswald Mosley*, p. 333.

16. Strong hostility to the Common Market was a major theme in the National Front's economic policies. See Martin Walker, 'The National Front', in H. M. Drucker (ed.), *Multi-party Britain* (London: Macmillan, 1979).

17. Powell's standpoint is shared by several committed economic liberals in the Conservative party. See, for example, John Biffen, *Political Office and Political Power* (London: Centre for Policy Studies, 1977).

18. Snowden threatened to resign when the government introduced the Import Duties Bill which imposed a general 10 per cent tariff, and he carried out his threat when the Ottawa agreements on imperial preference were negotiated.

19. See Skidelsky, *Oswald Mosley*, ch. 10, and his earlier study, *Politicians and the Slump* (Harmondsworth: Penguin, 1967). Mosley appealed for a time to a wide range of younger politicians from all parties, including John Strachey, Nye Bevan, Harold Macmillan and Robert Boothby. They were attracted by his new ideas and his personal dynamism. All abandoned their connections with him when his New party began to develop towards Fascism, which occurred once Mosley became convinced that he could not achieve what he sought through the existing party system.

20. Marxism had long been a formative influence on the Labour movement through, for example, William Morris and Eleanor Marx. It received enormous impetus from the Russian Revolution and from the formation of an independent Communist party in the 1920s. Some of the most important and widely read Marxist writings of the 1930s were the books of John Strachey. A British Marxist intellectual tradition began to form at this time.

21. The simple opposition between reform and revolution was never clear-cut. See Ralph Miliband, *Marxism and Politics* (Oxford University Press, 1977) for an examination of the problem.

22. Stafford Cripps became Minister of Economic Affairs in 1947,

but before a separate department could be established, Cripps became Chancellor of the Exchequer and his wider economic responsibilities were transferred with him to the Treasury. The Department of Economic Affairs, set up explicitly under George Brown to oversee the whole development of the national economy, including the work of the Treasury, was reduced to impotence after 1966, and abolished in 1969.

23. On trade, see, for example, the writings of one of the most influential intellectuals in the Labour Movement, G. D. H. Cole: for example, *Principles of Economic Planning* (London: Macmillan, 1935).

24. See E. Durbin, *The Politics of Democractic Socialism* (London: Routledge & Kegan Paul, 1940).

25. The most influential works were Anthony Crosland, *The Future of Socialism* (London: Cape, 1966), and John Strachey, *Contemporary Capitalism* (London: Gollancz, 1956).

26. The flavour of the programme is captured nowhere better than in the pages of Harold Wilson's *The New Britain* (Harmondsworth: Penguin, 1964).

27. By-election local government election losses were particularly severe. The government trailed the Conservatives by 24 percentage points in the Gallup poll in May 1968. Many Labour party activists had also been alienated by government support for the Americans in Vietnam, the tightening of immigration policy, and policies of pay-restraint and deflation.

28. The proposals were put forward in a White Paper (Cmnd 3888) *In Place of Strife* (London: HMSO, 1969). They were strongly opposed by the trade unions and by a considerable section of the Cabinet, and had to be withdrawn after the Whips had warned Wilson that the measure would split the party and might not pass the House of Commons.

29. Foremost among them were the women's movement, the campaign against the Vietnam War, and new tenants and community groups. The scope of the new movements are explored in Nigel Young, *An Infantile Disorder: Crisis and Decline of the New Left* (London: Routledge & Kegan Paul, 1977), and by David Widgery, *The Left in Britain* (Harmondsworth: Penguin, 1976). On the left-wing political parties see Peter Mair, in Drucker (ed.), *Multi-party Britain*.

30. An integral part of the New Left was not only the breaking down of old divisions and the birth of new movements, but the ending of the intellectual paralysis of Marxism which had been so marked a feature of the period of Stalinism and the Cold War. The renaissance of Marxism as a system of thought was shown

particularly clearly in Britain by the *New Left Review*, which established itself as a major international journal of Marxist theory, and by such new organisations as the Conference of Socialist Economists, which was established in 1970 and soon had more than 1000 members.

31. Its proposals which were based on the earlier 'social contract' between the trade unions and the Labour party included new legal safeguards for trade unions; price controls; a radical housing policy; the strengthening of public transport; a major redistribution of wealth; an end to prescription charges; an increase in pensions; industrial democracy; and the expansion of investment through the creation of a National Enterprise Board, controls on capital movements, and planning agreements.

32. The informal alliance between the TGWU headed by Jack Jones, and the AUEW headed by Hugh Scanlon, was the most notable expression of this shift.

33. During its 3½ years of office the Heath government declared five states of emergency: July 1970, national docks strike; December 1970, power station workers' strike; February 1972, miners' strike; August 1972, dockers' strike; November 1973, miners's strike.

34. Amongst their writings see particularly Michael Barratt Brown, *From Labourism to Socialism* (Nottingham: Spokesman, 1972), K. Coates and T. Topham, *The New Unionism* (London: Peter Owen, 1972), and Stuart Holland, *The Socialist Challenge* (London: Quartet, 1974).

35. Tony Benn's ideas are best studied in his collection of speeches, *Arguments for Socialism* (Harmondsworth: Penguin, 1980). See also his interview with Hobsbawm, *Marxism Today*, October 1980.

36. The Referendum campaign and results are analysed in David Butler and Uwe Kitzinger, *1975 Referendum* (London: Macmillan, 1976).

37. See David Coates, *Labour in Power* (London: Longman, 1980) for a full assessment.

38. See Crosland, *The Future of Socialism*.

39. In this sense the events of 1966 and 1976 reinforced the attitudes that had been shaped in 1931.

40. This wider conception of rights is most fully set out in T. H. Marshall, *Citizenship and Social Class* (Cambridge University Press, 1950).

41. See the evidence presented in John Westergaard and Henrietta Resler, *Class in a Capitalist Society* (Harmondsworth: Penguin, 1975); Peter Townsend, *Poverty in the UK* (Harmondsworth:

Penguin, 1979); and Frank Field *et al.*, *To Him Who Hath* (Harmondsworth: Penguin, 1977).

42. See, for example, the analysis put forward by Andrew Glyn and Bob Sutcliffe, *Workers, British Capitalism and the Profits Squeeze* (Harmondsworth: Penguin, 1972).

43. The most detailed advocacy of import controls has been made by the Cambridge Economic Policy Group. See their annual *Economic Policy Review* from 1975; also the summary of their position by Wynne Godley, 'Britain's Chronic Recession – Can Anything be Done?', in W. Beckerman, *Slow Growth in Britain* (London: Heinemann, 1978).

44. Ideas put forward most explicitly by the Cambridge Political Economy Group in their pamphlet *Britain's Economic Crisis* (Nottingham: Spokesman, 1975). See also the important study, *The Alternative Economic Strategy* by the CSE London Working Group (London: CSE, 1980).

45. The Industrial Reorganisation Corporation was set up by the Labour government in 1966 to encourage 'concentration and rationalisation and to promote the greater efficiency and international competitiveness of British industry'. It was abolished in 1971. The National Enterprise Board was established in 1974 but its power and funds were drastically reduced after the EEC Referendum in 1975, and its chief role became that of holding the government's shares in British Leyland and sponsoring a number of relatively small projects.

46. Interest rates had been held at 2 per cent during the 1930s, and despite the enormous pressure on demand they were held at that level in the 1940s so as to aid reconstruction.

47. Some of the more important statements on the Alternative Economic Strategy are The Cambridge Political Economy Group, *Britain's Economic Crisis*; CSE London Working Group, *The Alternative Economic Strategy*; Geoff Hodgson, *Socialist Economic Strategy*, Labour Party pamphlet, 1979, and Stuart Holland, *The Socialist Challenge*.

48. Among the critics are Andrew Glyn and John Harrison, *The British Economic Disaster* (London: Pluto, 1980); David Coates, *Labour in Power*; A. Cutler *et al.*, *Marx's 'Capital' and Capitalism Today*, vol. 2 (London: Routledge & Kegan Paul 1978) Conclusion; Alan Freeman, 'The Alternative Economic Strategy: A Critique', in CSE Conference Papers, 1980; and David Purdy's contribution to *Politics and Power I* (London: Routledge and Kegan Paul, 1980).

49. Critics like Cutler *et al.*, *Marx's 'Capital'*, who assert this give a very selective account of the strategy.

50. See Glyn and Harrison, *The British Economic Disaster*, David Coates, *Labour in Power*; Alan Freeman, 'The Alternative Economic Strategy: A Critique'.
51. This line of argument is pursued particularly by Freeman, 'The Alternative Economic Strategy: A Critique'.

Chapter 7: The end of decline?

1. See Alan Walters, *Britain's Economic Renaissance* (Oxford University Press, 1986); Geoffrey Maynard, *The Economy Under Mrs Thatcher* (Oxford: Blackwell, 1988).
2. CUCO, *The Conservative Manifesto 1983*, p. 7.
3. Ibid, p. 18.
4. CUCO, *The Next Moves Forward* (1987) p. 4.
5. Hugo Young, *One of Us* (London: Macmillan, 1989) ch. 11. See also Ian Gilmour, *Britain Can Work* (Oxford: Martin Robertson, 1983).
6. See Paul Mosley, *The Making of Economic Policy* (Brighton: Harvester, 1984). The historical and theoretical significance of the shift from Keynesianism to monetarism is assessed by Simon Clarke in *Keynesianism, Monetarism, and the Crisis of the State* (Edward Elgar, 1988).
7. William Keegan, *Mrs Thatcher's Economic Experiment* (London: Allen Lane, 1984).
8. *The Times*, 13 June 1980.
9. For a more detailed analysis see Andrew Gamble, *The Free Economy and the Strong State* (London: Macmillan, 1988). See also, R. Jessop *et al.*, *Thatcherism* (Cambridge: Polity Press, 1988).
10. Cento Veljanovski, *Selling the State* (London: Weidenfield, 1987); Andrew Gamble and Celia Wells (eds), *Thatcher's Law* (University of Wales Press, 1989); Cosmo Graham and Tony Prosser (eds), *Waiving the Rules* (Open University Press, 1988).
11. See Keith Dowding 'Government at the Centre' in Dunleavy P. *et al.* (eds), *Developments in British Politics 4* (London: Macmillan 1993) pp. 175–93.
12. Desmond King, 'The Conservatives and Training Policy 1979–1992; from a Tripartite to an Neo-Liberal Regime', *Political Studies* 41:2 1993, 214–35.
13. OECD, *Economic Survey 1987/88: UK* (OECD, July 1988) p. 8.
14. Ibid, p. 48.
15. Martin Holmes, *The First Thatcher Government* (Brighton: Wheatsheaf, 1985).

16. Nigel Lawson, *The British Experiment*, Fifth Mais Lecture, City University Business School, 18 June 1984.

17. Mancur Olson, *The Rise and Decline of Nations* (Yale University Press, 1982).

18. Geoffrey Maynard, *The Economy Under Mrs Thatcher*.

19. P. J. Forsyth and J. A. Kay, 'The Economic Implications of North Sea Oil Revenue,' *Fiscal Studies*, vol. 1, no. 3, July 1980, and 'Oil Revenues and Manufacturing Output', *Fiscal Studies*, vol. 2, no. 2, July 1981.

20. House of Lords, Select committee on Overseas Trade, Session 1984/5, Volume 1 Report (238–1), 30 July 1985, pp. 47–8.

21. See the Cambridge Economic Policy Group, *Economic Policy Review*.

22. Wynne Godley. 'The Mirage of Lawson's Supply-Side Miracle', *The Observer*, 2 April 1989. Godley pointed out that since 1982 imports of manufacturers had once again doubled while exports had risen by less than 50 per cent. He forecast that this would lead either to a sterling crisis or another severe bout of deflation. In either case the supply-side 'miracle' of 1982–7 would disappear. See also Ken Coutts and Wynne Godley, 'The British Economy Under Mrs Thatcher', *Political Quarterly*, vol. 60, no. 2, 1989, pp. 137–51. For an earlier negative verdict see C. F. Pratten, 'Mrs Thatcher's Economic Legacy', in K. Minogue and M. Biddiss (eds), *Thatcherism: Personality and Politics* (London: Macmillan, 1987).

23. R. Rowthorn and J. Wells, *De-industrialisation and Foreign Trade* (Cambridge University Press, 1987). See also the earlier collection of papers edited by Frank Blackaby, *De-industrialisation* (London: Heinemann, 1978), especially those by Ajit Singh and Alec Cairncross.

24. Perry Anderson, 'The Figures of Descent', *New Left Review*, 161, 1987, pp. 20–77.

25. Assessments of the economic policies of the Thatcher decade include Francis Green (ed.), *The Restructuring of the UK Economy* (London Harvester Wheatsheaf, 1989); Jonathan Michie (ed.), *The Economic Legacy 1979–1992* (London: Academic Press, 1992); Nigel Healey (ed.), *Britain's Economic Miracle: Myth or Reality* (London: Routledge, 1993); Stephen Wilks, 'Economic Policy', in P. Dunleavy *et al.* (eds.) *Developments in British Politics 4* (London: Macmillan, 1993) 221–45.

26. David Edgerton, *England and the Aeroplane* (London: Macmillan 1991); 'Liberal Militarism and the British State', *New Left Review 185* January–February 1991, 138–69.

27. Scott Newton and Dilwyn Porter, *Modernisation Frustrated*

(London: Unwin Hyman, 1988). See also David Marquand, *The Unprincipled Society* (London: Cape, 1987); Bernard Elbaum and William Lazonick (eds), *The Decline of the British Economy* (Oxford University Press, 1986), and Henrik Halkier, 'The Political Economy of Britain's Decline' in U. Ostergard (ed.), *Culture and History 9/10* (Copenhagen: Academic Press 1991) 105–36.

28. Perry Anderson, 'The Figures of Descent'.
29. Ben Fine and Laurence Harris, *The Peculiarities of the British Economy* (London: Lawrence & Wishart, 1985).
30. For different perspectives on Labour's evolution in the 1980s, see Paul Whiteley, *The Labour Party in Crisis* (London: Methuen, 1983); Barry Hindess, *Parliamentary Democracy and Socialist Politics* (London: Routledge, 1983); Geoff Hodgson, *Labour at the Crossroads* (London: Martin Robertson, 1981); Hilary Wainwright, *Labour: A Tale of Two Parties* (London: Hogarth, 1987); Eric Hobsbawm, *The Forward March of Labour Halted?* (London: Verso, 1981). See also Martin Smith and Jo Spear (eds), *The Changing Labour Party* (London: Routledge 1992).
31. Keith Middlemas, *Power, Competition, and the State: Vol. 3 The End of the post-war era: Britain since 1974* (London: Macmillan 1991).
32. Jim Tomlinson, *Can Governments Manage the Economy?*, Fabian Pamphlet 524 (London: Fabian Society, 1987).
33. Hugo Radice, 'The National Economy – a Keynesian Myth?', *Capital and Class*, 22, 1984, pp. 111–140.
34. David Baker, Andrew Gamble, and Steve Ludlam, 'Conservative Splits and European Integration', *Political Quarterly*, 64:4 (October–December 1993) 420–34.
35. Such a strategy is set out in Paul Hirst, *After Thatcher* (London: Collins, 1989).
36. Ron Martin and Peter Tyler, 'The Regional Legacy' in Jonathan Michie (ed.), *The Economic Legacy 1979–92*, 140–67.
37. John Grahl and Paul Teague, 'The Cost of Neo-Liberal Europe', *New Left Review*, 174, 1989, pp. 33–50.

Index